AF428425

FINDING MY VOICE

FINDING MY VOICE

THRIVING BEYOND PEDOPHILIA

HEIDI CRAIG

ISBN 979-8-9944049-0-4
Library of Congress Control Number: 2025928198

Cover design: Heidi Craig and Sofie Birkin

Printed in the United States of America

First Edition: April 2026

CONTENT WARNING

This memoir contains references to childhood trauma, including grooming, sexual abuse, emotional neglect, and complex family dynamics.

Please take your time, care for yourself as you read, and pause whenever you need to. Your well-being matters.

AUTHOR'S NOTE

This memoir is the story of my lived experience. It reflects the truth as I remember it, shaped by the emotions, perceptions, and understandings I carried at the time. Memory is complex, especially when it forms around trauma, and the passages in this book are written from the perspective of the child and young woman I once was, as well as the adult who later sought to make sense of it all.

Some scenes and conversations have been reconstructed to the best of my recollection. Certain timelines have been condensed, and some details have been altered to protect privacy. None of these adjustments change the emotional truth of my journey or the heart of what I lived through.

While this book tells my story, it is not written to accuse, condemn, or harm anyone. It is written to reclaim my voice, honor the girl I used to be, and offer connection to anyone who has carried their own story in silence.

Note: This memoir represents my personal memories, interpretations, and emotional truth. Others may remember events differently. Any similarities to real individuals are either coincidental or the result of subjective recollection.

With love and gratitude,
Heidi

PRIVACY & COMPOSITE CHARACTERS

This memoir is drawn from my lived experience. While the emotional truth remains unchanged, certain individuals in this book are presented as composite characters—meaning their traits, actions, and roles may reflect a blend of behaviors or moments across different times in my life.

In addition, names, occupations, physical descriptions, relationships, and identifying details have been changed or omitted to protect the privacy of the people involved. These changes do not alter the essence of my story, but they do help preserve the dignity and anonymity of individuals whose paths intersected with mine.

Some scenes are portrayals of the overall emotional reality rather than precise chronological accounts. Dialogue has been recreated from memory and is not intended to reflect verbatim conversations.

Where individuals appear in this memoir, they are portrayed solely through my perspective. Other people's memories, experiences, or interpretations may differ.

These adjustments are meant to safeguard privacy while allowing me to tell my story with integrity, honesty, and care.

"What was taken in the dark became the very light that led me back to myself."

—Heidi Craig

For the little girl I used to be—
you deserved safety, truth, and love.
This is for you.

For every survivor who learned to stay quiet—
may this book remind you that your voice matters.

For my sons—
my heart, my breath, my reason for rising.

CONTENTS

1

BEFORE I HAD WORDS FOR THE HURT

"We are not given a good life or a bad life. We are given a life. It's up to us to make it good or bad."
—Ward Foley

My name is Heidi Craig.
My father is a pedophile.
And this is my story.

I entered the world in a fight for breath.

Machines surrounded my tiny body—hissing, clicking, and flashing with indifferent rhythm as tubes fed air into lungs too weak to rise on their own. I was swaddled not in warmth, but in plastic and wires, sealed in a sterile box of blinking lights and beeping alarms. The scent of antiseptic hung in the air like a curtain, sharp and unforgiving.

My mother stood on the other side of that clear wall, watching with helpless eyes. Her hands reached through latex-gloved portholes, fingertips brushing skin she wasn't allowed to cradle. No forehead kisses. No skin-to-skin warmth. Only prayers. Only waiting. She was told I might not make it.

But I did.

Four weeks later, I was released—my body still soft with survival, my lungs barely catching up to life. My mother carried me out of that hospital as if I was made of glass. A fragile victory.

The house we returned to looked ordinary on the outside—stucco walls, tired windows, a lawn trying to grow—but it groaned under the weight of secrets.

Inside waited Hunter, my twin—my first mirror, my first tether—and my sisters, Misty and Lena. Misty was eight, old enough to dream in fairy tales. She knelt beside my carrier, eyes wide, fingers grazing the edge of my blanket as if she'd just unwrapped the most delicate gift.

"She looked like a doll," she would later say. "Like a princess just for me."

In her mind, I was something magical. She carried me around the house like royalty, brushing my cheeks with tiny hands and whispering stories meant for happy endings.

But our house didn't speak in storybook language.

The walls didn't hold magic—they held echoes. Old ones. The kinds that creep through floorboards and rattle picture frames when no one is looking.

Misty and Lena's father had left long before I was born, but his shadow lingered. My mother never spoke his name, but sometimes her silence said more than words. She'd flinch at slamming doors. Her voice would tremble when bottles clinked too loudly in the trash.

He had been cruel. Drunk. Dangerous. Love, when it came from him, left bruises. Eventually, she escaped—with two girls in tow and no map for what came next. The only place to land was her parents' home, but even safety can suffocate.

Under their roof, she wasn't seen as a woman rebuilding her life. She was treated like a girl who had failed. Their rules came wrapped in the language of concern: no smoking, no visitors, and no independence. Her mother watched her with suspicion, her father with quiet sorrow.

She stayed as long as she could. However, at twenty-eight, carrying more pain than possessions, she packed the car and drove to Texas, with hope buckled in the backseat. There, she met a man. My father.

He smiled when he talked to her. He said the right things. He held the door. He listened as if he cared. He didn't recoil at the idea of two daughters. He called them "beautiful girls." He called her "strong." He called their mess "a new beginning."

She wanted so badly to believe him.

After all the wreckage, here was someone handing her a promise with both hands. He told her she was safe now. That she was worthy of love.

Maybe he believed it. Maybe she did too.

She opened the door and let him in.

She didn't know she was letting the cold back in with him.

They moved fast. Most people don't when they're healing. However, trauma doesn't wait—it rushes in, dressed like comfort, pretending to be the answer.

I imagine her there, holding two newborns—one in each arm, the weight of their needs pulling at the edges of her strength—trying to build something real with shaking hands.

She needed to believe this time would be different.

She couldn't afford not to.

They brought us home to Colorado not long after we were born—back to the mountains, to the thin, familiar air my mother had grown up breathing. Maybe she thought being near family would bring comfort. Maybe protection. Maybe both.

However, no one saw it coming.

No one saw *him* coming.

From the outside, it looked like a fresh start. A new chapter. But inside, something was already unraveling. The walls held tight to secrets. Smiles at church, polite hellos at the grocery store—no one would've guessed what was building beneath the surface.

It didn't happen all at once.

It never does.

First came the warmth—soft words, easy laughter, and hands that seemed safe. Soon, however, the warmth cooled. The words stopped. His voice, once gentle, turned sharp around the edges. Promises withered into rules. Kindness folded into control.

It's strange how quickly love can change form. How fast the light fades.

We moved to Julesburg, the tiny farming town where my mother had been raised. Flat plains stretched for miles in every direction, broken only by the silhouettes of grain silos and weather-beaten barns. I don't remember how old we were, exactly. However, I remember the house.

Lake Street.

A modest four-bedroom, pale siding, with a cracked concrete walkway leading to the front door. The unfinished basement always smelled like damp earth and laundry detergent. A single lightbulb swung overhead in the laundry room, casting shadows that danced along the bare walls.

Misty stayed downstairs in the one finished room. Hunter and I shared the bunk beds upstairs—me on the bottom, him on top. Lena had the room next to ours, and sometimes I could hear her humming softly to herself at night.

My memories from that time come back in pieces—flashes of sunlight through half-closed blinds, the squeak of a box fan in the window, the cold sting of linoleum on bare feet.

But mostly, I remember being afraid.

There was a hum that lived inside the walls of our home—not the gentle kind, but something sharp and electric, like a wire pulled too tight. When the house was calm, it lay low and quiet. But when things shifted, when the air changed, that hum would rise like a warning.

I must've been five, maybe six, the night that sound became a scream.

I stood in the doorway between the living room and kitchen, with my small body tucked behind the frame, and my bare feet rooted to the cold linoleum. My fingers curled into the wood as if they might anchor me there. To the right was the dining table, and the garage door. To the left was the kitchen.

My mother stood in front of the door, trembling.

Stan, my father, was in the kitchen, his face twisted under the yellow glow of the overhead light. His eyes were wild. Unrecognizable.

They were fighting.

Or rather, he was screaming. His voice split the air, thick with rage and words I didn't fully understand but felt like knives anyway.

Then came the storm.

A crash. Another. Another.

The toaster flew first. Then the can opener. The blender. He grabbed everything off the counter—pots, pans, silverware and hurled them at her one by one. They didn't just hit the door behind her; they buried themselves in it. Loud, ugly, violent thuds—metal colliding with wood, over and over, like the house itself was flinching.

She tried to shield herself. Hands up. Shoulders curled. Her cries barely audible under the sound of his fury. She backed into the garage door, as if she could somehow disappear into it.

"Stop!" she pleaded.

He didn't want her pleas.

He wanted her fear.

And me?

I couldn't move.

I was frozen in place, shaking so hard my knees knocked together. I wasn't sure if I was standing or falling. Tears streaked my cheeks. I covered my ears, but nothing could block it out: the crash, her voice, and his rage.

Then came the warmth down my legs. A different kind of shame. The kind that doesn't wash off. The kind that settles deep in the bones.

Through it all, I saw her eyes—wide with terror, filled with something worse than fear. Apology. She was trying to protect us, and in that moment, she couldn't.

And I was too small to stop it.

That night didn't end when the screaming stopped. It lived on—in my dreams, in my chest—in the places inside me that still flinch at sudden sounds.

Stan never replaced the door.

It stayed there, battered, splintered, and full of jagged dents like bite marks in the wood. A quiet monument to everything that had happened. A scar, right there in the hallway, where anyone could see.

Not long after, my mom found the strength to leave. She packed us up—four kids—and moved us into a small apartment up the street. The floors creaked, the kitchen barely fit a table, but we could breathe again. It wasn't perfect. But it was ours. It was quiet.

Years later, I found myself back in that house. I can't remember why. Maybe curiosity. Maybe I needed to know it was real.

The walls had been painted. The furniture had been replaced. The kitchen felt smaller than I remembered.

But the door…

The door was still there. And so were the dents. They stared back at me like eyes. Like wounds that never healed. Because some rage doesn't leave bruises.

It leaves ghosts.

It leaves flinching hearts in grown children who still hear the blender hitting the door in their sleep.

The scars were still there.

And so was I.

I was a teenager when I finally learned the truth.

The *real* reason my mother left Stan.

Up until then, I only knew the fragments—the edges of a story never fully told. It lived in our house like a phantom, that story. You could feel it, more than hear it. It clung to the air like smoke after a fire—long after the flames were gone, the scent of danger still lingered in the drywall.

I thought I already knew. I thought the violence was the story.

The screaming that split open quiet afternoons.

The door slamming hard enough to shake picture frames.

The blender sailing through the air like a missile.

The holes he punched through the walls—always just inches from where we stood, as if that was supposed to be reassuring.

I thought that was the worst of it.

However, I was wrong.

Even as a little girl—five, maybe six—I *knew*. Not in words. Not in facts. But in my body. In my stomach.

It would twist when he walked into a room. I'd shrink into myself, eyes darting away. I couldn't explain it, but I knew something was wrong with the way his eyes followed us. The way his hands stayed a second too long. How his smile felt more like a trap than a comfort.

He was different when no one else was watching. Too affectionate. Too close.

I wasn't the only one who felt it. We didn't say it out loud. Not back then. But something passed between me and my sisters in the silence—a glance, a flinch, a tightening jaw. We carried a shared knowing, buried deep in our bellies.

It stayed quiet.

Until it didn't.

As I grew older, the shape of that sickness became clear. The words finally came, heavy and sharp.

I learned what those feelings really meant. I learned what he was. And I learned what he had done. The worst part wasn't the rage we saw.

It was the horror we hadn't.

The monster hadn't lived under the bed. He had lived in our house, the entire time.

What I hadn't known—what had been buried beneath years of silence—was that Stan had been sexually abusing my sister Misty.

He started when she was just eight years old.

Eight.

Still soft with baby fat and the smell of strawberry shampoo. Still building blanket forts and falling asleep with her stuffed bear, the one with the missing button eye. Still believing that goodnight kisses meant safety and that the adults in your life would never, ever hurt you.

However, behind one closed door, everything Misty believed about the world was taken from her.

As the abuse continued, Misty did what no child should ever have to do. She moved into the basement.

At the time, my mom thought it was just her way of becoming a teenager—pulling away, wanting space and independence. That's what everyone thought. However, the truth was far more devastating.

She didn't go down there for privacy. She went down there to protect us.

Specifically, Lena.

Misty believed that if she stayed closer to him—if she became more accessible—maybe, just maybe, he would leave her younger sister alone. She thought that if she gave more of herself, she could contain the monster. Keep him fed. Keep him away from the ones she loved.

It wasn't a choice. It was a sacrifice. One no child should ever be forced to make.

But Misty was just a little girl trying to negotiate with a nightmare. Trying to carry the pain so no one else had to.

The basement was cold year-round. It smelled like wet cement and mildew. The walls were unfinished, rough to the touch.

There were no windows. No stars. No sunrise.

Just shadows.

It should have felt like a punishment. But for Misty, it became a sanctuary, of sorts—a place where she could quietly disappear. Where she could absorb the darkness in silence, so it didn't spread upstairs.

At night, while the rest of us slept in our beds, Misty laid awake in the basement, waiting. That kind of decision—that kind of love—should never be required of a child. And yet, it was the only power Misty thought she had. She gave herself, so Lena might be spared. And in doing so, she bore more pain than most adults could fathom.

Misty gave everything she had to protect Lena.

She gave her childhood, her innocence, and her body.

She gave it all because she believed—desperately, dangerously—that maybe if she stayed close to him, if she absorbed enough of his violence, he'd leave Lena alone.

But monsters don't honor love.

They exploit it.

And one morning, everything shattered.

Misty came upstairs like she always did—quiet, careful, the soft thud of her feet on the stairs, the morning light spilling across the hallway floor. She told me later that something felt different the moment she reached the top step. The house was too quiet; still in that way that makes the hairs on your arms rise.

Then she saw the door to Lena's room cracked open.

And him. Stan. Inside.

He was hurting Lena, just as he had hurt her.

In that moment, Misty's entire world collapsed.

Her body locked. She couldn't scream. Couldn't move. She was paralyzed, caught between past and present, horror and disbelief. She said the cold rushed through her like water, as if she was being flooded from the inside out. Her lungs seized. Her limbs went numb. Her throat burned with words she couldn't form.

She had spent years suffering in silence. Years bargaining with her body to keep Lena safe. And now, with one glimpse, she knew—none of it had worked.

Everything she endured. Every time she let herself be taken. Every night she lain awake in that freezing basement praying for help…

It hadn't been enough.

Enduring the unthinkable…

Imagine that. Imagine being twelve, thirteen, fifteen— enduring the unthinkable—and doing it with a single, sacred hope: that you are shielding someone you love. And then discovering you had failed.

Not because you were weak, not because you didn't try hard enough; but because monsters don't care. They take what they want, when they want, from whomever they want. And no amount of suffering buys mercy.

Misty told me later she felt her heart break in that instant. Not just figuratively—but literally. She said she felt something in her chest snap. It was as if a thread that had been holding her together had finally given way.

And then came the guilt.

That unbearable, relentless guilt that clings like smoke and seeps into your skin. She blamed herself. Not Stan. Not the grown-ups who failed to see what was happening. Not the systems that allowed it all to go unnoticed.

No.

She blamed herself. Children—especially abused children—

carry their pain as if it's their fault. She told herself she should have done more. Stayed closer. Slept less. Given more. She believed that, if she had just tried harder, maybe she could have saved Lena.

That's the cruelty of abuse. It distorts logic. It rearranges blame. It convinces the most innocent people that they are responsible for the devastation left behind.

Misty should never have had to carry that weight.

She should never have had to play protector, sacrificial lamb, and silent witness to evil. She should never have had to trade her safety for ours.

And yet she did. She did it without question. Without thanks. Without rescue.

And my heart still aches for her. It always will.

Because the moment everything changed wasn't the day when Stan crossed another line. It was the day Misty realized that, no matter how much of herself she gave, he would never stop taking.

That morning, Misty couldn't carry it anymore.

The truth had become too heavy.

She sat frozen in the kitchen, watching the clock, with her heart thudding in her chest as if it was trying to escape.

Boots scraped across the floor. The front door opened. Then the door closed.

She held her breath as the sound of Stan's truck rumbled to life. Gravel crunched beneath the tires.

Only when the noise disappeared did she reach for the phone—hands trembling so badly she missed the buttons the first time. Her fingers shook against the plastic, her breath catching before a single word even formed.

She called our mother.

The second Rose answered, Misty broke.

Not just her voice—her whole being.

Years of silence erupted in gasping sobs. All of it poured out: every secret buried beneath years of fear, every sleepless night in the cold basement, every moment she had surrendered herself to protect Lena.

No more hiding.

No more pretending.

Just truth—raw and jagged, bleeding out between breaths.

On the other end of the line, our mother went quiet. Just for a moment. A breath. A beat where the whole world seemed to stop.

And then—"I'm coming," she said. "Don't move. I'm on my way."

Misty told me later she had never seen anyone move that fast.

Our mother flew through the door as if she was chasing a fire. Her keys were still in her hand, her face pale, her eyes scanning every corner as if she expected him to jump out. She looked panicked—wild with fear, but focused.

"Go downstairs. Pack a bag," she told Misty, her voice shaking, but steady enough to move mountains.

Then she moved—drawer to drawer, closet to closet—grabbing what she could, flinging clothes into trash bags, and shoes under her arms; her body moving on instinct alone.

She packed for Misty. For Lena. For Hunter. For me.

No tears. No time. Just motion.

Like a mother pulling her children from a burning house. Within minutes, we were in the car.

I don't remember the packing.

I don't remember walking to the car.

I don't remember the sound of the tires crunching over the gravel as we pulled away.

That's what trauma does.

It smudges the edges, softens the sharpest parts just enough to keep you from breaking.

However, I remember the silence.

I remember the seatbelt cutting into my chest, my hands folded stiffly in my lap. I stared out the window as the house shrank behind us. Stan's coffee cup was still sitting by the sink. Half full. Forgotten. The basement light was still on.

We left with nothing but what we could carry—no plan, no goodbye, only the weight of truth finally spoken and the quiet wreckage it left behind.

She drove us to her parents' house.

To safety—at least physically.

We were no longer under the same roof as the man who hurt Misty, and who hurt Lena.

However, nothing felt safe. Not really. That kind of escape doesn't come with relief. It comes with disorientation. With a silence so thick, it feels like a second skin.

No one talked much.

No one knew how.

There weren't any instructions for what came next.

All I remember is the stillness. The kind that settles after a storm—when the sky clears, but everything has changed. When the damage is done, and only the silence remains.

No one talked about what happened. Not ever.

There were no police, no charges, and no justice.

Stan was never held accountable.

So, the truth—unbearable, violent—was folded up, hidden away, and sealed beneath layers of fear and shame and silence.

It became a secret. Our family's secret. A wound that closed over but never healed.

In the weeks after our escape, the house changed. But not in the way you'd hope.

There was no righteous fury. There were no tears around the kitchen table. There was no space to lay our pain bare: just stillness, and heavy, aching, breath.

Like the entire house had exhaled once—and then never dared inhale again.

We didn't say his name. We didn't ask questions. We didn't speak about what he had done. There was no agreement, no declaration of silence. It simply settled over us—thick and invisible, like a fog we had walked into and from which we couldn't find our way out.

At dinner, the clink of forks on plates was louder than anyone's voice. The TV stayed on longer at night, with voices and laughter from sitcoms echoing through rooms that didn't laugh anymore.

If someone cried, it was behind closed doors. No one knocked. No one asked. We all knew better.

I learned quickly that the safest thing to do was stay quiet.

We were physically safe—but emotionally? Spiritually? We were scattered—shattered.

Each of us was pretending we were okay because we didn't know how to say we weren't.

In that silence, we started to disappear. Misty, once fierce and full of light, became hollowed-out by guilt too big for her frame. Lena, so young, so confused, had no words for what had been done to her. And me—I watched. I listened. I studied the tension in my mother's jaw, and the way her eyes flicked away any time the past came too close.

The silence wasn't just in the room.

It was *in* us.

Slowly, it rewired the way I understood the world. I learned that love doesn't always protect. That sometimes the people who say they love you are the ones who look away when truth becomes too heavy to hold. I learned that secrets, left unspoken, don't disappear. They root down. They wind through your relationships, through your self-worth, and through your sleep.

I learned how to smile with my mouth while my eyes stayed haunted. And I learned how to be quiet—too quiet.

The truth never left. It just went underground. It lived on in our bodies.

It was there in the way Misty flinched when a cabinet slammed. It was there in how Lena's voice would go small anytime she asked for something. It was there in how I sometimes woke in the middle of the night with my heart racing and no idea why.

It followed us into the future. Into the walls we built. Into the ways we guarded ourselves. Into the bracing—for disappointment, for danger—even on peaceful days.

Because when a secret that big is buried inside a family, it doesn't stay buried. It becomes a language, even when no one speaks it. We never spoke of it again. However, the silence never ended.

It still echoes—in the hollow spaces of our story. In the questions I never knew I was allowed to ask. In the things I only understand now because I've lived in their shadows for so long.

That silence is still with me. It has a weight. A sound. A temperature.

Some nights, when the world is still, I can feel it again—humming just beneath my skin.

The brain has a way of shielding us from pain that's too much to hold. So, there are parts I don't remember. Big pieces of my early childhood are gone.

Softened. Blurred. Erased.

However, trauma doesn't vanish. It fractures. It burrows. It hides beneath the surface, pulsing like a second heartbeat. And the fragments that *do* come through—they're enough.

A dim hallway.

The creak of a door.

The weight of dread before a hand even touched me.

The way my body knew how to freeze before I ever learned what that word meant.

I don't have the whole picture. Just flashes. A smell—cheap cologne and sweat. A whisper—*"This is our secret."* The sensation of vanishing into myself. Those fragments.

They are more than enough.

My father was a pedophile. Not a man with "a troubled past." Not someone who made mistakes.

A predator. Calculated. Repetitive. Unrepentant.

He preyed on his wives.

On their children.

On *us*.

On *me*.

And on the countless little girls of the women he dated, seduced, and married.

It wasn't accidental. It was a pattern. A method. He knew how to pick them—women with wounded hearts and wide-open hopes. Women who needed love, who wanted family, and who longed for stability.

He moved in with soft smiles, gentle eyes, bedtime stories, and warm dinners. He braided hair. He called us his "little angels." He gave out affection like candy—until you realized it came at a cost. He made monsters look like family.

That confusion—*that* cruel, deliberate confusion—is what devastates the soul the most. Because when the person hurting you is the one who tucks you in at night, the world stops making sense.

Love becomes a weapon. Touch becomes danger. And home becomes the place you learn to fear the most.

His crimes weren't just physical. They were emotional, spiritual, and existential. He didn't just violate our bodies. He violated our *sense of being*. He twisted our trust. He taught us silence before we ever learned how to speak the truth. But the silence…it was never empty.

It had shape.

It had weight.

It moved through our house like smoke—visible and invisible all at once.

It taught us how to look away.

How to stay quiet.

How to survive.

What I remember most isn't the moments. It's the *feeling* that lived inside them. That low, buzzing hum beneath the surface of everything. That quiet sense that something was off—even when the room was calm. That feeling of holding your breath for no reason you could name. That feeling of looking into your father's face and knowing, in a place too deep for words, that what lived behind his smile wasn't love.

Even now, as I name him for what he was—*a predator*—I feel the fog lift.

Not all the way, but enough. Because truth has a way of unraveling silence. And just because something was once unspoken, it doesn't mean it has to stay buried forever.

There are signs, if you know how to see them.

Predators are good at looking like caretakers. They wrap their sickness in affection—warm hands, soft tones, and a father's smile that doesn't quite reach the eyes. Stan knew how to blend in. and how to make his darkness look like devotion.

He'd call us over—"Come sit on my lap."

So, we did.

We were small. It seemed sweet. Normal. The kind of thing daughters were supposed to do. But his hands didn't rest. They moved, slow, lingering, and too low.

His fingers traced our spines in long, possessive strokes. I didn't know what was wrong—I just knew I wanted to pull away. But I stayed, and I smiled, because that's what good girls did.

Sometimes he'd ask us to rub his back.

His skin slick with sweat. His voice low, almost tender.

"You're my favorite," he'd whisper, as if it was a secret.

As if I should feel lucky.

And I did, for a moment. But underneath the warmth was something sour, something that twisted in my gut.

I didn't know the word *grooming*. But my body did. It *knew*.

He liked to watch us dance. He'd sit in the middle of the living room—legs spread, leaning back in his chair—and say, "Spin for me."

We would. We twirled. We giggled. We thought we were making him happy.

However, we weren't dancing. We were performing, being observed, studied, and watched like prey.

He took pictures, too. Not the kind that live on fridge doors or inside dusty albums—messy, joyful snapshots of real childhood. No—his were staged.

"Smile bigger."

"Sit up straight."

"Tilt your head—there. That's perfect."

I remember one photo, with my hair in pigtails, and my knees pressed together. I was wearing that pink dress I hated—it pinched under my arms and rode up when I sat. I kept tugging it down.

However, he said I looked "beautiful." So, I smiled, because I didn't know what else to do.

Stan never dated women without children: more specifically—without *daughters*. Young ones, always. It was his preference. His pattern.

He didn't just charm the women—he studied them.

He looked for loneliness.

Fatigue.

That thin crack in the armor.

Then, he slipped in. With gentle eyes. With compliments. With promises of family and stability. He made them feel safe, wanted, and loved.

Once he was in—once he was trusted—he turned to the children.

That was always the sequence:

First the woman, and then the child. Every house he lived in had one room that felt…wrong.

It wasn't just empty.

It was *off*.

Too still.

Too cold.

Too quiet in a way that made the hairs on your arms rise.

Always one room.

Always the same: a bare mattress on the floor. No blankets. No lamp. No furniture. Just the sagging mattress and silence. The door was never shut, just slightly ajar—an opening you instinctively avoided. As a child, I didn't know why. Only that I wasn't supposed to go in there. Sometimes, I'd walk past and catch a strange smell—sweat, fear, and something unnamable.

Now I know.

Now I understand what that room was.

What it was *for*.

And the knowing makes me sick.

Stan didn't just take up space. He *controlled* it. Rooms shifted when he walked in. Voices dropped. The air changed. People adjusted their breathing to match his moods.

He didn't always need fists to make you afraid—though he used those too. More often, he used his words like blades.

He humiliated. He isolated. He turned love into something conditional and cruel. He told people they were broken—then offered himself as the cure.

He called it *discipline*.

He called it *love*.

But what he really did was break people, and feed on the pieces.

It wasn't just the girls. It wasn't just the women. He hurt the boys too. He didn't want sons. He wanted soldiers. Quiet. Controlled. Stripped of softness.

Boys who learned early that tenderness was weakness and emotion was a sin.

My twin brother, Hunter, was one of them.

He didn't get spared. He got *targeted*.

Stan's cruelty toward him was surgical—sharp, direct, constant. He screamed with no warning. Belittled him for existing.

If Hunter spoke, he was talking back.

If he was quiet, he was being sneaky.

If he cried, he was weak.

If he flinched, Stan hit harder.

And the beatings—they weren't spankings. They were rage, unleashed. I remember the sound more than the sight: the slap of skin. The thud of impact. The breath that caught in Hunter's throat and never became a scream.

He wouldn't scream, not because it didn't hurt, but because he thought if he stayed silent, it would end sooner.

It rarely did.

He started walking differently around the house—small, careful, his steps barely audible. He had his shoulders hunched, and his fists clenched at his sides, like he was trying to hold himself in. Or hold himself *together*.

Stan mocked his tears.

"Such a little bitch," he'd sneer. "Grow up. Be a man."

Hunter was six. There's a kind of violence that steals more than safety. It steals *self*.

Hunter stopped asking for hugs. He stopped drawing—the thing he used to love most. One day, I found his sketchbook in the trash. Every page was torn in half. It was stuffed under the kitchen sink like something shameful.

When I asked why, he shrugged. "They were stupid." But I knew what he was trying to erase.

Even after we escaped, the damage stayed.

In his avoidance of eye contact.

In the way he flinched at loud noises.

In how he always had to know where the exits were.

He couldn't take compliments, and he wouldn't accept

praise. If you said something kind, he'd change the subject, as if he didn't deserve it. Like if you *really* knew him, you'd take it back.

He didn't carry his pain on the outside. But that doesn't mean it didn't bleed.

Stan didn't just hurt him. He broke something inside him. And then he convinced him it was *his* fault.

Predators don't always look like villains. Sometimes they stand in broad daylight—laughing, hugging, and handing out candy. They look like caregivers. Coaches. "Nice guys."

They know exactly what they're doing. They *rely* on looking normal. They rely on your discomfort to keep you quiet.

Stan would put his arm around me in public and ruffle my hair. He'd call me his "little angel."

Strangers smiled and nodded. They said things like, "You're so lucky to have a dad who loves you like that." And I smiled too, because I was supposed to.

But inside, I was screaming.

Begging someone—*anyone*—to look closer.

To see how stiff I got under his hand.

To ask why I watched the *door* more than I watched the room.

No one ever did. No one ever said, "Are you okay?" No one said, "You don't have to go with him if you're scared." So, I stayed quiet.

Silence felt safer than not being believed.

Here's what I need you to understand: grooming doesn't begin with abuse. It begins with trust, with affection, and with words like *special*. It begins with secrets that feel like sugar but rot like poison.

It starts with boundary-testing that seems harmless—until it isn't.

By the time a child feels uncomfortable, they're already too far in to know how to ask for help.

And if they *do* speak up—they often doubt themselves. They second-guess what they felt and wonder if it was "bad enough" to matter.

Because the world has taught them that discomfort is not evidence.

That adults are always right.

That proof is required.

But children don't make this up. They don't say these things for attention. They speak when the truth becomes too heavy to carry alone.

So, if something feels wrong—speak up.

If your gut twists—trust it.

If a child is too quiet, too jumpy, too guarded—ask why.

And when they answer—*believe them*.

Don't question the story just because it's hard to hear. Don't look away because it makes you uncomfortable.

Instead, lean in. Because it is *always* worth it:

—to protect a child,

—to preserve their innocence,

—to defend their safety.

You have to save them, even if it's just by saying, "I see you. I believe you. I'm here."

I wish someone had said that to us.

Just once.

Do you know what that could have changed?

2

I WAS NOT SPARED

In my family, there was a quiet assumption that, because I was Stan's biological daughter, I had somehow been spared. That his sickness had boundaries. That I was safe.

But predators don't recognize boundaries.

They exploit them. And the truth is, I don't know the full extent of what he did to me. I only have one memory. One night. But it is enough.

I was seven.

Hunter and I were spending the weekend at Stan's house. It was one of those rare moments where things felt… normal. We asked if we could sleep in the living room, curled up on the carpet in front of the soft flicker of the TV. I remember the hum of the static, the low murmur of a late-night movie, and the warmth of my twin brother beside me. For a moment, I felt safe.

But safety never lasted long in that house.

I woke in the middle of the night, groggy and disoriented, to the sensation of being lifted. Stan's arms were under me—firm, certain. He carried me as if I was something precious. Or something he owned.

I didn't speak. I didn't move. Terror had locked my body in place.

I kept my eyes shut, pretending to sleep. That was the only plan my brain could offer: stay still, stay quiet, stay invisible.

He brought me into his bedroom and laid me on his bed. The mattress dipped under his weight as he climbed in beside me.

He pulled my nightgown up to my neck.

And then he laid on top of me.

The weight of him stole my breath. His skin was damp. His breathing heavy. His presence was massive, suffocating.

I didn't dare open my eyes.

My heart was pounding so loud I was sure he could hear it and feel it. And all I could think was, "If he knows I'm awake, he'll hurt me. If I scream, he'll kill me. If I run, he'll find Hunter. And he'll kill him too."

The fear wasn't just for me. It was for my brother—my other half—still curled up in the living room, unaware that the world had just turned upside down.

That fear swallowed me whole.

I stayed frozen. A statue made of flesh and panic. I don't know how long he stayed there. It felt like hours. Days. A lifetime.

Eventually, he got off me.

He pulled my nightgown back down, rolled over, and fell asleep—as if nothing had happened. As if I was nothing.

I lay there, paralyzed. Eyes wide open now, staring at the ceiling fan as it turned in slow, lazy circles. The room smelled like sweat and silence.

I didn't cry. Not yet. I was too afraid even for that.

I kept playing escape plans in my head. Each one ended the same way—with him catching me. Hurting me. Hurting Hunter.

So, I stayed.

Eventually, exhaustion dragged me under.

The next morning, I was still in his bed.

The sun came up like it always did. Stan made pancakes like he always did. He smiled, and joked, asking us if we wanted syrup.

I sat at the kitchen table, silent. Every bite turned to ash in my mouth. I wanted to scream. I wanted to run. I wanted to go home.

But I said nothing, because I didn't think anyone would believe me.

Not Hunter. Not my mom. Not even myself.

So, I did what so many children do.

I buried it. I shoved the memory into a corner of my brain and told it not to move. I told myself it was a dream, that it wasn't as bad as I thought, that maybe it hadn't even happened.

And Stan did the same.

He never spoke of it. Never looked at me differently. Never acknowledged what he had taken.

But my body remembered.

My body never forgot.

I positioned myself carefully—strategically—on the floor in front of Hunter. We were lying lengthwise in the living room, the same as the night before, but this time I made sure my body was between Stan and my brother. I thought if he tried to move me, he'd wake Hunter. And if Hunter woke up, Stan would stop. He'd be scared off. He wouldn't hurt me. My brother's presence would protect me.

I was seven years old, building a fortress out of hope and proximity. It was the only power I thought I had.

But when I woke up the next morning, I wasn't on the living room floor. I was in Stan's bed again.

And this time—there's nothing…no memory. No image. Just a heavy, suffocating blankness in my mind where something should be. It is as if someone ripped the page out of the story and left the jagged edges behind.

I've tried for years to recall it. To pull something from that void. But all I find is blackness. A silence that hums. A knowing without language.

My body remembers. And my heart remembers.

The tightness in my chest when I hear a certain tone of voice. The way I flinch at sudden movements. The way I shrink around men, even ones I trust. The instinct to stay small. To stay quiet. To please, to appease, to survive.

Over the years, that blank space has whispered things I didn't want to hear. It tells me that something happened.

Something worse.

Something I still don't have the strength—or safety—to fully remember.

And that uncertainty is its own kind of torture.

You question yourself. You doubt what you can't prove. You try to rationalize the fear away, to stitch logic over wounds that were never visible.

But the body doesn't lie.

I've asked myself the hard questions.

Did he…?

Could he have…?

I don't know.

And yet—I do.

Not in facts.

But in feeling.

In the way my throat closes around certain memories. In the nightmares that don't have images but still leave me breathless. In the way I once looked into the mirror and didn't see a little girl—I saw a body that had already been taken.

I was not spared.

I was not safe.

And even when no one saw it—even when I couldn't see it—I was surviving the unimaginable.

Sometimes, survival doesn't look like running.

Sometimes, it looks like stillness.

Silence.

Blank pages.

But even in that silence, I was fighting to live.

The only other memory I have from that time is hazy, but it sits heavy in my chest like a stone I've never been able to put down.

I was around eight years old.

It was one of those nights that should have blurred into the rest—quiet, forgettable, and uneventful. I was around eight. Stan had been dating a woman named Claire. She had two kids—a boy named Mike and a little girl named Becky, who was about seven. That night, Hunter and I were staying over at Stan's place. Claire and Stan went out to dinner, leaving us—four kids—alone in the house.

Just kids, alone, in a house that never felt safe.

We were all in the living room, curled up on the floor, with cartoons flickering on the screen. A bowl of dry cereal passed between us. Becky had been laughing earlier—full, easy giggles—chasing Hunter through the kitchen with a plastic sword. She wore a unicorn sweatshirt, her long braids bouncing behind her. For a moment, it felt like any other weekend night. Like maybe this time, things would just be normal.

But then the room shifted.

I don't remember the show that was playing or what time it was—only that suddenly, everything felt too still. I glanced over at Becky, expecting another silly face or a whisper—joke.

But she wasn't smiling.

She sat stiff, her knees pulled to her chest, her eyes trained on the carpet. When she looked up, the sparkle in her eyes was gone—replaced by something fragile. Frightened.

Her voice came out barely above a whisper. "He's been doing things to me." The words shattered the air like dropped glass. My lungs emptied before I even realized I'd stopped breathing.

Becky's eyes darted to mine—wide, pleading, and terrified. It wasn't just a confession. It was a lifeline. A desperate offering from one child to another. She was handing us the weight she could no longer carry, hoping we might know what to do with it.

I did. God, I did.

Because I knew that voice. I knew that kind of quiet.

It lived inside me too.

My hand found hers. I don't remember the exact words, just that we cried with her. We told her we were sorry. We held her in the only way we knew how—as kids who had no power, but too much understanding.

And yet…that was all we did.

I wanted to scream. To run outside, and to yell until someone—anyone—listened.

However, fear wrapped its hands around my throat, the way it always did. I was terrified. Terrified that if I spoke up, Stan would find out. And if he found out—he would hurt her. He would hurt me. He would hurt everyone I loved.

Hunter sat beside me, his expression blank. Then he shook his head slowly.

"I don't think that's true," he said.

His voice was distant, almost mechanical. Like he needed the lie to feel real. Like he couldn't let himself believe it—because if he did, everything else we had buried would crack wide open.

And something in me broke.

If Hunter—my twin, my anchor—couldn't believe her, how could he ever believe me? So, I said nothing.

Not about Becky. Not about what had happened to me. Not even that I believed her.

We didn't scream. We didn't run. And we didn't save her.

The cartoon kept playing. Someone poured more cereal. But the air was thick now. The innocence was gone. The silence had grown fangs.

I never saw Becky again.

She disappeared from our lives like a dream you wake up from too fast—smeared at the edges, slipping through memory.

But I think about her, all the time.

I wonder what it cost her to speak the truth that night. And I wonder if anyone ever listened to her.

If anyone came for her. If she's okay.

Because that night, in that house, when she reached out with everything she had left—we let her fall.

And I've carried that ever since.

Shortly after that night—the one that changed everything— Stan sold the house and disappeared.

No warning. No explanation. No goodbye.

It happened quietly.

No slammed doors. No packed bags. No dramatic goodbyes. Just…gone.

One day, Stan's car sat in the driveway like always—its hood still warm from errands we hadn't been invited to join. His boots were by the door. His toolbox in the garage. His coffee cup—half-drunk—still sitting on the counter.

And the next day, the car was gone. The boots. The tools. The cup. All of it.

It was as if the man himself had evaporated, leaving behind nothing but the scent of engine oil and old cologne.

No one explained. No one called a family meeting. No one said his name.

The adults moved around like shadows, their mouths tight, their voices clipped. The TV played louder. The lights stayed on longer. But no one said, *"He's not coming back."* And I didn't dare ask why.

So, I made up stories. Maybe it was my fault. Maybe he saw the way I looked at him—the fear I hadn't hidden well enough. Maybe he knew what I remembered.

Maybe he was punishing me.

Or maybe—just maybe—he was protecting himself.

The silence didn't bring comfort. It brought questions— and fear. The kind of fear that doesn't go away just because the monster is no longer in the room. Because monsters have a way of lingering. Even in their absence.

Especially in their absence.

I kept bracing for the sound of tires on gravel. For the jingle of keys. For the weight of his footsteps in the hall.

I waited for the punishment I was sure would come. For the smile that always came before the storm.

Even though he was gone, I was still terrified. Maybe more than ever.

Years passed. And still, I waited.

Then, sometime in my twenties, the truth came out quietly—like a secret passed through a crack in a wall.

Stan hadn't left on his own. He'd been *run* out.

He'd been told to go. Told never to come back.

I don't know who said it. I don't know what they saw or how they knew.

But someone had seen enough, heard enough, *or believed enough.*

And they did what none of us—none of the children— ever could.

They made him leave.

When I heard those words, something inside me stopped moving. A frozen part of me thawed, just a little. Because for so long, I had wondered if anyone saw us. If anyone *ever* would.

And someone had.

I don't know their name. I don't know their face. But I imagine her sometimes.

A neighbor.

A teacher.

A mother who saw the wrongness in his eyes and didn't look away.

I picture her standing on a front porch, with her spine straight, and voice steady.

"We know what you are," she says. "And you're not welcome here."

In that image, I find a kind of healing. A kind of hope. Because for so long, we were just children, clutching our stories in the dark—waiting, aching, for someone to turn on the light.

And maybe, finally…someone did.

3

A LIFE ON THE RUN

My mother was married and divorced six times over the course of her life.

With each new relationship came a new place, a new last name to remember, and a new chapter that promised stability but never delivered it. As a child, I didn't just grow up in chaos—I moved through it. Constantly. I never knew what it felt like to truly settle. We were always packing—and always leaving.

The first sign was always the suitcase.

Then the trash bags.

Then the promises.

"This one's going to be different," my mother would say, yanking open drawers and folding our lives into plastic. "This time, we'll have a yard." "This time, the school's better." "This time..."

I'd nod. Because that's what I'd learned to do.

By the time I was ten, I'd stopped counting how many cities we'd lived in. The welcome mats blurred. The wallpaper changed. But the pattern stayed the same—new man, new town, new last name to memorize. I moved

39

through childhood like a ghost in transit. Always arriving. Never staying.

We were never still long enough to belong to anything.

I didn't celebrate birthdays with classmates. I didn't hang posters in my room. I never unpacked all the way. My memories lived in cardboard boxes marked *Heidi's Room*, sealed with tape that barely held anymore.

At each new school, I learned the layout fast—bathrooms, exits, which lunch table to avoid. I kept my head down, and my voice soft. I smiled just enough to not seem weird, but not enough to be noticed.

The shoes never fit in. The accent didn't match. The hand-me-down jeans sagged at the knees. I became easy prey—an outsider before I even opened my mouth.

I learned to eat lunch with a book open, with my eyes fixed on the page so no one would see I was alone. I heard the snickers and saw the glances. I felt the burn of being laughed at as if it was branded on my skin. The girls rolled their eyes, and the boys whispered, just loud enough to hear.

I was sensitive. I still am. But back then, sensitivity was a liability.

So, I got smaller, quieter, and softer in all the ways that didn't look like strength. I said what they wanted me to say. I laughed when they laughed—even when it was at me. Especially when it was at me.

I learned how to be present without taking up space, how to survive by being the version of me that wouldn't get noticed…or hurt.

I never had a best friend for longer than a season. I never made it to the second slumber party. I never decorated a locker—because just as I started learning the names of the hallways, we were gone again.

And always, my mother chased the next chapter like it held salvation.

Another husband. Another apartment. Another blank slate.

I think she believed, deep down, that love could fix everything—that the *next one* would stay, that *this town* would feel like home.

But for me, every beginning was just another ending in disguise.

At night, I'd draw houses in the margins of my school notebooks—not just any houses—*mine*. It had two stories, and shutters. A porch light that always stayed on. A dog curled up by the front steps, never wondering if we'd come back.

I gave the street a name. I even made up a best friend who lived next door. Someone who always knocked before coming in. Someone who never moved away.

It was the only place that didn't disappear.

The only place that felt like mine.

I was nine the first time I saw Bob Smith standing in our kitchen.

He was tall and broad-shouldered, with a quiet presence that filled the room without demanding it. He wore a badge on his belt, grease under his fingernails, and carried himself like someone who knew how to fix things. He smiled at my mom as if she was the only person in the room.

That night, we had dinner at the table—all of us. Real food, not just cereal or drive-thru bags. Bob passed the mashed potatoes. My mom laughed. Hunter and I sat stiff in our chairs, unsure what to do with the sudden quiet that didn't come from fear.

It looked like something from a sitcom—siblings under one roof, a man who came home after work, the smell of dinner in the oven. Normal. *Almost.*

Bob had two sons of his own. We were a blended family in theory—two broken halves trying to look whole. My mother believed in the illusion. You could hear it in her voice, the way she said *we* instead of *me and the kids*. The way her shoulders dropped like she might finally have a partner.

Bob brought order with him. Routines. Bedtimes. Rules that didn't come with threats. He didn't yell. He didn't hit. He showed up. But I didn't see stability. I saw danger wearing a friendly face.

To me, he was just another man crossing the threshold. Another question mark with a key to the front door. And I had already learned what men with keys could do.

The first time he told me to do something, I spat it out like poison: "You're not my dad."

And I meant it.

I slammed doors. Rolled my eyes. Made silence into a weapon. I gave him weeks of cold stares and clipped answers. I wanted him to leave. I needed him to.

It wasn't rebellion.

It was armor.

I had learned that, if you trust someone, they vanish. If you soften, they strike. If you need them—they hurt you.

So, when Bob came with kindness and no agenda, when he offered presence without pressure, I didn't lean in. Instead, I recoiled.

One night, I hid around the corner and heard him talking to my mom. "I don't know what I'm doing wrong," he said. "I try. I really try. But she won't let me in."

He was right. I wouldn't.

Letting him in meant hope. And hope was a trap.

They were together off and on for over fifteen years—married, divorced, married again. Like love was a door that never learned how to close gently.

But Bob stayed longer than most. Even when I ignored him. Even when I threw up walls so high no one could see me behind them. Even when I made it clear with every gesture that I didn't want him there—he didn't leave.

Back then, I couldn't see the man trying to build something sturdy out of splinters. I only saw the threat of more splinters.

Now, I see it more clearly.

I see a man who showed up with hands open, not fists closed. A man who made dinners. Picked us up from school. Put gas in my mom's car. A man who tried—genuinely, consistently—even when I gave him every reason not to.

I don't know if I ever said thank you.

I don't know if he ever knew that I noticed. That I watched. That even as I pushed him away, some small voice inside me whispered, *Maybe this one is different.*

But I couldn't afford to believe that then.

So, I didn't.

Fifth grade found me in Cooper—another dusty dot on the map of my childhood. Another school, and another new last name scribbled on a fresh file folder. I had already grown used to the drill: show up, keep your head down, and try not to draw too much attention.

But something shifted that year.

Eric noticed me.

Eric was funny, golden-haired, magnetic. The kind of boy who made teachers smile and classmates lean in just to be near him. One day at recess, he slipped me a folded piece of notebook paper that said, "Will you go steady with me? Check yes or no." My heart raced. I checked yes.

We chased each other on the playground. Walked home on occasion. It wasn't serious—we were ten. But it felt like a beginning. Like maybe, for once, I wasn't the outsider.

Then Andy moved to town.

He was new, too. Sweet. A little shy. He liked me. When he asked if I'd go steady with him, I hesitated. I didn't want to hurt either of them. So, I told them both the truth: *I need time to think.* It was honest. Kind, even.

I thought kindness would count for something. But life doesn't always reward kindness.

A week later, the sun was scorching the pavement as if it wanted to sear footprints into the ground. Hunter and I walked barefoot to the community pool, hopping between patches of shade and hot cement. I remember the relief of cool water on sunburned shoulders, the sudden weightlessness as I dove under.

For a moment, I felt free.

Then they came.

A pack of girls from school—smiling as they swam toward me. Too many smiles. The kind that stretch just a little too wide. I smiled back, uncertain. Before I could speak, they lunged.

Hands grabbed my shoulders, pushed my head down.

Water surged into my nose. My arms flailed. Laughter echoed above the surface while my body thrashed beneath it.

When I finally came up, sputtering, choking, I gasped, "Stop! I can't breathe!"

One girl leaned in, close enough to smell the sunscreen on her skin. "You deserve to drown," she hissed. "Playing games with Eric and Andy."

My body froze. My lungs burned.

I was ten! Still playing with Barbies. Still asking my mom to braid my hair before school.

And yet, there I was—held underwater by girls who had decided I was dangerous. A problem. A threat.

Hunter got to me. I don't remember how. Just the grip of his hand, the urgency in his voice, the way I clung to him as we walked home. My hair was dripping. My swimsuit was clinging like a second skin made of shame. My sobs hiccupped out of me, loud at first, then smaller, and quieter, until I was just shaking.

He didn't say a word.

Neither did I.

The next day, it was over. Eric stopped talking to me. Andy pretended he'd never asked. Their faces—once warm—were now cold, and unreadable.

And I was left blinking at the sudden vacancy.

I hadn't lied. I hadn't played anyone. I had just needed time.

However, it didn't matter.

What mattered was that I'd been chosen—and then unchosen. Somehow, that made me guilty.

Something shifted in me that day. A tiny fracture deep in my core, too quiet to notice at the time, but growing steadily year after year. It whispered lies that would burrow in and take root.

Your voice causes trouble.

Your choices hurt people.

Love can turn on you. So, stay small. Stay agreeable. Stay wanted.

I didn't have the language for it back then.

I just knew I stopped raising my hand in class. I stopped telling the truth if I thought it might upset someone. I stopped trusting my gut.

Because that summer afternoon wasn't just about boys, recess games or poolside drama. It was the first time I learned that being chosen didn't mean being safe.

It was the first time I realized…girls like me could be drowned.

•　　•　　•

Sixth grade didn't just hurt me. It hollowed something out.

I walked into that year already unsure of who I was—too quiet, too eager, and too much of a question mark in a world that had already made up its mind. The halls felt colder, the lights brighter, and the silence sharper. And it didn't take long for the others to decide who I would be.

That girl.

The one who flirted with two boys. The one who thought she was special. The one no one would sit with.

It didn't matter that I was kind. It didn't matter that I told the truth.

The whispers followed me like shadows down the hallway. The stares stung more than slaps. And the laughter—cutting, loud, never mine—followed me into every classroom, every lunch period, and every bathroom stall where I tried to cry quietly enough not to be heard.

I stopped raising my hand, stopped speaking unless directly called on, and stopped making eye contact.

I memorized the safest corners of every room—the ones near windows, the ones farthest from the girls who sneered when I walked by. I held back tears until nightfall, when I could bury my face in a pillow and let it all pour out in silence.

Some mornings I woke up with my jaw clenched so tight, it ached until dinner. But I never told anyone. Not really. How do you explain that the place meant to shape your future is teaching you how to disappear?

The note landed on my desk like a dare.

A folded square of notebook paper, passed with too much ease from one hand to another. When I opened it and read the words—*"Come to my slumber party Friday?"*—my heart skipped. The handwriting was girly and neat. The names at the bottom belonged to girls who had spent the last year perfecting the art of tearing me apart one glance at a time.

Still, something inside me fluttered. A tiny, desperate hope. *Maybe they changed their minds. Maybe they want to be friends now. Maybe I could belong.*

That night, I packed with care. My favorite pajamas—clouds and rainbows, worn soft from so many washes. The popcorn balls my mom and I made together, still warm and sticky. Pink sponge rollers in my hair. My softest sleeping bag. I stood at the door like it was Christmas.

I wanted to believe. God, I wanted to believe.

Their smiles greeted me at the door—but they were the kind that didn't reach their eyes. We walked into the living room. I barely had time to unroll my sleeping bag before the first words hit.

"You're disgusting."

"You should never have been born."

No laughter. No punchline. Just silence. The kind that swells and warps the air around you.

I stood there frozen, the sleeping bag limp in my hands, my breath caught in my throat. My skin burned with humiliation, my cheeks hot with disbelief. I searched their faces for kindness, for regret—for anything human.

Nothing.

I reached for the phone with trembling hands, dialing home with fingers that couldn't stay still. My voice cracked when I finally said it: "Please come get me."

There was a pause. Then her voice—flat, distant.

"If you want to leave, you can walk."

It was nine p.m. Outside, the world was black and wide. I was ten. Alone, and terrified. But I walked.

No, I ran.

I ran into the night with shame slicing through me like wind. My pajamas clung to my skin. My heart hammered like it might crack my ribs open. Every sound made me jump. Every flicker of movement made me look back. But I kept going, because staying had become unthinkable.

I don't remember reaching the front door. Just the weight of my hand as it pushed it open, the wetness on my cheeks, and the quiet click as the door shut behind me.

I stood in the hallway—shaking, breathless—suddenly aware that something inside me had gone missing.

And I wasn't sure it would ever come back.

That year felt like walking through a storm with no umbrella—a constant downpour, with no shelter in sight. But then, one afternoon in spring, as I was walking past the main office, a flier fluttered on the window—*Seventh Grade Cheer Tryouts*.

I froze. My heart did a little flip.

I stared at it for a long time, chewing on the inside of my cheek. I could already hear the laughter if I failed, already feel the sting of whispers. But something inside me—a flicker, a spark—urged me forward.

That evening, I stood barefoot in the backyard, the grass damp and cool under my feet, chanting into the wind and practicing clumsy cartwheels under a sky that didn't care if I made the team or not. Each jump, and each shout felt like trying to shake the heaviness off my chest.

Tryout day, my stomach was a war zone. My hands trembled. But I smiled anyway. I shouted louder than I ever had. I nailed the routine—not perfectly, but with everything I had.

When the results were posted, my fingers shook as I traced the list. And there it was. My name.

I had made it.

I stood there, wide-eyed, feeling taller than I ever had.

For the first time in what felt like forever, I had *something*. A reason to stand proud. I was fitted for a uniform. I couldn't stop talking about it. I memorized every stitch of my name on the roster as if it were proof I existed.

For a moment, I was someone. For a moment, I was seen.

And then—two weeks before school started—Mom sat us down on the couch, her voice too calm, too practiced.

"We're moving to Montana." Just like that, it was gone.

The uniform.

The team.

The spark.

I didn't throw a tantrum. Didn't cry. I just folded my dreams into a cardboard box and packed, as I'd done a hundred times before.

But something grieved. Quietly. It felt like watching the only door out of a burning house slam shut.

That move didn't just pull us out of one place and into another—it shifted something between Hunter and me.

We had always been close in the way twins often are. When we were little, he could speak for me before I even opened my mouth. "She wants chocolate," he'd say with certainty. And he was always right.

When he broke his arm one day, I felt it. I didn't know where he was or what had happened, but a pain bloomed in my body like a siren. Hours later, he walked in with a cast, and I just nodded as if I'd known all along.

We didn't need words. We just *knew*.

But somewhere along the way, that unspoken thread began to fray. Maybe it was the instability. The noise. The chaos that kept chasing us from house to house, man to man, and goodbye to goodbye. Love started to feel like competition—for attention, for air, and for space.

And we fought.

We raced home after school just to lock each other out. Slap fights left red marks on our cheeks. Screams echoed through thin apartment walls, loud enough for the neighbors to complain. And they did. A lot.

But under the yelling, there was something else. Something wordless. A grief too heavy for kids to carry. We didn't have the tools to say we were scared. We didn't have the words to explain why everything felt like drowning.

So, we fought.

Because it was easier than admitting we were hurting. Easier than saying we felt forgotten. Easier than naming what we couldn't fix.

Still, even in the middle of slammed doors and ugly words, there were moments. Like the night I had a nightmare. I tiptoed into his room, barely whispering his name. And without even opening his eyes, he lifted the blanket and made room for me.

We didn't hate each other. We just didn't know how to *love* each other while we were both gasping for air.

The bond stretched. Thinned. But it didn't break. Because even then, he carried pieces of me. And I carried pieces of him.

That year hurt in every direction. But the worst part was that no one noticed.

Not the teachers who watched me grow smaller with each passing week. Not the girls who turned their backs with a glance. Not even my mom, lost in her own quiet storms. Not even Hunter—standing right beside me.

I was a soft, quiet, lonely girl—trying to carry more weight than any child should ever be asked to hold. I wanted someone to ask. To look a little closer. To stay. But no one did.

So, I stayed small. And I walked through the dark, alone.

•   •   •

It was during this chapter of my life that I first came to understand the bittersweet weight of love—and the aching, hollow silence of loss. And I learned it from two souls who never spoke a single word.

We had a dog and a cat back then. Their names have faded with time, like smudged ink on the edges of an old journal. But what they gave me—the way they loved me, held me, healed me—and it still echoes in the quiet places of my heart.

Our dog was just a puppy then, a black blur of energy and devotion. He adored us—Hunter and me—with a loyalty so fierce it felt holy. Every day after school, he'd be waiting at the front door before we even turned the corner, tail whipping back and forth like it might lift him off the ground. The moment he saw us, he exploded—spinning, barking, hopping on hind legs, losing his mind in the purest joy.

No one had ever been that happy to see me.

In a world that often felt cold and confusing, he was my warmth. He made things feel okay.

It happened on a warm afternoon. I was on the trampoline, chasing the sky, when I heard the high school across the street release its wave of students. Laughter floated through the air. A few of them saw our dog and called to him. Everyone knew him. Everyone loved him.

He bolted.

His ears flapped like wings. His legs stretched in full sprint. He looked so happy, like he was flying.

He never saw the car.

But I did.

There was a sound I'll never forget—a thud, a sickening crunch, then a sharp yelp that split something open inside me. The world slowed. My breath caught. My body moved before my mind could catch up—I leapt from the trampoline and ran.

He was crumpled on the pavement, his tiny chest rising, falling…then still.

I fell to my knees and pulled him into my arms. His fur was warm. His eyes were already dimming. I rocked him back and forth, sobbing, begging, whispering, "Stay, please stay. I love you. Don't go. Please."

He took his last breath in my arms.

I didn't want to let go. I couldn't. I held onto him as if love could be stronger than death. My mother had to carry us both inside—me clutching his body like a baby blanket, wailing in a voice I didn't know I had.

For weeks I cried. Everything reminded me of him—the leash by the door, the spot he used to curl up in, and the silence. I didn't understand how the world could keep moving when he was gone.

That was the first time I truly understood grief—not just the word, but the bone-deep emptiness that settles in your heart when someone you love disappears.

And then…one morning, a whisper of hope.

I woke to a quiet sound—soft *mews* at the foot of my bed. Still half-asleep, I crawled toward it, the covers heavy around me. There she was—our cat—curled into the blankets. She was a soft, affectionate orange tabby with eyes like honey and the gentlest soul I'd ever known. Her body curled protectively around four tiny, pink-nosed kittens. She had given birth while I slept.

She had chosen me.

Out of all the places in the house, she chose my bed. Me. My breath. My warmth. My presence.

When I looked into her eyes, she didn't look away. There was a silent understanding in her gaze, something ancient and kind. I felt it in my chest—the quiet magic of being trusted. Of being needed.

In the middle of heartbreak, she brought life.

I didn't know how to name it then, but I know now: that

was grace. That was love showing up again—not loud, not with fireworks—but quietly. Soft paws and slow blinks. Tiny lives that fit in the palm of my hand.

She gave me something to hold on to.

She gave me hope.

The summer of 1981 brought with it a new beginning—one I didn't know would both lift me and break me in the same breath. My stepdad, Bob, my mom, Hunter, and I packed our lives into boxes and drove off to Freemont, Montana—a town so small you could blink and miss it on the highway. One grocery store. One bar. A post office. A library. That was it.

I was nervous that first day of school, stomach tight with hope and fear. All I wanted—more than anything—was to be liked. To be seen. I remember walking into my first class, the whisper of my footsteps on the linoleum, and eyes turning to me like spotlights. I forced a smile, sat down, and turned to the girl in front of me.

"Hi, I'm Heidi. Nice to meet you," I said, stretching out my hand.

She shook it—and from then on, we were best friends.

Just like that, something clicked. And for the first time in a long time, I felt like I could just be.

I didn't know exactly who I was yet, but in Freemont, I didn't feel the need to hide. I could be quirky, bright, awkward—even weird—and no one laughed. I wasn't invisible or torn apart by sideways glances. I had friends who liked me for me. Teachers who believed in me. I fell in love for the first time. I had my first kiss under a Montana sky.

I felt seen. I felt safe.

I felt...home.

•   •   •

The snow crunched beneath our boots, and our breath came out in puffs of white as we gathered outside Mrs. Jones' porch. Our cheeks were flushed pink from the cold, voices shaky from giggles and nerves as we huddled close to sing.

"Silent night…holy night…"

When we finished, the porch light flicked on, and there she was—Mrs. Jones—her silver curls tucked beneath a knitted cap, eyes glassy with emotion. She pressed something into my mittened hand. I opened it slowly. A crisp fifty-dollar bill stared back at me.

Fifty dollars.

More money than any of us had ever held.

We squealed. Spun in circles. Giddy with the thought of what we could buy. However, as we stood there, still and breathless in the glow of her porch light, something shifted. The joy fluttered, then fell flat. A silence settled between us—not awkward but knowing.

Christmas wasn't about getting. It was about giving.

Back at my house, we huddled at the kitchen table, smoothing out a piece of notebook paper. One of us scrawled *Merry Christmas* across it in red pen. I folded the bill into the note, tucked it in the envelope we'd used for lyrics, and later that night, tiptoed back to her house to slip it into her mailbox.

That was the kind of town Freemont was.

It made you want to be better.

And I was better there.

But Freemont would also be the place where I learned the most devastating truth of all—that my mother wasn't who I thought she was. That the pedestal I'd placed her on had cracks I hadn't seen. And it would come crashing down.

I was eleven, maybe twelve.

My hair was my everything—long, soft waves of brownish blonde that spilled past my waist. When people complimented it, I stood a little taller. Their words made me feel real. I felt seen, and beautiful.

One Saturday morning, sunlight poured through the trailer windows in golden stripes. Mom sipped her coffee and glanced at me.

"We're going to get it trimmed today," she said casually.

Just a trim. I nodded, trusting her completely.

At the salon, she leaned in and whispered something to the stylist. I didn't think twice. I sat in the chair, swinging my feet, watching dust motes dance in the air.

Then the mirror turned away.

Snip.

My heart stuttered.

Snip. Snip.

Long strands of my identity slid to the floor in slow-motion feathers.

Panic bloomed in my chest. I couldn't breathe.

"Mom?" I whispered, my voice trembling.

She didn't look at me. "Calm down. It'll be fine. You look great."

When the chair finally spun around, I blinked at the stranger in the mirror.

My hair was gone.

I looked like my twin brother. I looked like a boy. I looked like someone I didn't recognize.

My throat closed up. Hot tears blurred my vision. I sobbed—loud, messy, heart-shattering sobs that filled the room.

Mom's expression twisted. Embarrassment. Disapproval. "Be quiet," she hissed. "You're making a scene."

"Why?" I choked out. "Why did you do this?"

She rolled her eyes, her voice sharp and flat. "Because I'm tired of dealing with it. The knots. The tangles. I'm done."

Not love. Not care. Just…convenience.

In one hour, she cut away the one thing that made me feel beautiful. The one thing that made me *me*. For weeks, I didn't leave the house. I couldn't. I imagined the look on my friends' faces—their laughter, the whispers, and the pity. I felt erased, stripped down to nothing. A version of myself I didn't choose.

It took a year for the girl in the mirror to start feeling like me again. It only happened once my hair began to grow back. Just as those fragile pieces of me began to settle back into place, a little light broke through.

Her name was Isabelle.

That summer, she arrived on our doorstep with a squeal and a diaper bag. She was two years old. Tiny curls stuck to her forehead like little question marks. Glitter clung to her cheeks. Joy clung to her laugh.

Misty had her young—nineteen and already worn down by life. Her marriage was falling apart. Money was tight. She asked Mom to step in for a while, and just like that, Isabelle came to live with us.

She saved me.

She called me "Dee-Dee," her voice soft and giggly, and every time she said it, I melted a little more. She climbed into my lap as if it was her throne. She draped spaghetti-covered fingers across my arms and traced invisible shapes on my skin when she was tired. She followed me every-where. A shadow made of sweetness and need.

I dressed her, fed her, and carried her on my hip as if she was an extension of my own body. She looked at me like I was her world.

And somewhere along the way…she became mine.

For the first time in what felt like forever, I felt whole.

But summer never stays.

When Misty came to take her home, Isabelle wrapped her arms around my neck and wouldn't let go. Her tiny fingers clutched my shirt as if they could hold off goodbye. I forced a smile. I kissed her forehead.

When the car pulled away, I sat on the porch steps and sobbed into my hands.

She hadn't just been my niece. She had been my anchor. Now, I was drifting again.

Not long after, my mother tried to cheer me up. It was a grey afternoon, the kind that stretches long and quiet. She drove me to the edge of town, to a hill I'd never noticed before.

"There it is," she said, nodding toward the horizon.

And there it was—a house that looked like a dream. Three stories. A wraparound porch. Tall windows that watched like eyes. It sat high above the world, wrapped in a mist that made it seem magical.

"Bob's looking into buying the cement factory," she said, eyes twinkling. "We're thinking about this house."

My breath caught. My heart lifted. I saw it all: birthday parties on that porch. Sleepovers. A window seat just for reading. A room of my own with space for my dreams.

That night, I couldn't sleep. I told everyone at school. I held the dream like a lantern in the dark. However, dreams in my world always had timers.

Two weeks later, she sat me down, her voice low and dull. "We're moving back to Julesburg."

Just like that, it was over.

No castle. No cement factory. No Fremont. No home.

I sobbed so hard I thought my ribs would crack. I didn't just lose a house—I lost a life. A beginning. A place where I had started to believe in goodness again.

Everything I loved kept slipping through my fingers.

And I started to wonder if maybe…I was never meant to hold on to anything at all.

•   •   •

The car slowed to a stop, the tires crunching over gravel like a sigh of surrender. I don't remember the exact day we arrived—but I remember how it felt.

Like being dragged backward through mud.

Like slipping into skin I'd already tried to shed.

The air in Julesburg smelled different—dry, metallic, and laced with something older, something forgotten. The kind of cold that seeps into your bones, as if even the wind had learned how to whisper disappointment.

I stood in the doorway of our new home, clutching a box that suddenly felt too heavy. Something inside me shifted that day. A quiet kind of despair settled in like dust on windowsills no one bothered to clean.

Hunter didn't say much. He just paced more and looked out windows as if he was searching for something. Or maybe someone. A few weeks later, his room was empty. He'd packed his things and left for Texas to live with our father, Stan.

I stayed behind—alone with the echoes of the girl I used to be, trying to remember how to keep moving forward when everything inside me wanted to disappear.

His silence left a hole, but life didn't pause for mine.

The next Monday, I was back in school. The same chipped lockers. The same bathroom stalls etched with gossip and cruelty. And the same hallways filled with whispers that stung like static under my skin.

Each morning, I stood in front of the mirror, trying to gather myself like armor. However, my chest always ached. My eyes gave me away.

Time didn't move back then—it trudged. One dragging footstep at a time.

I wasn't living.

I was surviving.

4

A FAMILY I NEVER KNEW

Years later on a balmy summer evening, the air hung heavy with the scent of jasmine drifting through my open window. I was sprawled across my bed, the soft hum of the fan circling above me as "We Built This City" by Starship poured from my boombox. The world felt simple for a moment—just music, summer air, and the faint hum of streetlights outside. And then—like a loose thread tugged at the hem of truth—a quiet revelation unraveled everything I thought I knew.

The phone rang. It was my twin brother. His voice carried that usual easy calm, but his words shattered the stillness around me. "You know," he said, almost casually, "we have other siblings."

For a split second, I couldn't breathe. A chill rushed over my skin, goosebumps rising like tiny whispers of truth. My heart began to race, each beat echoing with a thousand questions. Other siblings? In that moment, I knew—without hesitation—I had to meet them.

I had siblings.

Not just Hunter. Not just the familiar bond of growing up side-by-side.

There were others.

An older half-brother. A half-sister. A stepmother. Two stepsisters. Even a baby half-sister. A whole hidden family I had never known existed.

The news hit like a cold wave—sudden, breathless. But tucked inside that tidal surge of shock was something else. Something warm. A tiny ember.

Hope.

For the first time in what felt like forever, I didn't feel so alone. Maybe somewhere out there, someone else shared my eyes. My blood. My ache. I started to wonder—did they know about me? Had they ever imagined me, the way I now imagined them?

I clung to the idea like a lifeline. I had to meet them— even if it meant stepping into the shadow of the man who had once shattered me.

The summer of 1984, I asked my mom if I could visit Texas. I was fourteen. The night before the trip, I barely slept—too many what-ifs were crowding the corners of my mind.

The plane touched down in Galveston, and my heart pounded like a fist against my ribs. At the gate stood a tall boy with warm eyes and an easy, lopsided grin.

Stan Jr.

Our eyes met—and something inside me settled.

He didn't feel like a stranger. There were no awkward pauses. No need to explain who we were to each other.

We laughed. We *clicked*.

I hadn't known something was missing until I found it in him.

And then…he appeared.

Stan.

My father.

One glance and my stomach dropped. My legs turned to water. Every cell in my body screamed, *run.*

But I didn't.

I stepped forward. I hugged him. Because I thought I was supposed to.

His arms around me were stiff—foreign. Like hugging cardboard. His cologne stung my nose, masking something sour underneath.

He looked like a father in the shape of a stranger. Like someone trying to play a role he hadn't earned.

Fear twisted in my gut. But tangled up in it—curiosity. A tender ache I couldn't shake. I still wanted to believe maybe…just maybe…this visit could offer something worth holding on to.

Not from him.

From *them*.

Later that morning, we pulled into a driveway lined with cracked cement and tall grass. This was where Izzy lived—my half-sister. Fourteen, just like me. I had rehearsed what I might say. How I'd smile. Whether she'd hug me back.

But she never came to the door. I stood there—heart pounding, palms sweating—waiting for it to open. It didn't.

The porch light clicked on, then off again. I stared at that door like it might blink.

It never did.

She wouldn't meet me. She wouldn't even look at me. I wasn't the one who betrayed her mother. I wasn't the one who disappeared. But still, I carried the weight.

I've never met her—not even once. We remain strangers, tethered only by blood and the wreckage left behind by our parents' choices.

That summer felt like unwrapping a gift with shaking hands—wonder inside, yes—but also, shards. Pain. Absence. Realization. I had found pieces of myself I never knew were missing. But some pieces…I'd never get to hold.

The sun was just beginning to dip as the car pulled up to

a modest house with chipping white paint and a tiny front driveway. I clutched my bag tighter.

This was it. The moment I'd meet the rest of them. The door creaked open. There it was—taped to the wall in big, bold letters drawn in marker and love:

Welcome Home, Heidi.

I froze. Warmth surged through me so fast it made my throat ache. They made That…for *me.*

Stacy pulled me into a hug that felt like sunlight. Solid. Steady. Real. I liked her instantly. Behind her, wide-eyed and bouncing, were three girls—Sharon, Suzi, and baby Stephanie. They ran toward me with open arms, giggles tumbling from their mouths.

We became a pile of tangled limbs and laughter on the living room rug.

I didn't care about titles. "Half." "Step." None of that mattered.

They were *mine.* My sisters.

When Hunter arrived and wrapped me in a hug too, something clicked into place.

For one perfect moment, I wasn't just visiting.

I *belonged.*

Summer shimmered with light and noise—sandy toes, shrieking laughter, and dance parties in pajamas. We were alive. I let joy in. Until the day it fractured.

Stan and Stacy were at work. Hunter and I were babysitting. Morning passed in a blur of cereal, cartoons, and couch forts.

Then we started arguing.

I don't remember why. I just remember stomping out the front door and slamming it behind me. The minutes passed.

Then I heard the screen door creak behind me. I turned around—and froze.

A gun. Pointed at my face.

Time stopped.

Hunter's eyes locked onto mine. And I saw it—something fractured. Dangerous. Real. He wasn't joking.

I closed my eyes. *God*, I whispered silently, *if this is it, I'm ready*.

Silence.

Then…the click of the safety. The lowering of metal. He turned around. Walked inside.

I collapsed onto the porch, my knees buckling beneath me, sobs ripping from my chest. Minutes later, he returned. His face was pale, and he had open arms.

"I'm sorry," he whispered, again and again.

That night, I told Stan what had happened.

I didn't know the cost of my truth.

Years later, I learned Stan had beaten Hunter for it. And suddenly…everything made sense.

The distance. The outbursts. The silence.

Hunter had been carrying his own kind of pain all along—hidden bruises and invisible wounds. While I was burying shame, he was burying fear.

And when I found out—I wept. Not soft tears, but shaking, bone-deep sobs that felt like they'd never end. After that day, something shifted.

The house didn't feel the same. Not in any obvious way—just a lingering discomfort, like a draft you can't find the source of. It began with the kitchen junk drawer. I'd been digging through it, looking for a pen, when my fingers brushed across glossy paper.

Photographs.

The girls—my sisters—smiling, posing.

Too posed.

The tilt of their chins. The way their arms draped just so. The forced softness in their eyes. My stomach twisted before my mind could explain why. They weren't nude. But they weren't right.

One afternoon, when Stacy was at work, my father picked up his camera.

"Let's do a photo shoot," he said, with a syrupy smile. "I want to capture your essence. You girls are just so beautiful." At first, it sounded sweet. Almost fatherly.

But then came the directions.

"Stand like this."

"Hands on your hips."

"Lie across the couch."

"Turn your head."

"Dance for me."

His voice was smooth—too smooth. Every syllable landed like a fingerprint on my skin. I nodded. I moved. I danced.

But inside, everything screamed.

My arms swayed, my feet followed the rhythm, but my smile was a mask—tight, trembling, and wrong. I didn't know how to say no. I wasn't even sure if I was allowed.

He always wanted one of the girls on his lap. His hand moved up and down their backs, slow and deliberate. They sat too still. The room was too quiet.

Something heavy clung in the air, like the truth itself was holding its breath. And then…it stirred.

That buried part of me I had long tried to forget.

The same unease that had lived in my small body at five or six.

The same tightness in my chest.

The same silent rule: go still, go quiet, don't draw attention.

I had come to Texas searching for family.

And in that moment, something shattered again.

The house in Galveston stood tall, lifted on stilts like most homes near the coast. From the outside, it looked like any other—weather-worn, sun-bleached, and ordinary.

But beneath it…was something else.

Where other families might keep beach chairs or bicycles, ours had an enclosed lower level. No latticework. No airflow. No signs of life. I wandered down once, under the excuse of laundry. The fluorescent bulb flickered as I passed through the washroom, its hum growing louder the deeper I went.

Then—I saw it. A narrow door. Slightly ajar. Behind it: a single room.

No windows. No shelves. No color.

Just a mattress on the floor.

No sheets. No blanket. No pillow.

Just that mattress.

The silence in that room buzzed.

I didn't need to touch anything to feel the wrongness of it. I didn't need proof. My body already knew. Even at fourteen, I knew.

That room wasn't for sleeping. That room was *wrong*.

I had come here craving connection. Craving the pieces of myself I'd never known. And for a while, I thought I'd found them—laughter in the living room, sisterhood on the porch, bedtime stories that felt warm and real. But under that warmth, there was shadow.

And I couldn't unsee it.

I couldn't unknow it.

When summer ended, I sat at the airplane window, cheek pressed to the cool glass. The clouds below blurred like tears I refused to let fall. I should've been excited to go home. But grief sat on my chest like a stone.

I was leaving behind my sisters—Sharon, Suzi, baby Stephanie. And Stacy's steady warmth. The laughter, the dancing, and the light.

I didn't want to go. But I couldn't stay.

Not with *him* there.

I had no evidence. No scars to point to. No words strong enough to pierce through adult denial. All I had was a knowing, something in my bones.

In the way my breath caught remembering his voice behind the lens.

The cold mattress in the room below.

The predatory way he watched the girls.

And worse—the terror that he was *hurting them*, too.

I wanted to scream. To break down doors. To yank them into safety with my bare hands. But I was just a girl. I was fourteen, scared, and small.

So, I stayed silent. And I left.

The goodbye I gave was quiet. Polite. A wave. A hug.

But inside, I was shattering.

I had to let go of them—my sisters, my stepmother, and the fragile slice of family I had longed for my whole life. I carried that ache home like a secret. A wound with no language. A grief no one could see. Because loving someone and having to walk away is a kind of heartbreak that stays lodged inside you. It settles deep—in your spine, your breath, your bones.

It waits.

Back in Colorado, I unpacked my suitcase, folded my clothes, and folded the truth right along with them.

I didn't tell anyone.

I didn't know how.

So, I swallowed it. Pressed it down. Tried to walk forward as if nothing had happened.

But silence doesn't stay still.

It grows heavier when no one's listening.

5

DROWNING IN SILENCE

The first day of high school in 1984 felt like stepping onto a minefield.

I clutched my backpack straps with white knuckles, breath shallow as I crossed the threshold. The walls were the same color. The lockers still groaned when slammed. But I had prayed: *God, please, just let this be different. Please don't let me be invisible again.*

But Julesburg hadn't changed. The whispers came fast, biting at my heels like snapping dogs. "Look who's back."

Their laughter followed me through the hallways— sharp, cruel, echoing off the linoleum floors. I became what they needed me to be. I nodded too quickly. Laughed too loud. Said yes when I wanted to say no. I was a puppet trying to guess the next move that might earn a sliver of approval.

Every afternoon, I came home in tears. I'd close the door to my room and collapse onto my bed, muffling sobs into my pillow. Each day, the weight on my chest pressed heavier.

One afternoon, after a particularly brutal walk home filled with taunts and shoulder checks, I stormed into my room, trembling, with my cheeks streaked with tears. The door creaked open behind me. My mom stepped in.

Arms crossed. Expression unreadable. She didn't ask if I was okay. She didn't reach for me. Instead, her voice dropped like a stone. "What did you do this time?"

The air left my lungs. I stared at her, stunned, words trapped in my throat. *What did* I *do?* I wanted to scream, *I was just born!* However, I swallowed it—like all the other times.

That moment carved something deep inside me. I couldn't trust her. Not with my pain. Not with my truth, and not even with my tears.

Volleyball. Long bike rides. And Blake.

Those were my lifelines.

Blake had the kind of smile that softened the noise. He'd show up early at my door just to say, "I love you," with his voice warm as flannel. He made me feel like the world wasn't always cruel. Like maybe I mattered.

We never had sex. We didn't need to. We were soft with each other. Safe.

And then Chandler Jenkins looked at me.

Senior. Quarterback. Golden-boy glow and cologne-soaked arrogance. When he smiled my way, something inside me sparked. Hope? Longing? Desperation?

Suddenly, I wasn't invisible.

Blake was my comfort, but Chandler was a ticket. A passport into the world I thought I wanted. I told myself it was what I had to do. I chose Chandler.

Blake's face crumpled when I told him. His eyes—once so steady—dimmed right in front of me. I pretended it didn't matter.

But it did.

A week later, a senior girl with frosted lips cornered me in the hallway. "Hey, Heidi," she sneered. "You might wanna check the senior lounge."

My heart thudded as I skipped class and made my way there. On the table, carved in pencil: *"Heidi Lincoln gave Blake Hopkins head!"*

The words blurred.

My knees buckled.

I scrubbed at the table until my hands burned, erasing and erasing, as if I could rub my shame out of existence. But it clung to me—hot, pulsing, and acidic. My face flamed. My ears roared. My stomach turned inside out.

I felt humiliated. Betrayed. Exposed.

And worst of all—I believed I deserved it.

Shame seeped into my bones. It told me to shrink. To shut up. To say thank you when someone noticed—even if it hurt.

So, when Chandler called again?

I answered.

He pulled me in, deeper and deeper, with honeyed words and hard hands.

"I want you," he whispered. "If we do this…you'll be mine."

I wasn't ready. I told him so. But his voice curled around my fears like smoke, slipping through the cracks of my self-worth. He promised love. He promised belonging.

So, on a cold, snowy night, I climbed into his bed.

It was quick. Clinical. Over before my heart caught up.

There was no affection. No magic. No whispered promises or lingering touch. Just the weight of him on top of me, the sound of my heart pounding in my ears, and the soft crack of something breaking inside me. No softness. No tenderness.

Afterward, I lay still, pulling the blanket over my chest like armor. My eyes traced the ceiling, trying to make sense of what had just happened. I had crossed into some invisible adulthood, but it didn't feel sacred. It felt hollow. It felt lonely.

I waited for something. A touch. A smile. A single word.

But silence took up all the space between us.

I closed my eyes and wished—*Maybe now I'll matter. Maybe now I'll be chosen.*

But even then, I knew.

This wasn't love. It was desperation wrapped in hope. It was me giving away pieces of myself, chasing the illusion of being wanted.

Days passed. Then weeks.

When he finally called, my heart jumped. Maybe he was ready. Maybe it meant something. He asked to meet at his dad's office.

I arrived, heart pounding.

He didn't say hello. Just looked at me and said:

"Take off your clothes."

I did.

We had sex again.

Afterward, he looked at me with eyes like stone. "You're not my girlfriend," he said. "I don't want to see you anymore. You're an embarrassment."

His words sliced through me like broken glass. I felt sick. Used. Dirty. I got dressed in silence, trembling, and walked out the door with my dignity shredded and nothing but shame clinging to my skin.

By Monday, everyone knew. The whispers were louder. The smirks sharper. *He took her virginity.* I became the joke, the punchline, the hallway echo. I walked with my head down, eyes blurred, breath caught in my throat.

And then came Abe Carter.

My "friends" said he liked me. That he told them so.

I wanted to believe it. Needed to.

So, when he said yes to the Sadie Hawkins dance—a tradition where the girl asks the boy—I floated. I bought matching shirts—red and blue stripes. The clerk let me borrow one to show him. When I held it up and he smiled, I felt a flicker of something I hadn't felt in weeks.

Hope.

On the night of the dance, I curled my hair. I applied my makeup slowly, carefully. I wore my favorite jeans and Adidas sneakers. I looked in the mirror and almost recognized the girl staring back.

At Abe's house, the lights were off. I rang the bell. Nothing. Knocked. Walked around back. Still nothing.

Confused, I drove home and called him.

"I don't like you," he said flatly. "I never planned on going."

The world tilted. My cheeks burned. Tears blurred the road as I drove to my mom's work, headlights smearing across my vision.

She hugged me. Told me I'd feel better in the morning.

But I didn't.

That Monday, taped to my locker was a message: *"Dances are not for LOSERS."*

The message was clear. They never liked me. I was alone.

After Chandler. After Abe. After the sign on my locker, something inside me snapped. I stopped trying to protect myself. I started offering up my body like currency. If they wanted attention, I gave it. If they wanted more, I said yes.

I thought if I gave enough, someone might finally stay.

But with every "yes," I lost a little more of myself.

I became a shell, dressing up my pain as confidence. Mistaking validation for love. Mistaking desire for worth.

I didn't want to be invisible anymore. I didn't want to feel *anything*. So, I kept giving myself away—piece by piece, kiss by kiss—hoping someone would see through the mask and choose me. But love built on fear fades fast.

And I was fading right along with it.

•　　•　　•

The announcement came just as the school year ended, tossed out as if it meant nothing. "We're moving."

The words landed with a dull thud in my chest—familiar, predictable, and still somehow crushing.

This time it was Davis, California. Another new town. Another "fresh start." But those resets no longer felt like hope. They felt like survival—like pressing restart on a game I never asked to play, one I was always losing.

The summer of 1986 greeted us with sun-scorched sidewalks and the sharp smell of asphalt baking in the heat. My mom had taken a job managing an apartment complex on the edge of town. Bob was still trucking—gone more than he was home.

Boxes were unpacked, drawers filled, and routines forced into place. But none of it felt new. Just another version of the same old story.

I wandered around like a ghost those first days. My body was in California, but pieces of me were still scattered in every town we'd left behind—fragments left in locker rooms, on front porches, and with broken friendships.

I didn't trust easily. Not anymore. My smile was tight. My heart braced. I kept myself small and hard, like a stone tucked deep in a pocket.

And then—I saw her.

Samantha.

Sam.

She was lounging on a sun-bleached pool chair as if she owned the sky, with her legs stretched out, Walkman headphones wrapped around her curls, and sunglasses low on her nose. She looked like freedom.

She lived just a few doors down with her older brother. She had just graduated. She worked at a trendy retail store in town. She wore confidence like perfume.

To me, she was magic.

She saw me watching from across the courtyard and waved. Just like that, she let me in.

Sam took me under her wing without asking why I needed shelter. She taught me how to tease my hair just right, how to walk into a room like I belonged there, how to flirt without folding. But more than that—she saw beneath my armor. She looked straight through my layers of defense and didn't flinch.

She didn't judge the cracks. She loved me right through them.

Our days blurred into late mornings and lazy afternoons, stretched out by the pool, legs draped over lounge chairs, wet towels drying in the sun. We whispered dreams into the summer breeze—boys, music, and the lives we swore we'd one day live.

Laughter curled between us like smoke. We told secrets with ease, our voices soft and safe. And somewhere in all that light, I began to loosen up.

To believe that maybe—just maybe—I wasn't broken beyond repair.

That summer, for the first time in years, I didn't wake up dreading the day. The air felt sweeter. The sun felt warmer. Even my reflection looked different—like someone worth loving might be hiding behind my eyes.

But in my world, happiness could never last.

One afternoon, when the sky was too blue to hold bad news, Sam dropped it casually. "We're moving."

My heart plummeted.

I begged her not to go. Begged like a child—like someone drowning, and reaching for the last hand that ever felt like safety.

We stood in the parking lot on her last day, with arms wrapped tight, and silence stretching between us. I pressed my face into her shoulder, breathing in the soft scent of her shampoo, the warmth of her skin against mine. I tried to memorize it—her, this, *everything*.

And then…she was gone.

The taillights of her car blinked once, then disappeared into the blur of summer heat.

The complex felt quieter after that. Every corner echoed. The pool shimmered but felt colder. I still laid in our usual spots, but it was never the same. Alone again—but holding onto the memory like a shell I could still crawl inside.

That summer had kissed me in a way no one else had. The light wrapped around me like a soft blanket and whispered, *you're allowed to feel good.* For a little while, I sparkled.

Even *I* believed it.

But when the first bell of junior year rang, I didn't sparkle anymore.

I had already begun to shut down.

I moved through the halls of Davis High like a ghost—feet hitting the same linoleum tiles as everyone else, but somehow never leaving a mark. I didn't try out for sports. I didn't join clubs. No one called my name in the crowd. I just floated, hollow and unnoticed, like I was waiting for something—anything—to either break me or save me. I didn't care which.

The loneliness wasn't loud. It was quiet, and heavy—a slow erosion. I could feel it gnawing at the edges of me. I was untethered, bruised in places no one could see.

And then came Carol. She didn't walk. She crashed through the world as if it owed her something. Black leather skirts that clung to rebellion, jangling earrings that danced with every turn of her head, a nose ring that glittered like defiance, and a purple mohawk that dared anyone to question her. She didn't whisper through the halls—she roared. Carol didn't apologize and didn't explain. She existed loudly, and I couldn't look away.

Her name came with rumors. Drugs. Boys. Trouble. But when she stopped in front of me—me, the invisible girl—and said, "Wanna hang out after school?" something inside me cracked open.

I didn't say yes because I trusted her. I said yes because I was starving, for attention, for connection, and for someone to look at me and not look through me. I wanted to be seen. Just once.

I lied to my mom. I told her I had a library study session. Instead, I slipped out the side doors and found Carol waiting near the curb. A beat-up van idled nearby, music pounding through rusted speakers. Two older guys leaned against it, beers already in hand.

We climbed in, the windows down, the wind wild in our hair. Gasoline, cigarette smoke, and something sharp—danger, maybe—filled my nose. Laughter bounced off the metal walls of the van as we sped down roads I didn't recognize.

We ended up near a run-down barn, half-swallowed by weeds and time. The guys cracked open beers like they were sodas, tossing them to us like party favors. I drank. Not one. Not two. Five. Maybe six. My limbs grew syrupy. The world tilted.

Then came the joint.

I didn't touch it. I didn't need to. The van filled with smoke so thick it clung to my skin like fog. I felt it seeping in—through my clothes, my pores, my bones. The laughter got louder. Then quieter. Then distant.

And then—nothing.

Memory fractured after that. What came next lived in blurs and half-thoughts. Later, I was told I'd made out with one of the guys. Sloppy. Messy. He left a mark—so dark and strange it looked like a bruised map of some faraway country. Russia, maybe. On my neck. Real classy.

I must've stumbled into the apartment like a wrecking ball. Knocked over a lamp. Mumbled nonsense. Blacked out on the couch or maybe the floor. I wouldn't remember any of it.

But my mother would.

Morning light sliced through the blinds like judgment. My skull pulsed with every heartbeat. My mouth felt like cotton. Then—her voice. Sharp. Cold. "Get up! Now!"

I cracked one eye open. I groaned. "Why are you so mad at me?"

She stormed into my room, fury radiating off her like heat. "You came home reeking of booze and pot!" she spat. "I had a friend over—you made a complete fool out of me."

Her words hit like slaps. I sat up too fast. The room span.

"I didn't smoke," I murmured. "I just drank a little…" She didn't let me finish.

"They're not your friends," she said. Her voice was flat. Final. A gavel dropping.

Something inside me shifted—quiet and irreversible. The door between us didn't slam shut. It just…clicked. And I knew I wouldn't be able to open it again.

She didn't believe me. Didn't trust me. Maybe never had. But now, I could feel it in my bones: she was done. Still, she made me go to school that day.

So, I went. A scarf knotted tight around my neck, trying to hide the evidence of the night I couldn't remember. The shame sat thick in my stomach, heavier than the hangover. I didn't feel sick. I felt worthless.

Because somewhere deep down, I knew I hadn't just messed up.

I had lost her. Her respect. Maybe even her love.

She never forgave me for that night.

And from that day on…she stopped trying.

Not the shouting. Not the smell of beer or smoke. Not even the hickey.

What broke me was the silence that came after.

•   •   •

By the time the school year ended, we had packed up again—boxes taped shut, trash bags stuffed with clothes, and another unfamiliar address scratched on a sticky note. This time, Sacramento.

Another apartment. Another city. Another high school. Another shot at pretending I was okay.

My mom had taken a new job managing a different complex. She slipped into her routine like she always did—filling out paperwork, yelling at maintenance guys, walking units—and I was left, once again, to figure out how to exist in a place that didn't feel like mine.

The high school I was zoned for sat just a few blocks away. From the outside, it looked like any other campus—but inside, I would've been one of only two white students. I wish I could say I approached it with openness, with the kind of curiosity that bridges differences—but I didn't. I was sixteen. I was scared and insecure. I hadn't grown up around much diversity, and I didn't know how to belong anywhere—especially there.

So, I did something bold. Something desperate.

I went to the district office—alone. I sat in a plastic chair with sticky armrests, filling out a transfer request form with sweaty hands and a pounding heart. I didn't even know if they'd say yes. But they did.

The new school was across the city, in a completely different zip code. I thought getting approved would be the hard part.

Then I asked my mom if she'd drive me. Or let me borrow the car. She didn't even look up. "No," she said. "If you want to go to school across the city, you're on your own." Then, as if she were commenting on the weather, she added, "You'll also need to start buying your own groceries. And if you want to do anything—clubs, sports, friends—that's on you too."

Just like that, love became conditional. Affection came with invoices. And I learned, without anyone even saying it, that needing too much made you a burden.

So, I did what I had to do. I got a job. Because survival doesn't care if you're sixteen. And apparently, neither did she.

I found a telemarketing gig—cold-calling strangers, pitching time-shares I'd never seen, reading from a script in a cheerier voice than I felt. I hated it. Every second. But I stuck with it. Because quitting wasn't an option.

My alarm went off at five a.m. every day. I laced up my sneakers, stepped outside into the dark, and ran. The streets were still. The air was sharp. Streetlights blinked overhead as I moved through the silence like a girl trying to outrun her reality. The run was the only time I felt like I belonged to myself.

Back home, I'd shower, pull on thrifted jeans and a faded hoodie, and walk four blocks to the bus stop. Morning light barely brushed the sky. The bus ride took two hours. I'd sit by the window, watching Sacramento yawn awake—coffee shops flickering to life, people rushing, car horns rising like a song—and wonder if anyone knew I existed.

I got off three blocks from campus. Made it to school by eight a.m. Because of my credit load, I only needed a half-day.

At noon, I was back on the bus, headed to work. Four hours of fake smiles and scripted lines. Then another long ride home, the same stops in reverse.

By the time I stepped through the apartment door, my legs ached, my mind was foggy, and my spirit dragged behind me like a torn coat.

No one was ever waiting for me. There was no "How was your day?" And there was certainly no "I'm proud of you."

Just silence.

Dinner was usually Cup O' Noodles—fast, cheap, and microwavable—and Diet Pepsi. I'd sit cross-legged on my bed, with my homework balanced beside me, and the glow of the TV casting shadows across an empty room.

There were no sleepovers. No volleyball games. No late-night phone calls with friends.

Just a sixteen-year-old girl learning how to survive in a world that had no place for her. And somewhere in the middle of all that motion—I started to disappear.

Not just to fade.

To unravel, thread by thread.

A few weeks into school, the nurse called me out of class. She said I needed a physical on file. I nodded. Took the form. Folded it up. And like I did with most things by then, I handled it myself.

I sat on the exam table alone, legs dangling over the edge, the paper beneath me crinkling with every nervous shift. When the doctor pressed the stethoscope to my chest, something in his expression shifted. Barely. A crease between his brows. A pause that lasted just long enough to notice.

"I hear a murmur," he said, voice low and clinical. "I'd like to run some additional tests."

I nodded again. Like I understood. But I didn't. Not really.

I walked home with the word *murmur* repeating in my mind like a warning. Something about my heart wasn't normal. That's all I heard.

That night, I told my mom.

She didn't even look up from whatever she was doing. She didn't ask a single question or show the smallest flicker of concern.

A cold weight sank into my chest.

I was terrified. And she couldn't even pretend to care.

Bob happened to be home that week. When I mentioned the hospital visit, he offered to take me. I said okay. But when we pulled into the parking lot, I turned to him and said, "Wait in the car."

Not because I didn't want support. Because I wanted hers. And when she wasn't there, I punished him for it.

Inside, I lay on the table, with my heart thudding beneath a thin hospital gown. The screen showed it all—my heart pulsing in black and white, strange, beautiful, and vulnerable.

When the doctor came back, he explained it clearly: Mitral Valve Prolapse. MVP. "It's common," he said. "Nothing to worry about. It won't change your life."

But I was sixteen. And all I heard was: *Your heart isn't right.*

I swallowed. "Am I going to die?"

He softened. "No," he said gently. "You're not going to die."

With that, the breath I'd been holding escaped—quiet and shaky. I walked out to the parking lot and opened the car door. Bob was still there, just like he had said he would be. He didn't ask questions: he didn't say anything at all.

He just…stayed.

"I'm okay," I said, voice thin. "I'm not going to die."

He nodded. We sat in silence for a while before driving home. The test said my heart was fine. But I couldn't shake the feeling that something inside me was still broken. Not because of MVP, but because I was carrying it all alone.

A couple of weeks later, Hunter moved back from Texas.

He rolled into our cramped apartment with a duffel bag and a worn smile, dropping his things by the couch—the same couch that would become his bed. The hallway closet, once half mine, filled with his clothes overnight. There were only two bedrooms, but nobody talked logistics. Not that it mattered.

The moment he walked through the door, something in her shifted. My mom lit up. Laughter spilled out of the kitchen again, rich and familiar. They talked for hours at the dinner table, voices soft at first, then rising in bursts of shared jokes and stories I wasn't part of. I watched from across the room as she hugged him—arms wrapped tight, face pressed into his shoulder like she'd been holding her breath until he came home. A week later, a used truck appeared in the parking lot. His.

No rent. No curfews. No rules. Just love.

I watched it all unfold like a stranger watching life happen through a window—close enough to see, but not to be seen.

Hunter had dropped out of his freshman year. He had no job, no early alarms. And no long bus rides. Meanwhile, I was waking up in the dark to lace up sneakers, riding the city bus two hours across town, clocking into a job I hated just to afford groceries, and holding my life together with duct tape and willpower.

And still, I was the one fading into the background.

I was trying so hard to be enough. And somehow, it made me invisible.

One warm afternoon, sunlight spilled across the courtyard, rippling across the pool in lazy glints of gold. I spotted her stretched out on a lounge chair, with a paperback resting in her hands, and sunglasses shielding her eyes. She looked peaceful and detached.

I walked over and sat beside her, hoping maybe this moment—quiet and sun-soaked—would be different.

"Can we talk?" I asked, my voice barely louder than the breeze.

She didn't flinch or look up.

"I'm busy," she said, flipping a page. "Go away."

So, I did.

That night, I found her at the sink, with her sleeves pushed up, and fingers scrubbing a plate. The warm scent of soap filled the kitchen, but the silence between us chilled the air. My feet carried me forward before I could change my mind.

I stepped into the light and wrapped my arms around her.

She froze. Her back stiffened. Then she pushed me away like my touch burned. "Why do you hate me so much?" The words tumbled out, cracking as they landed. "I'm sorry—for Davis. For messing up. For making things harder. I'm sorry."

She didn't raise her voice. She didn't scold or accuse. Just a simple, quiet: "I'm not upset with you. I do love you." But her voice was hollow: the kind of empty that echoes. Because love doesn't forget you exist.

Love doesn't stop asking where you are, or if you're okay.

Love doesn't look through you like smoke.

She stopped asking where I went. She stopped caring if I came home and stopped noticing me at all. She never asked about school, work, or what it was like to live every day in survival mode. I wasn't allowed to bring friends over—not that anyone was knocking. But it didn't matter. The silence in our apartment was louder than any house party ever could be.

And the space between us? It widened like a crack in the foundation. Not just emotionally. Everything.

Eventually, I stopped trying.

No more reaching for affection. No more wondering what else I could do to make her see me. I folded inward, tucking my hope into corners where even I couldn't reach it. Something inside me hardened, not in anger, but in resignation.

I was alone.

And even though my heart still beat—strong enough to survive, steady enough to pass every test—something deeper inside me had gone quiet.

Because being held at arm's length by the one person you need the most doesn't just feel like rejection.

It feels like vanishing.

Senior year arrived like a life raft tossed into deep water.

I was still exhausted from the chaos of the years before, but something shifted when I walked onto campus that fall. I found them—*my* people. A small group of girls who didn't look through me or past me. They saw me. And they stayed.

They were bright, wild with laughter, soft with kindness, full of messy, beautiful life. I didn't have to try with them. I didn't have to explain or perform. I could just *be*—messy hair, quiet mornings, cracked jokes, sleepy eyes and all.

Around them, I could breathe.

After years of trying to wedge myself into spaces where I didn't fit, these friendships felt like sunlight spilling through a half-open window—warm, unexpected, and almost too good to believe. I leaned into it slowly, like a person relearning how to feel warmth without flinching.

School became my anchor. The hallways echoed with predictability. The clatter of lockers, the hum of morning announcements, the quick bursts of laughter between classes—it all wrapped around me like a rhythm I could trust. No matter what was happening at home, school gave me something solid. Something real.

A small part of me braced for it to vanish. But another part—quiet and stubborn—held on tight. For the first time in years, I felt like I belonged, like maybe I was worth keeping around.

Even with everything stacked against me—the moves, the instability, and the noise at home—I'd always managed to get good grades. School had been my one reliable measure of worth. Put in effort, see results. It made sense.

Until Algebra II and Trig.

The numbers taunted me, rearranging themselves on the page like puzzle pieces that refused to fit. I stayed up late scribbling through homework, hoping it would suddenly click. It never did. And when my report card came, the D glared back at me like a slap. My stomach dropped.

I stared at the paper, willing the grade to change. It didn't. Graduation felt like it had slipped from my fingers. I begged my teacher for a passing grade. Pleaded, really. And somehow—maybe out of pity or grace—he said yes.

That D was the lowest grade I'd ever earned. But it meant freedom. It meant I wouldn't be stuck. It meant I hadn't failed completely.

On the weekends, I found my refuge.

Julie's house was everything mine wasn't—warm, welcoming, alive. Her mom hugged me without hesitation. Her dad joked with me as if I belonged. We'd sit around the dinner table, passing plates and stories, and I'd pretend—just for a little while—that this was my life too.

I'd breathe in the scent of home-cooked food and soak up every laugh, every soft gesture, as if I could press them into my skin and carry them back with me.

Then came Cole.

He was older, a sophomore at Sacramento State. Confident. Smooth. With Cole, I didn't feel like an afterthought— I felt *chosen*. Seen. Special.

We spent weekends wrapped in each other, building a fragile world where I could forget how lonely I was. However, that world came with its own cracks. With Cole came drinking. With drinking came everything I'd tried to bury—every rejection, every ache, every wound I'd stopped pretending wasn't there.

One afternoon by the river, it all came loose.

We were drinking and laughing, with the sun warming our skin. Then I saw him glance at another girl—just a glance. But jealousy boiled up, fast and ugly. I snapped. Accused. Demanded. He rolled his eyes, said I was being ridiculous, and drove off—just like that.

I stood there, stunned. Wind tugging at my shirt. Strangers' laughter in the background. My heartbeat thudding louder than everything else.

He just left. And with him went the illusion of mattering.

I walked home in a daze, each step heavier than the last. My breath tight. My thoughts spinning.

The apartment was silent when I walked in.

I opened the fridge. Grabbed a six-pack. My hands moved on autopilot. Beer cans clinking. The butcher knife gleaming under the fluorescent light.

I locked my bedroom door, curled onto the floor, and held the cold steel in my palm. I didn't want to die. I just didn't want to feel like this anymore.

The silence was deafening. My thoughts pressed in like fog.

Then I reached for the phone.

My fingers trembled as I dialed the suicide hotline. I didn't know what I was looking for. Maybe just to be heard. Maybe for someone, anyone, to say, *You're not invisible.*

A woman answered. Her voice was soft, steady, and kind in a way I hadn't heard in years.

I cried harder the moment I heard her speak.

She asked questions gently, and patiently. I told her everything—the fight with Cole, the ache in my chest, the knife I couldn't stop looking at.

She didn't rush me. Didn't panic. She just kept me tethered with her voice, with her presence. I didn't know she had already sent help.

So, when I heard the knock on the front door, my breath caught.

"I have to go," I whispered into the phone. "Maybe it's Cole. Maybe he came back."

But it wasn't Cole.

I opened the door a crack—and there they were: two police officers. They were stone-faced, and stern.

I panicked and tried to shut the door, but they pushed it open.

One officer grabbed my arm, the other disappeared down the hall. I heard him rustling through my room.

"Found the knife. And beer cans," he called out. I froze. My legs went numb. "I didn't mean it," I cried. "I wasn't actually going to do anything."

But it didn't matter. The cuffs were cold against my wrists. My scream was torn from someplace deep—wild and primal and terrified.

My mom came flying out of her room, startled, barefoot in her robe.

"They're taking me!" I yelled. "Tell them I'm okay! Tell them I didn't mean it!"

But she said nothing.

Just stared.

And the neighbors—curtains fluttering, blinds peeled back—watched me being dragged out like a criminal.

The shame was unbearable. It flushed my skin, stung my eyes, and filled my lungs with humiliation.

I had embarrassed her. Again.

I was the problem. Again.

•　　•　　•

The metal bit into my skin, cold and tight. I shifted in the back seat of the squad car, wrists shackled behind me, trying not to cry. My cheek pressed against the window, fogging the glass with shallow, uneven breaths.

From the front seat, one of the officers glanced back. "It's a shame," he said, as if he was making casual conversation. "You're such a pretty girl."

I blinked. His words hit like acid splashed across an open wound.

As if that made any of this better.

As if beauty could excuse pain.

As if a soft face was supposed to make what I'd done... less.

I turned away, wishing I could sink into the seat and disappear. The upholstery scratched against my skin. My insides buzzed with humiliation. I wasn't even a person to him. Just a face. A file. A body in cuffs. Seen—and still invisible.

They wheeled me in strapped to a gurney, one wrist cuffed to the rail. The hallway lights pulsed overhead—too bright, too white. My pajama top clung to me as if it knew I didn't belong there.

People passed by without stopping. A nurse glanced at the clipboard, not at me. An orderly adjusted a curtain. Eyes moved over me as if I was a strange exhibit—curious, but not urgent.

I kept mine fixed on the ceiling. *One tile. Two. Three. Breathe. Don't cry.*

They poked. Prodded. Took samples. My body obeyed, limp and quiet. The drug test came back clean. It didn't matter. They wheeled me in anyway...

The mental health unit was dim, the air stale with sterilized sorrow. The lights buzzed overhead like distant hornets. No warmth. No sound but the soft hum of doors locking behind me.

They left me in observation. Cameras in the corners. Mirrored glass on the walls. I sat cross-legged on a thin mattress, wrapping my arms around myself, not sure whether I was more afraid of being alone or being watched.

Then, she walked in.

Bandaged wrists. Faded hoodie. Her eyes met mine and didn't flinch. She sat beside me like she'd done it a hundred times.

"I've been here a week," she said, calmly, as if describing the weather. "Tried to end it."

We didn't trade names, just pieces: fragments of pain spoken in quiet tones. There was something steady in her voice, something I needed.

For hours, we whispered into the air between us—confessions without judgment. I didn't have to explain. She already knew. In that sterile room, I didn't feel crazy. I felt understood. I felt seen and heard.

The psychiatrist's office was tidy and professional. His chair creaked as he sat across from me, flipping through a chart like he might find the answer in its pages.

He asked questions.

"Do you feel safe?"

"Do you still want to harm yourself?"

"Why didn't you call someone?"

Each one fell into the space between us, and I caught them as if I was taking a test. Careful. Detached. My voice came out hollow, like it didn't belong to me.

He nodded, eventually. Closed the folder with a quiet snap.

"You're safe to go home," he said, like that settled it.

But home didn't feel real anymore. I couldn't call my mom. The silence between us had thickened into something immovable.

And my friends? What could I possibly say?

So, I called Cole.

When he walked through the double doors, his eyes locked on mine and stayed there. His face twitched—shock first, then something softer. Guilt. Love. Maybe both.

"I'm sorry," I whispered. My voice cracked. "I didn't mean to scare you. I didn't want to hurt myself. I just…I can't drink anymore. It messes with my head. I mess everything up."

He didn't answer right away. Just stepped forward and pulled me into him. His arms wrapped around me, and I collapsed into the safety they offered.

"I love you," he murmured.

And for just a breath—a single heartbeat—I believed I might survive this.

When we pulled into the driveway, she was already waiting, with her arms crossed, and eyes unreadable.

The porch light flickered above her, casting shadows across her face.

"Why didn't you call me to pick you up?" she asked flatly.

I stood frozen, with my discharge papers in one hand. My mouth opened, but nothing came out. The words were stuck somewhere behind my ribs. She didn't wait for a response.

The door clicked shut behind her. We never spoke of that night. Not once. Not about the cuffs. Not the hospital. Not the ride home.

It dissolved into the space between us, unspoken but heavy.

I buried it deep. I didn't tell anyone—not even the friends who once promised I could tell them anything.

The shame clung to me like smoke.

Silence was safer than the truth.

•   •   •

The lease hadn't even warmed beneath our feet before we moved again—another apartment, another so-called fresh start. It had two bedrooms.

But not for me.

Hunter got the extra room, his posters already taped to the walls. I got the sofa. My clothes lived in cardboard boxes along the living room wall—unopened, unlabeled, slowly collapsing under their own weight. I had stopped bothering to unpack. It felt pointless, and temporary, as if I was just visiting someone else's life.

Each night, I curled into that couch's sagging cushions, with the springs groaning beneath me. The TV flickered across the dark room while I pulled a blanket tight around my shoulders—not for warmth, but for comfort.

It didn't matter how soft the fabric was. The silence was louder. The message was clear. *You don't belong. Not in this room. Not in this house. Maybe not anywhere.*

Mom rarely spoke to me, and when she did, it was clipped, and functional. Like asking a roommate if they'd paid the water bill. The space between us stretched wider by the day—tight with tension but empty of words.

Still, I had my girls—my circle of four who held me together like threads in a fraying seam. They were loud, funny, and full of life. With them, I didn't feel so misplaced.

One afternoon, after school, one of them asked us to meet at her house. We flopped onto her couch, expecting gossip, maybe a secret crush or a fight with her mom. But when she sat down, everything about her was different— she had tense shoulders, and hands twisting in her lap. No sparkle in her eyes. No teasing smirk.

"I'm pregnant," she said. "And I'm getting an abortion."

The room held its breath.

We looked at each other. No one moved. I opened my mouth, trying to summon something comforting, something wise—but all that surfaced was a rush of panic… and judgment I didn't want to admit.

That won't be me, I thought. *I can't let that happen. I won't be that careless.*

She asked us to be there for her afterward. We all nodded. Of course, we did.

Two weeks later, we crammed into a cheap hotel room she'd rented, passing chips back and forth, watching reruns, and pretending everything was normal. She laughed easily—too easily, maybe—but there was a lightness in her. Like the weight she'd carried had finally been set down.

I asked if she was going to tell her parents. She nodded. Said she planned to.

A few weeks later, she showed up with her backpack slung over one shoulder and nowhere to go.

"They kicked me out," she said.

Just like that, she was living on her own—cooking dinner, paying bills, and navigating the world like an adult, while the rest of us were still worrying about finals and prom dresses.

That's when it hit me.

We weren't invincible.

We were girls one moment…and then we weren't.

Innocence doesn't disappear all at once. It unravels, one hard truth at a time.

The school year blurred by in a mess of deadlines, cap and gown fittings, and senior pranks. But for the first time in a long time, I felt steady, and accomplished.

I had survived. I was graduating. And I was proud of myself.

I started to imagine my own celebration—the kind Lena had. Her graduation had been like something out of a movie: purple and white balloons bobbing in the yard, cake layered with violet frosting, flowers braided into her hair. Laughter. Music. Family packed shoulder to shoulder in joy.

I dreamed of that day for myself.

In April 1988, I sent out my graduation announcements with trembling hope, imagining hugs from my sisters, my grandparents clapping from the stands, maybe even Mom stringing streamers across the apartment walls.

I didn't follow up. I didn't ask. Because moms just... know. Right?

However, as the date got closer, the silence pressed in around me. A week before graduation, I finally broke. "When is everyone coming?" I asked, pretending not to notice how tight my voice sounded. "Where are they staying?"

Mom didn't even look up from what she was doing.

"No one's coming," she said flatly. "And you're not having a party."

I stood frozen in the kitchen doorway, my breath caught in my throat.

"Why?" I managed.

"They're too busy. Can't afford the trip." Her tone didn't change. The conversation was over before it had even begun.

Something inside me cracked.

I had built the moment up in my mind—a day wrapped in validation, in finally being *enough*. And with a few careless syllables, it was gone.

Graduation came anyway. I wore my cap and gown with a forced smile, walked across the stage while the auditorium thundered for other kids—kids whose families showed up. In the stands, Mom, Hunter, and Cole sat together, polite and distant. I spotted them once but didn't wave.

After the ceremony, Mom handed me a card and a small heart-shaped locket. It sat in my palm like a farewell. For a moment, I wondered if it was her way of saying, *"I love you."* Then she looked me dead in the eye and said, "You have two weeks to find someplace else to live."

I blinked. "Are you serious?"

"Dead serious."

I didn't ask for a reason. I didn't need one. I had become her burden. Her embarrassment. And now, with the last parental obligation checked off, she was done.

Two weeks later, she used her connections as a property manager to place me in a small studio across the city—bare walls, chipped tiles, and second-hand everything.

That was the day the word *Mom* stopped making sense. She wasn't lullabies and scraped knees anymore. She was Rose now. Just Rose.

I asked once—just once—if she could help with rent. Her response came quick and cold: "Absolutely not."

That was it. That was all I needed to hear.

I made a promise to myself in that empty room: I will never ask her for help again. I won't give her another chance to leave me wanting.

She wasn't my mother anymore, just the woman who gave birth to me.

So, I sat on a threadbare couch in a city that didn't know my name, the locket still tucked in my palm like a cruel joke and felt the ache of being unwanted.

That was the moment I stopped waiting to be chosen.

If no one was coming to save me, then I would have to learn how to save myself.

6

SEARCHING FOR SOLID GROUND

Eighteen and out on my own, I expected freedom to taste like fresh air and open roads.

Instead, it smelled like stale air and burnt toast.

Each morning, I woke to the low, persistent hum of the refrigerator in my cramped studio apartment. The walls, dimly lit and thin as paper, pressed in around me. The silence was the worst part—thick and unmoving, like a fog that never lifted. I had once imagined independence as something powerful. This felt more like abandonment.

At the movie theater, I poured popcorn and wiped down counters while fluorescent lights buzzed overhead. The buttery scent followed me home, woven into the seams of my hoodie, and the roots of my hair. I was taking a few classes at American River College, trying to stitch together a future—but the weight of solitude pressed against my chest like water filling my lungs.

Even surrounded by friends, I felt it—that hollow, echoing ache. Most of them still lived at home, their lives cushioned by the small, invisible kindnesses of family. Parents who cooked meals, checked in, and sent care packages. My life was a different kind of quiet: cold floors, microwave ramen, and bills I barely managed to pay.

Once a month, I picked up the phone with fingers crossed and my heart in my throat.

"Hi, Grandma. Hi, Grandpa…"

And every time, without fail, a check arrived in the mailbox.

It was never just money. It was light in a dark hallway. It was proof that someone still saw me. That I wasn't invisible after all. They had always been steady presences—my mother's parents. Their love didn't come in grand gestures. It came in consistency, in care offered without condition. My grandfather, especially. I never called him "Dad," but deep down, he filled that space.

His love felt like a porch light that had been left on—just in case I ever found my way back.

Six months in, with independence hanging by threads, the phone rang. "We'll buy you a plane ticket to come home to Colorado," my grandfather said, his voice low and even. For a moment, I couldn't speak. My breath snagged in my throat. I pressed a hand to my chest, trying to hold something in—or maybe keep something from breaking loose. The bed creaked beneath me as I sat down, the sound brittle in the quiet room.

I hadn't even realized how badly I needed to hear those words. Until now.

"We'll help you get into an apartment," he continued. "Help you get a car. All you have to do is enroll in community college."

I didn't ask questions. I didn't bargain.

It wasn't just an offer.

It was a rescue.

A way out of sagging ceilings, gas station dinners, and the heavy silence that filled the gaps my mother's love never reached. A way toward something solid. Something that resembled home.

The weekend before I left, Cole and my friends planned a trip to Tahoe.

I hadn't realized how much I needed them—how much I needed that kind of laughter—until we were curled up under blankets, passing around peppermint schnapps, and laughing so hard our stomachs ached. The fire popped and crackled, with shadows dancing across our faces as we took turns telling ghost stories, too spooked to head to bed.

No one said it out loud, but we all knew.

Tomorrow meant goodbye.

That morning, I stood outside the condo, arms wrapped around each of them as if I could anchor something in place. We whispered promises—We'll visit. We'll call. This won't change anything.

But even as I nodded through the tears, a quiet truth settled in my chest.

What if it did?

What if this was the last time?

Driving away with Cole, the ache settled behind my ribs. I held on to the belief that we'd stay close—that what we had was strong enough to last.

A week later, I boxed up what I could carry and stored the rest. Cole drove me to the airport, and the drive was quiet. Not awkward—just understood. Neither of us needed to fill the silence. We were already bracing for the end.

Our goodbye was soft. Heavy. No shouting, no blame—just a shared sadness between two people who had once loved deeply and knew they couldn't stay tethered to something that was already letting go.

When I looked into his eyes, I saw it.

We were a chapter. And we had reached the final page.

•　　•　　•

I never told Rose I was leaving.

Not because I forgot, but because I couldn't.

I didn't believe she'd care. And worse: part of me couldn't bear to find out if I was right. Some quiet, aching part of me still wished she'd stop me at the airport gate. Ask where I was going. Tell me not to leave.

But I already knew better.

Her silence had spoken loud enough. I didn't need another demonstration of how little space I took up in her world.

So, I gave her nothing. No goodbye. No letter. No opening for disappointment. I left without turning back, with what was left of my heart packed tight inside me—something fragile I had to carry on my own.

The hum of the plane filled my ears as I leaned into the window, with clouds shifting outside like pulled cotton. I had hours to sit with everything I was feeling.

Relief.

Fear.

Sadness.

Hope.

They came in waves—no rhythm, no warning—crashing over me again and again. I pressed my forehead to the cool glass, trying to steady my breath, trying to believe this was the beginning of something better. A reset, or a second chance. But underneath the swirl of hope was that familiar ache—like I was drifting again. Always floating from place to place, always packing my life into boxes and starting over. Never quite grounded. Never quite home. I didn't know what would happen next.

I knew one thing.

I was going to try—try to build something real. Something that felt like mine.

I still didn't know where home was. But as the plane began its descent, the land rising up to meet me, I let myself believe—maybe for the first time—that I was flying toward it.

When I stepped off the plane in Colorado, I scanned the crowd with hesitant eyes. Then I saw them. My grandparents. Arms open. Eyes warm. No hesitation. They pulled me into a hug that wrapped around every part of me—the seen, the unseen, the barely-holding-it-together. It poured warmth into places I didn't know had gone cold. For the first time in a long time, I didn't feel like I was just arriving somewhere.

I felt like I had come home.

The drive to their house was quiet.

Not the kind of silence that cuts or stiffens the air.

The kind that feels like an exhale. Like safety. Like being with people who don't need you to explain your pain to understand it.

Even so, something gnawed at me.

I glanced over at my grandmother. Her hands were folded neatly in her lap, her gaze soft on the road ahead. "Why didn't you come to my high school graduation?" I asked gently.

She paused. Her fingers twitched slightly. Her eyes glossed over, and she turned to me with a trembling jaw.

"I wanted to be there," she said. "But...Rose called. She told us not to come. Said there wasn't enough room." The words sliced through me, sharp and slow. I blinked, unsure if I'd heard right. "She called the whole family," she added, voice cracking. "Told everyone the same thing."

I turned toward the window, but the world outside had already begun to blur. My throat tightened. My chest ached.

She reached for my hand, her own shaking now. "I knew something wasn't right. I should've come anyway. I'm so sorry." In that moment, I felt it—the full weight of what had been stolen from me.

It wasn't just a ceremony.

It was love.

It was celebration.

It was the chance to be seen.

Something hot began to rise in me. Not loud. Not explosive. Just steady and burning.

Fury.

Grief.

Betrayal.

I saw myself again—on that stage, gown clinging to my knees, and heart pounding. My eyes scanning the crowd. Waiting. Hoping. Believing. Believing they'd show up. Believing I mattered.

Rose had taken that from me. Not just the celebration. She had stolen the belief that I was worth showing up for.

I made a quiet decision in the silence of that moment—one that settled deep into my bones. I would not speak to her again. Not for a long time.

And it would be five years before I did.

That first week, I stayed tucked inside the warmth of my grandparents' home—their voices soft, their presence steady—as I enrolled at Aims Community College in Greeley.

Each step forward felt shaky, like learning to breathe again after nearly drowning. Unsteady, but possible.

I found a small bedroom for rent in an apartment shared with two other girls. When I moved in, I carried only a single box of essentials and a quiet hope that maybe—just maybe—this was the place where my life would finally shift.

I told myself I was ready. Ready for a new beginning, and ready to build something of my own.

I dived into my classes with a kind of fierce determination, grasping at the chance to rewrite my story. I clung to lectures, assignments, textbooks—anything that might tether me to a life of which I could be proud.

But loneliness has a way of finding you, even in a crowded room.

My roommates were polite. We exchanged smiles, passed each other in the kitchen, made small talk about coffee creamers and class schedules. But our conversations never cracked the surface. There were no movie nights, no whispered confessions at two a.m.—just the soft shuffle of strangers occupying the same square footage.

I lingered in doorways longer than I needed to. Laughed a little too loud at nothing. Waited for an invitation that never came.

I wanted to belong. And I tried. But most nights, I lay in bed listening to muffled voices behind closed doors, feeling like a guest in someone else's life. By mid-semester, the weight of everything—the pretending, the isolation, and the exhaustion—pressed heavy against my chest.

I dropped three of my classes. I told myself it was just temporary. That I needed to breathe. That it wasn't giving up—just letting go of what I couldn't hold. I kept two—not because I had it all together, but because I needed something to hold on to. Some thread of purpose. Some small, trembling proof that I was still trying.

But inside, I felt untethered.

Like a leaf tossed into the wind—weightless, spinning, unsure of where I belonged or how to land. No one noticed I was falling. And I was too tired to explain.

The next few years slipped by in fragments.

A blur of temporary jobs, short leases, and community college classes I couldn't seem to finish. I packed and unpacked my life more times than I could count, always trying to build something—anything—that felt like mine.

But every time I laid a foundation, it cracked beneath me.

My only steady lifeline was my grandparents. Whenever money got tight—and it always did—I'd call. My voice would tremble as I asked for "a little help." I always said I was borrowing it. But I never paid it back.

And still, they never said no. They never asked when I would. They just showed me love, with no conditions, and no judgment. Just the quiet, constant grace of two people who kept showing up, even when I didn't feel like I deserved it.

One afternoon, I made the call again. My voice cracked as I explained that I needed help covering the electric bill. Grandpa didn't ask questions and didn't hesitate. He just said he'd send a check.

Two days later, it arrived. Just like always.

This time, I didn't use the money to keep the lights on. I used it to buy birth control pills.

It felt like the right decision—grown-up, responsible, and necessary. But as I stood at the pharmacy counter, guilt burned in my chest. I could already feel the weight of what I was about to do—not just the purchase, but the silence I would keep about it.

I had promised them, long ago, that I would wait until marriage. I had said it so many times, with childlike certainty and Sunday-school conviction. They were devout Lutherans, active in their church, their lives shaped by scripture and tradition.

I loved them and respected them. I didn't want to disappoint them. So, I lied.

And when I opened the pill pack that night, I felt a strange ache—like I was choosing myself...and betraying them at the same time.

It wasn't the pill that hurt.

It was the space between who I was and who they believed I'd be.

What I hadn't counted on was Grandma's meticulous

nature. She kept journals of every household expense—rows of handwritten notes in her careful script. Each check sent to the grandkids, each promise made, tracked and filed with quiet precision.

She must have noticed the overlap—two "electric bills" in the same month.

The knock at my apartment door came the next day. When I opened it, my grandfather stood there. There was no anger in his face, just something still and serious—steady in a way that felt heavier than shouting ever could.

My stomach dropped. I didn't need him to say it. I already knew why he was there.

He looked at me with calm eyes, his voice low and even.

"What did you use the money for?"

I froze.

My throat closed. My chest tightened. I wanted to lie again. To dodge. To disappear. But I couldn't. Not to him. Not again.

"I bought birth control," I said, barely louder than a whisper.

His expression didn't shift much. But something in his eyes dimmed—just slightly.

Not rage. Not shame.

Disappointment.

Quiet, but heavy.

"I'm not upset about what you used it for," he said. "I'm upset that you lied to us. Don't ever lie to us again."

The words struck something raw. Shame surged up fast, hot and choking. My eyes stung before I could stop them. Tears spilled over as I nodded, silent.

I'm so sorry," I whispered, my voice barely a thread. It was one of the worst feelings I'd ever known. It was not because I had lied. It was because I had hurt *him*—the one man who had never once turned his back on me. The one who had always answered and always shown up.

I didn't care about the money. I cared about the look on his face. In that moment, I felt something sacred break between us—his trust—something I had always believed was unshakable.

And I made a silent promise. I would never lie to him again. Because hurting someone who truly loves you... that's the kind of pain that doesn't fade.

After months of drifting—untethered, unsteady, like a leaf caught in the gutter with nowhere to land—I found myself staring at something I never imagined.

Two pink lines.

I was pregnant, and terrified.

There was no plan, no partner, and no steady ground beneath my feet. Just the sinking realization that I had failed again—failed to be careful, failed to build anything real, failed to make it out clean.

I couldn't tell my grandparents. Not after the lie. Not after the check. Not after watching disappointment wash across my grandfather's face like a tide I couldn't pull back.

I wasn't ready to carry that weight again.

The father was a guy I met at a college party. One night. One reckless decision. I had missed a few birth control pills—barely thought about it at the time. But now here I was. At the age of twenty, I was broke, alone, and pregnant by someone I barely knew.

When I told him, he didn't blink.

You should get an abortion," he said, in a flat and matter-of-fact way—like he was commenting on the weather.

The air shifted. The floor beneath me tilted. The world grew strangely quiet, except for the pounding in my ears.

He didn't ask what I wanted and didn't ask how I felt. He had already made up his mind. The truth was that I didn't know what I wanted either. But I knew how I felt—scared, ashamed, and completely alone.

So, I didn't argue. I just nodded, small and silent.

There was no money. No backup plan. I couldn't keep my own lights on without a borrowed check. How could I care for someone else?

We made the appointment at Planned Parenthood. I told myself we were just going to get information. But deep down, I knew.

I was already walking a path that felt like it had no exits. I couldn't imagine bringing a baby into this chaos. I didn't even know who I was—how could I possibly raise someone else?

And then it hit me—hard. I remembered my friend from high school. The day she broke down and told us she was pregnant. That she was getting an abortion. Back then, I judged her. Quietly, but sharply. I told myself I'd never be that careless. That naïve. That stupid.

God, I understood now. One mistake. One vulnerable moment.

It didn't make her a bad person.

And it didn't make me one either.

But it did make everything heartbreakingly complicated.

I didn't tell my grandparents or Rose. I didn't really tell anyone. It felt too dangerous—like if I said it out loud, everything would shatter. So, I carried it alone, like a lead weight strapped across my chest. At night, I'd lie awake, hands pressed against my belly, wondering what was happening inside me. Wondering if that tiny spark of life could already feel my fear.

I was only a few weeks along, but it already felt like I was vanishing beneath the enormity of it. Some days, I almost convinced myself it wasn't real. Other days, a sudden wave of nausea or lightheadedness pulled me back into the truth.

I searched clinics late at night when the world was quiet.

Read stories. Imagined myself walking through those doors, sitting in the waiting room, going through with it.

But every time, I stopped. It was not because I was sure I wanted to keep the baby, but because I wasn't sure I could live with the alternative.

Eventually, I made the appointment—for a week later. Each day leading up to it felt like a war inside me. My stomach cramped constantly. I spotted blood. I told myself it was stress. That I was fine. But deep down, I knew.

My body was trying to speak when I couldn't find the words.

I had been raised Lutheran. Baptized Catholic. I hadn't been to church in years, didn't believe most of what I'd been taught—but the guilt and the questions lingered. Was I killing a child?

Would God forgive me?

Was I damned?

The night before the appointment, my body gave out. I got violently sick—vomiting and shaking. My back throbbed. My belly twisted in pain. I collapsed on the bathroom floor, curled into myself, too weak to move, and too wrecked to cry.

The tiles were cold against my skin. I lay there for what felt like hours.

I didn't know if I was losing the pregnancy or if my body was simply folding under the weight of everything I hadn't said. All I knew was that something inside me had shifted.

And nothing would ever be the same.

The morning of the appointment, we pulled up to the clinic under a gray, washed-out sky. That's when I saw the protestors. They were lined up shoulder to shoulder along the sidewalk, their signs raised high like weapons.

Their voices tore through the cold air, amplified by megaphones and moral certainty: "Protect babies!"

"Choose life!"

"God is watching!"

I froze. My hands went numb on my lap. My breath caught in my chest. I couldn't move, couldn't blink, and couldn't face them. The shame slammed into me like a wave I hadn't braced for—rushing in fast, flooding every inch of me.

I turned away from the windshield. "We can't go in that way," I whispered.

He circled around to the back of the building—there were no signs, no stares, no shouting voices. Just a quiet door, and a different kind of dread.

I stepped inside, trembling. But their judgment followed me. It didn't need a megaphone anymore. It echoed from somewhere inside my own heart.

I asked to use the restroom. The nurse pointed down the hall, and I moved like a ghost through the fluorescent light. When the door clicked shut behind me, I collapsed onto the toilet, my entire body trembling. I doubled over, vomiting into the trash can, waves of nausea and fear hitting all at once.

Then a cramp—sharp and deep—ripped through me. I gasped and clutched my sides. Something inside me twisted, like it was trying to claw its way out. And then I looked down. I stared, frozen. The toilet bowl was filled with blood.

In that sterile clinic bathroom, I miscarried the baby I had come there to abort. Pain bloomed through my abdomen, but it was nothing compared to what was breaking inside me.

In a strange and terrible twist of fate. I had made a choice I wasn't sure I could live with. And life—or something else—had made another one for me.

When I walked out of that clinic, I was not the same girl who had walked in. Something inside me had shifted, broken open.

There wasn't clarity, and there wasn't peace. But there was something else—a quiet knowledge that I had been changed in a way that couldn't be undone.

So, I went home—aching, emptied, and forever changed.

The years slipped by, and then something unexpected happened, I found myself speaking to Rose again. I still couldn't call her "Mom." That word felt too soft—too sacred for someone whose love had felt like a guessing game. But the silence between us, once thick and absolute, began to shift. Just slightly. A small crack in the wall. And for that, I had my grandmother to thank.

It was a cold, snowy afternoon in Colorado—the kind of cold that blankets everything in silence and makes time feel suspended. I was curled up on the couch, a worn blanket tucked beneath my chin, when the phone rang.

Grandma. Her voice came through the line steady and warm, like the low hum of a lullaby I hadn't heard in years.

"Heidi," she said softly, "it's time to let go." I didn't answer. I couldn't. My throat tightened. "Let go of the anger. The resentment. The pain that's been living in your bones for too long. It's not for her. Forgiveness isn't for Rose—it's for you."

I closed my eyes.

"You deserve peace, baby. And forgiveness…that's where it begins."

Outside, snow pressed gently against the window. Inside, something stirred.

By then, Rose had moved back to Colorado. We lived in the same state again. But the distance between us wasn't measured in miles. It was measured in silence.

Somehow, in that moment, I heard her—not just the words, but the weight behind them. Her knowing. Her heart. Her fierce, quiet love.

Before I could second-guess it, I whispered a promise into the phone.

"Okay…I'll call her."

The moment I hung up, my hands trembled. My heart pounded as I scrolled through my contacts. I hesitated over her name. Then dialed her number.

Each ring felt like a countdown I couldn't stop.

And then—"Hello?"

"Hi, Rose…it's Heidi."

"Heidi! How are you?"

"I'm…okay. Would it be possible to see you in person? I'd like to talk." There was a pause.

"Sure. How about lunch on Sunday, at my place?"

"Okay. See you then."

The call ended, but the silence lingered—thick and pressing against my ribs. I stared at the phone long after we hung up, wondering what I had just done.

Seeing her again felt like stepping into a storm I wasn't sure I could survive. My walls were high. My body remembered things my mind had worked hard to forget.

Sunday came. I stood at her door with my heart in my throat and every muscle drawn tight. When she opened it, she smiled as if nothing had ever happened.

"Come on in," she said, cheerful—casual. As if no years had passed. As if there weren't whole oceans of pain between us.

We sat in her living room and talked about easy things—weather, work, what we'd been up to. Small talk, floating above the truth. But I hadn't come for the weather.

At some point, my voice broke through the script we were playing.

"Why did you stop loving me?"

The question landed hard between us.

She looked at me with the same eyes I remembered from childhood. Calm. Unmoving.

"I never stopped loving you," she said. That was it. There was no explanation or apology. Just that.

I left her house feeling…hollow. The door had opened, but the room was still empty. Yes, we were speaking again. But our words echoed inside a space still aching from everything unsaid. Still, beneath the emptiness, something fragile stirred.

Hope. It was wobbly, uncertain and unsteady. But it was there.

Hope that maybe—just maybe—this was the first step toward something real.

I called Grandma when I got home and told her how it went. She was proud of me. Her voice bright, full of joy. I wanted to feel that too.

But the truth was that I wasn't there yet.

Did I forgive Rose that day? I told myself I did. I wanted to believe it. However, real forgiveness doesn't show up all at once. It doesn't arrive neatly wrapped in a single lunch or a brave phone call. It doesn't live in a sentence that leaves you colder than before.

Real forgiveness takes time. It takes years of untangling your shame from your worth. Years of learning how to hold your broken parts with grace. Years of forgiving the girl you used to be…before you can ever truly forgive the one who made her feel unlovable.

For a few years, I drifted through life like a shadow—present, but untouchable. My body moved through the motions: class, work, home. Conversations. Dates. Smiles. But nothing stuck. Nothing felt real.

It was like watching my life from outside a window—so close I could trace the glass with my fingers, but never quite step through.

People talked about purpose. About passion. About dreaming. But we didn't talk about things like that at our dinner table. College. Careers. Futures. That kind of imagining belonged to other families. Other girls. Not girls like me. I wanted more—but wanting was all I had. I didn't know how to build a life I had never seen.

Still, there were flickers of light in the fog. Misty was one of them. She lived nearby in Fort Morgan, raising her child on her own—her days full of work and motherhood—but she always made room for me. We'd sneak away to our favorite restaurant, splitting nachos, sipping Bloody Mary's, letting time slow under the weight of laughter and sisterhood. In those moments, something inside me softened. I felt known. For a little while, I wasn't lost.

Lena, my other sister, saw what I tried to hide—what I couldn't hide.

At the time, I was stretched thin between two dead-end jobs: cleaning motel rooms by day and shining cowboy boots at a country bar by night. I was still clinging to a few college classes, but barely.

I was exhausted in every possible way.

She was working as a branch manager at Home Savings of America and told me there was an opening at the Fort Collins branch—a teller position. Her offer felt like a lifeline tossed into deep water.

She believed in me when I couldn't believe in myself. I applied and got the job. I moved to Fort Collins. I even enrolled at Colorado State University and finished a semester. But the money wasn't enough. Rent, books, food—it all added up faster than I could keep up. I dropped out again. Quietly. Ashamed.

I made myself a promise: I wouldn't ask my grandparents

for help. Not again. I'd already disappointed them once. That was enough.

So, I focused on work.

After a year, I took a job with First Bank of Fort Collins. I started in the drive-thru, and something shifted. The young women I worked with were bright, hilarious, kind. We clicked. For the first time in a long time, I felt like I had real friends. There was laughter. Light. Belonging. However, beneath the surface, something darker was at play.

My manager was only a few years older than me—but it felt like breaking me down had become her full-time job.

She mocked my clothes. My voice. My background. Anything she could sink her teeth into, she used against me. And she did it in front of customers, in front of my coworkers—who said nothing. Their silence was as sharp as glass.

She told me I had to join the branch's softball team, or she'd fire me.

So, I joined.

I held it all in, smiled through it, and acted as if it didn't matter. But at night, I cried. My body tensed at the sound of my alarm. My dreams turned dark—visions of her car exploding when she opened the door.

That's where I was. Eaten alive by quiet rage and unspoken wounds.

Then came the vice president. He started trying to set me up with various clients—offhand comments, introductions, suggestions cloaked in charm.

One afternoon, right before closing, he called me into his office. His tone was casual, but something about it set me on edge. He told me he had someone for me to meet—a "well-established" client going through a separation. Twenty years older. Two small children.

I didn't feel like I had a choice. So, I said yes.

We met at a quiet Italian restaurant in town. He was wealthy, confident, and charming in the way that comes with money and practiced attention. He wasn't unattractive. He was polite enough. But something in me curled inward.

Still, when he asked me out again, I said yes. How could I say no? The man who arranged the date was my boss. Declining felt risky—like it could cost me more than just another awkward night.

The second date was at his new condo. One of many, he said. The place was beautiful, modern…and cold. Like him. Dinner was fine. Small talk, decent food. I tried to relax. Then he made his offer. He told me I could have the condo—if I moved in. If I belonged to him. "You'd never have to work again," he promised. But there would be rules."

Rules…

He listed them one by one, calmly, like negotiating a lease. A curfew. Limited friends. Available to him, whenever and wherever he wanted.

And last—"You'll need a boob job." I sat in silence, the air sucked from my lungs. He smiled like he was offering me a gift. But it wasn't a gift.

It was a cage.

I stood slowly, politely. I was quite composed.

"I'm not for sale," I said. Then I left—I was dignified on the outside. But the moment the door clicked shut, I ran to my car.

A few days later, everything shifted. I stepped out of the vault after closing and caught them—my manager, lips pressed against the vice president. Married. Both of them. No words were exchanged.

None were needed.

We all knew what had just happened.

The next morning, I requested a meeting.

There was no anger, and no drama: just truth.

I told him the harassment had to stop. No more set-ups. No more manipulation. If it continued, I would contact a lawyer. My voice didn't shake. My message was clear.

The next day, my manager called me into her office. Her eyes were burning. Don't you ever pull something like that again," she hissed.

I met her stare and replied calmly, "I want the VP or someone from HR in the room for this conversation."

She froze, then backed off—slowly. But not before spitting, "Watch your back."

I smiled. "You watch yours."

She stayed cold, but the power she had over me? It loosened. I could breathe again.

The mornings felt lighter. The days didn't just pass—they grew. I moved from the drive-thru to the front counter. Into customer service. Then into opening new accounts.

It wasn't a finish line. But it was a beginning.

And that's when Bert Cobb walked through the door.

We worked in the same orbit. He worked across the lot at the Kinko's next door and moonlighted as a DJ for a local radio station. I'd seen him around, usually through the drive-up window, always with a cocky smirk, always a little extra with whatever he was doing.

Tall. Lanky. A little awkward. Not really my type. Then again, I wasn't entirely sure I had a "type" anymore.

One afternoon, he strolled into the bank lobby. I was helping a customer. My coworker at the next window looked up and called, "Can I help you?"

He smiled politely. "No thanks—I'll wait for her," he said, nodding toward me.

My coworker raised an eyebrow. I pretended not to notice. When I finished, he walked up to my window without a word and slid a folded piece of paper across the counter. Then, without missing a beat, he turned and walked out.

My coworker leaned toward me, wide-eyed. "What the heck was that?"

"I have no idea," I said, heart ticking faster. I unfolded the note. It was handwritten—an invitation to his place on Thursday night to watch *Friends* and *Cheers* with a few friends. Cute. Casual. Unexpected.

But then my stomach dropped. My coworker had a thing for him…or at least I thought she did.

I walked back to the teller line and asked her, straight up, "Do you like Bert Cobb?"

She wrinkled her nose. "Absolutely not. Go for it."

So, I did.

That night, I called him. "I'll be there Thursday," I said, smiling despite myself.

When Thursday came, I checked the address—and froze. He lived right across the street from me. Too close. I didn't want him knowing exactly where I lived. Not yet. What if he turned out to be a weirdo? A stalker? So, I looped around the block and came in from the opposite side of the complex, pulling into a parking spot as if I hadn't just mapped a detour to protect my personal space.

I could hear the party before I even reached the door— laughter, clinking glasses, the telltale slur of voices several margaritas deep.

I wore jeans and a cropped shirt—just a hint of skin. Not scandalous, but enough to make him gasp when he opened the door.

The apartment was thick with pot smoke. The blender was already spinning out the next round of drinks. It was only seven p.m., but the crowd was deep into the night. I stayed for an hour. Smiled. Chatted. Kept my distance. When I stood to leave, Bert followed me to the door, with protest in his eyes.

I smiled, waved goodbye, and walked out.

He was sweet. A little chaotic. Not my type.

Definitely not my type.

A week passed. Then another half. I hadn't called him. Didn't plan to. Then the phone rang. "Why haven't you called?" he asked.

I paused. "I guess I'm just not that interested."

He didn't flinch. Just dinner," he said. "Tonight. Me and you."

I hesitated. Then I said yes.

When I walked into the restaurant, there he was—again—with a full table of friends, laughing and drinking. He smiled and raised his glass like it was no big deal.

I stepped closer, with my voice low. "I thought this was just the two of us."

"They just showed up," he shrugged.

I smiled, tightly. "Well, you enjoy your night. I'll see you around." And I left.

I ignored his calls after that. I figured we were done. But we weren't.

Instead of giving up, Bert started sending poems—actual poems—through the drive-thru tube at the bank. Each one tucked between folded paper, accompanied by a Tootsie Roll. Every couple of days, a new note would arrive. They were sweet, awkward, and surprisingly sincere.

I didn't respond. But something inside me began to shift.

Every evening after work, I ran the same two-mile loop—my own little escape. One night, as I rounded a familiar comer, I spotted someone up ahead.

Bert.

He turned, sounding breathless. "Mind if I run with you?"

I slowed down. "I didn't know you were a runner."

"I love it," he said, matching my pace.

What I didn't know then was that it was a lie. He hated running. Absolutely hated it. But that night, he showed up anyway.

And something in me softened. Maybe it was the effort. Maybe it was the way he kept showing up—genuine, goofy, unafraid. Whatever it was, I let him run beside me. And somewhere in that second mile, I realized—maybe he was my type after all.

Maybe I just didn't know what I needed…until someone kept showing me.

The first three months with Bert felt like a dream—one of those soft-focus montages in a romantic comedy, all laughter and golden light.

We went on dates that left me breathless with laughter, snuck into parties like we didn't have jobs to show up to the next morning, and drank like nothing could ever touch us. He kissed my forehead as if it meant something. Wrapped his arms around my waist like I belonged there. Whispered, *"I love you"* with a warmth that melted through my skin.

When he asked me to be his girlfriend, something inside me lit up. It felt like being chosen—like being picked first. Like maybe I finally mattered.

But then…something shifted. It was quiet at first, and subtle, like a hairline crack in glass. I spotted the red flags, but I painted them white. Told myself it was nothing. That he was still the same person from the beginning—the one who made me feel like I was everything.

I wanted so badly to believe I was still that girl. That we were still *us*.

He started with little comments.

"You spend too much time with your friends."

"They don't really get you."

"They're a bad influence."

However, when I tried to join him and his friends, I became invisible—hovering at the edge of conversations while he flirted with other women right in front of me. As if I wasn't even there.

I'll never forget one college party in particular. I wanted to look perfect for him. I spent the whole afternoon curling my hair, brushing on makeup with careful precision, slipping into a yellow halter dress that made me feel radiant. I paired it with crisp white sneakers and a jean jacket—cute, playful, and ready for anything.

He picked me up. We drove together in silence. I told myself he was just focused, tired, whatever. As soon as we arrived, he disappeared.

No hand on my back. No whispered drink order.

Just a solo march to the kitchen, a quick pour of rum and Coke—for himself—and then he vanished downstairs. I stood in the middle of the living room, blinking. Trying to look like I belonged.

I poured myself a beer. Smiled at strangers. Made awkward small talk that dissolved in seconds. I ended up curled on the edge of a sofa, trying to disappear into the cushions.

An hour passed. Then another. Finally, I got up. Room to room, I searched for him—until I reached the basement. There he was. Bent over a pool table, hand on the back of a tall, beautiful blonde. Their faces inches apart. Laughing. Flirting. So wrapped up in each other they didn't even notice me.

My face burned. My throat tightened. My heart pounded so loud I could barely think.

I walked up and tapped her on the shoulder. "Excuse me—this is my boyfriend," I said, grabbing his arm.

The girl laughed. Bert turned to me as if I'd just crashed his party. "You're overreacting," he snapped. "She's just a friend. Back off." Then, as if I'd vanished—he turned back to her and took the shot. I stood frozen in place, everything inside me shattering.

"I want to go home," I whispered.

He didn't even look at me. "If you want to leave, then leave."

So, I did. I walked upstairs, back to the couch. Curled into myself. Humiliated. Gutted. And waited. Two hours later, he finally came up and agreed to drive me home.

In the car, I was boiling with rage, hurt, and humiliation.

I wanted to scream. *Why did you bring me just to abandon me? Why did you humiliate me? Why do you make me feel so small?*

But I didn't scream. Because he beat me to the story.

"You're being too sensitive."

"You're overreacting."

"You're acting crazy."

The worst part was that I believed him.

I didn't know who I was yet. I didn't have boundaries. I didn't know how to say, *This isn't okay. I deserve more than this.* So, instead, I apologized. I begged him not to break up with me. I clung to him as if losing him would mean losing everything.

That night, I went home with him. We had sex. I told myself it meant we were okay again. That we'd fixed it.

But when I woke up the next morning, I didn't feel loved. I felt empty.

And I was just grateful he hadn't left.

Over time, a pattern formed. Disrespect. Tears. Apologies. Me, crawling back.

We built a rhythm—twisted, toxic, and familiar, like second-hand smoke.

I knew it was poisoning me.

But I kept breathing it in anyway.

7

THE COST OF IGNORING MYSELF

By then, we'd been together nearly a year and were living in a small, cluttered apartment that felt more like his than ours. When Christmas rolled around, Bert asked if I wanted to fly to Santa Barbara to spend the holidays with his family.

My heart fluttered.

This felt big: it was like a turning point.

Meeting his family wasn't just a holiday invitation—it was a sign. A step toward something deeper, and more permanent. Maybe it was even something real.

I called my grandparents, unsure how they'd react. I told them about the trip, about Bert, and about what it meant to me.

They didn't hesitate.

"Go," they said. "Enjoy Christmas. Make memories."

Their blessing made it feel official.

I threw myself into preparation with the kind of energy only a girl desperate to be accepted can summon. I spent nearly a month searching for the perfect gifts—something thoughtful for his mom, something fun for his dad, something stylish for his older sister.

It was just the four of them, and I wanted them to like me.

No—I *needed* them to.

I picked out outfits for every moment—Christmas Eve dinner, Christmas morning photos, church, and lazy afternoons in the kitchen. I imagined myself folding myself into their family. Laughing with his mom over cookie dough. Talking music with his dad. Finding common ground with his sister.

The plane tickets were booked, the gifts were wrapped, and I was ready.

One week before we were set to fly, the phone rang.

I was in the kitchen, with my hands in warm sudsy water, washing dishes. Bert answered from the living room. His voice was casual at first, then it changed—softer, quieter, the way someone talks when they're trying to calm a storm.

"It'll be fine," he said. "She'll be fine."

I paused, with a dish still in my hand, soap clinging to my knuckles.

He was telling his mom, Bertha, I was coming for Christmas. And it sounded like…she didn't know.

My stomach dropped.

When he hung up, I turned off the water and dried my hands slowly. "Is everything okay?" I asked.

He shrugged, sounding casual again. "She's just stressed about one more person being there at Christmas."

I blinked. "But…I thought they already knew I was coming?"

He waved it off. "Don't worry about it. Just help her bake cookies when we get there. That'll help."

I tried to nod. To smile. To convince myself it was no big deal. But something inside me twisted.

He had invited me.

Planned it.

Booked the flights.

And yet, his best friend Bob was going too—and no one seemed to have a problem with him. Just me.

Why?

The feeling crept in slowly, like cold seeping under a door. I felt like an afterthought. Like a burden. Like maybe…I wasn't really wanted there at all.

My gut tightened. I tried to shake it, but the unease clung to me like static. "I don't know," I said carefully. "It just…it doesn't feel right."

He didn't even look up from the couch. "You're overreacting."

"I just don't want to go somewhere I'm not welcome."

He sighed. "You're reading into things again. It'll be fine."

I nodded slowly, the warning still echoing inside me. But I wanted to believe him. Because if I didn't, I'd have to face something for which I wasn't ready.

And maybe this wasn't the fairy tale I kept trying to make it.

A week later, I boarded the plane with Bert—bags packed, gifts wrapped in tissue and ribbon, heart trembling somewhere between hope and dread.

I told myself this was what love looked like.

It was choosing someone, even when it hurt, even when it felt like you were chasing their approval in someone else's home.

However, underneath it all, a quiet truth pulsed in my chest. *Something isn't right.*

Still, I smiled as we touched down in California. Nerves fluttered as we stepped into the terminal. This was it—I was about to meet Bert's dad. Dick had driven all the way from

Santa Barbara to pick us up. It felt important, as if I was being invited deeper into his world.

I clung to that hope as we made our way to baggage claim. I stood at the carousel, watching bags loop past like lazy fish in a stream. One by one, strangers claimed theirs and walked away, chatting, laughing.

Mine never came.

I waited. I re-checked the tag and scanned the screen again. Nothing.

I was dressed in jeans, a lightweight blouse, and flats. My swimsuit. Toiletries. Carefully selected outfits. All of it still circling the sky on the wrong plane.

I swallowed hard and tried to laugh it off. These things happen, right?

Bert and Bob collected their bags without a hitch. Of course, they did.

We were told to check back in two hours.

I nodded and forced a smile, the first crack splintering beneath my ribs.

"Let's hit the beach," Dick said cheerfully, already energized. "The waves are perfect today."

I blinked. "I don't have a swimsuit."

I waited for the offer. The obvious solution. A quick stop at a store. A ten-minute detour. But no. "We don't want to waste surf time," Bert said. Bob nodded in agreement.

I sat on the beach in my jeans, as the sun climbed to eighty-five degrees. Sweat clung to my back. Sand stuck to my ankles. My blouse, wrinkled and damp from the flight, clung to me like a reminder: I wasn't ready for this.

I watched the three of them paddle out, whooping and laughing as they caught wave after wave. I sat alone on a faded towel, sunscreen-less, sunburn forming across my forehead.

Unclaimed. Uninvited. Just like my suitcase.

Hours passed. When we finally returned to the airport, I was sticky, exhausted, and quietly praying for a small mercy.

But my bag still wasn't there.

"It'll be delivered in three days," the clerk told us.

I nodded. Inside, I was already gone.

The drive to Santa Barbara should have been scenic. It runs down the winding coastline, with salt air, and golden light. But the beauty blurred behind the rising hum of cracked beer cans and louder laughter.

Dick had a cooler wedged between the front seats. As soon as we pulled away from the airport, it was open season.

Bert. Bob. Dick. Crack. Guzzle. Laugh. Repeat.

I sat in the backseat, clutching the door handle as if a seatbelt couldn't save me. My heart stuttered with every swerve. My eyes stayed fixed on the road ahead, silently counting mile markers between prayers.

Please let us make it there. Please just get me through this day.

By the time we pulled into the driveway of Bert's childhood home, the car reeked of sweat, salt, and alcohol. They stumbled out, red-faced and slurring. I stepped onto the curb, my legs stiff and sore. My blouse was still damp. My hair was limp from ocean air and dried sweat. I felt dirty, forgotten, and utterly alone.

And it was only the first day.

I took a deep breath. This was it—my first time meeting Bert's family. I was still reeling from the chaos of the day: no luggage, no swimsuit, and no sleep. But I told myself it would be worth it. I wanted so badly to make a good impression.

I smoothed down my jeans, wiped the sweat from my forehead, and followed Bert up the walkway, with the wrapped box of gifts still tucked under my arm like a shield. With every step toward the front door, I rehearsed what I'd say, how I'd smile. Be gracious. Be helpful. Be…enough.

The door swung open.

A wave of people spilled out—laughing, talking over one another, loud and buzzing with holiday energy. Perfume, aftershave, and oven heat wafted past me like a wall. I barely had time to take it all in when his mom stepped forward, her eyes scanning me in a glance so quick it felt like a reflex.

"She's bigger than in her pictures," she said.

She sounded flat, and unapologetic. It was loud enough for others to hear.

The smile on my face froze—half-formed, half-fallen. I laughed, too quickly, too brightly, hoping if I pretended it didn't hurt, maybe it wouldn't. Maybe it was just her sense of humor. Maybe I'd misheard. Maybe…

No. I hadn't.

Still, I told myself, *Don't let her get to you. You're okay. Just laugh it off. Play it cool. Prove her wrong.*

So, I laughed, even though it was shallow, and shaky. And I stepped inside.

The house was packed. Voices echoed off tiled floors and vaulted ceilings, kids darted through legs, adults balanced wine glasses and paper plates, and conversations collided midair. I was introduced to what felt like dozens of people—names I couldn't hold on to, faces blending together in the blur of chaos and judgment. Every "nice to meet you" felt laced with something else. Something I couldn't name, but my body recognized it. My skin prickled. My shoulders tightened. I was on alert.

All I wanted was to take a shower, and to exhale.

But there was no room for retreat. No one offered. No one noticed.

Dinner brought some relief. I felt slightly more human with something warm in my stomach. The rhythm of passing dishes and awkward small talk helped quiet the pounding in my head. When someone suggested a game of poker after dessert, I jumped in. *Be a good sport. Be easygoing. Show them you're fun. Worthy. Good enough.*

Just as I settled at the table, Bert's sister Olga tossed something across the room. It landed in my lap.

A Christmas stocking.

At first, I smiled—until I looked closer. Written in sparkly glue and glitter was my name…added hastily at the very bottom of a long list of other women's names, each one crossed out.

Olga smirked.

"Bert brings home so many girls, we had to make space for you."

The room erupted in laughter.

I laughed too.

Or I tried. The sound caught in my throat, shallow and dry. My cheeks burned. I nodded, pretending it was fine, pretending I could take it, and pretending I wasn't shrinking inside.

But the jokes didn't stop. Little jabs, passed around like appetizers. They laughed at the stocking, at me, at how I dressed, and how I spoke. I smiled and sipped my drink and told myself not to cry.

Eventually, I excused myself. I found the guest room and shut the door. As soon as it clicked behind me, the mask fell. I collapsed into bed—still in the same clothes I'd flown in—and let the tears come: silent, hot, endless.

Bert didn't come to bed until three-thirty a.m.

When he finally stumbled in, reeking of alcohol and cheer, I pretended to be asleep.

I had never felt so far from home.

The next morning, I woke up with a swollen face and a hollow chest. The lump in my throat hadn't budged. My jaw ached from clenching it through smiles. I needed comfort— just a thread of kindness to hold onto.

I slipped outside with my phone and called my sister.

As soon as I heard Misty's voice, I broke. The words tumbled out in sobs, raw and messy—about the comments, the stocking, and the way they made me feel like I was nothing.

"I feel trapped," I whispered.

And I was. I didn't have enough money for a hotel or to change my flight. I'd committed to this trip without a back-up plan. And now, here I was—stranded in a house full of strangers who didn't want me.

Misty's voice cracked. "I'm so sorry, sis…just hang in there, okay?"

It was simple. But it was everything. She still saw me. She still cared.

When I hung up, I stood in the stillness of the patio, staring out at the trimmed hedges and the neighbor's Christmas lights blinking quietly through the mist. I wanted to go home. To my loud, messy, imperfect family—the one I used to think I needed distance from. Funny how pain rearranges your priorities.

But I couldn't go. Not yet.

Later that morning, someone casually informed me—without asking—that I'd be spending the day hiking with Olga and Fern, Bert's cousin. Everyone else was going golfing.

No one asked if I liked hiking. No one invited me golfing. I was just…assigned.

I told myself fresh air would help. Nature could soothe. Maybe the trees would listen, even if no one else did. But the moment we got in the car, the tone was set. Olga turned and asked, "Why don't you have a family of your own to spend Christmas with?"

Fern snorted with laughter. They didn't wait for an answer.

During the hike, they walked several paces ahead, whispering and laughing. Their words floated back just loud enough for me to catch fragments. My name. My clothes. My quietness.

I was invisible…and also the joke.

After the hike, someone suggested grabbing fast food. I perked up—finally, something simple and normal.

I asked if we could stop by a bank so I could transfer money from savings to checking. I didn't want my card to be declined.

As I stepped out to use the ATM, I heard Olga's voice through the open window. "Can you believe it? She doesn't even have enough money."

More laughter.

When I returned and said, "Okay, I'm good," they exchanged a look.

"Actually," Olga said, smirking, "we're just gonna head home and eat leftovers. You know…since you're broke."

I bit the inside of my cheek so hard it nearly bled. I refused to cry in front of them.

Then she turned and added, "You're not going to cry, are you?"

I stared out the window. Silent. Sinking.

Back at the house, I found Bert and pulled him aside. I told him everything—with my voice trembling, the words heavy and raw.

He sighed. "They were just joking. You're being too sensitive. That's just how they are."

It gutted me. Again.

Not once did he defend me. Not once did he validate what I felt. I was alone in this—again.

That night, like the ones before, I cried myself to sleep. Quietly. Carefully. My pillow caught the tears I wouldn't let them see.

I asked myself, *Why can't I speak up? Why am I so afraid?*

The shame was suffocating. I didn't just feel small—I *was*

small. Shrinking with every whisper, every side glance, and every joke at my expense.

In that house, I had no voice, or at least, none that mattered.

Christmas morning arrived with none of the magic I had hoped for.

I watched from the couch, quietly clutching a mug of coffee as Bert's family tore into the gifts I had poured myself into—each one carefully chosen, thoughtfully wrapped, topped with bows I had tied by hand. I had imagined this moment so many times: laughter, gratitude, and maybe even a warm hug or a thank-you that felt sincere. Instead, I sat frozen as someone held up the scarf I'd spent hours picking out and muttered, "Well,…this is different."

Polite smiles. A few nods. A shrug. And just like that, the box of gifts I had carried like a peace offering became just more clutter to push aside.

I told myself not to care. But it stung. I had tried so hard—too hard—to make a good impression. To be likable. To be worthy of a seat at their table. And still, I was met with cool indifference and the hollow ache of invisibility.

Numbness settled in where hope used to live.

I poured myself a drink, trying to quiet the hum beneath my ribs. Normally, alcohol helped me disappear—just enough to smooth the sharp edges. But not this time. The wine clung bitterly to my tongue. Even that failed me. It only made the ache louder.

The house reeked of booze. Empty bottles filled every bin and lined countertops like trophies. Four massive trash cans overflowed with beer and liquor bottles, and the recycling bins groaned under the weight of excess.

Someone chuckled and said, "Recycling doesn't come

'til next week. Guess we've got room for round two." Laughter exploded around me. I forced a smile, even though every cell in my body wanted to disappear.

I couldn't believe how much they drank—how it never seemed to catch up to them. They woke up each morning, bright-eyed, loud, and effortlessly cheerful, as if the gallons of alcohol were nothing more than a vitamin supplement. I watched them, dazed, wondering how they did it. How they normalized so much chaos and still held it together as if it was all just part of the show.

This wasn't just dysfunction. This was something else—something colder, and sharper. It wasn't messy in the human way I was used to. This was a high-functioning, alcohol-fueled machine, polished to a shine and hollow at the center.

And I was trapped in it.

*Just two more days...*I whispered it to myself like a prayer. Two more days and I could go home. Two more days and I could breathe again without flinching.

But even the countdown did little to calm the rawness beneath my skin. I felt like I was walking barefoot on glass—every joke, every smirk, and every sideways glance slicing a little deeper. The bruises weren't on my skin, but I felt them all the same.

That evening, we were invited to dinner at Uncle Pete's house. He was Bert's uncle, and for the first time in days, I felt a flicker of hope. Pete seemed...normal. Grounded. When he greeted me, he looked me in the eyes—really looked. No smirks, no scrutiny, just something honest. Something that felt a little like kindness.

Over dinner, the conversation flowed easily. I found myself speaking up, letting down my guard, confiding in Pete how out of place I felt. How difficult it had been to feel welcomed. He listened without interrupting. He nodded slowly and said something that made my breath catch: "You two should stay here tonight. We've got plenty of space—and it might be good for you to have a break."

I said yes before Bert could get a word in.

We slipped back into his parents' house just long enough to grab our bags. I didn't say goodbye. I couldn't bear to put on the smile again.

At Pete's house, the air felt different. Lighter. The guest room was warm, the bed freshly made. I stood in the middle of that room for a long moment, soaking in the quiet. For the first time since we'd landed, I didn't cry myself to sleep.

It felt like safety. Or at least the illusion of it.

The next morning, I padded softly down the hallway in borrowed socks, lured by the smell of fresh coffee. The promise of comfort pulled at me.

But just as I turned the corner toward the kitchen, I heard Pete's voice.

"…Well, she made such a big deal about staying at your place that I didn't really have a choice, did I?"

I stopped. The words lodged in my throat.

My chest caved in on itself. The flicker of hope I had held onto like a lifeline was snuffed out with a single sentence.

I turned around without a sound and walked back to the guest room. My face flushed with humiliation. My hands trembled. I sat on the edge of the bed, trying to steady my breath, trying not to cry.

When I told Bert what I'd overheard, he didn't get angry. But he didn't comfort me either.

He sighed and said, "See? We should've just stayed at my parents' house like I told you."

No softness. No understanding. Just a reminder that I was, once again, the problem.

That night, we packed our things and drove back to the house that had been chewing me up since the moment I stepped inside. Each footstep through the front door felt heavier than the last.

I didn't speak or cry. I just kept counting down the hours until I could finally leave. I woke to the sound of waves crashing somewhere in the distance and sunlight filtering through the blinds in lazy streaks. For the first time in days, my chest didn't feel tight. My eyes didn't sting. I wasn't holding back tears or bracing for the next subtle jab. It was our last day in California.

Relief bloomed through my ribs like warm air after a deep breath. Tomorrow, I'd be home. Home. The word pulsed like a lifeline. No more cold stares from Bertha. No more sugar-coated cruelty from Olga. No more playing invisible in a house full of people who treated me like background noise.

I stretched beneath the sheets, savoring the stillness.

Don't overthink, I told myself. Don't ruin it. Just hold onto this lightness as long as you can.

But even in the quiet of that morning, I was—tense—because every moment in California had been a hidden landmine, and I never knew what might blow next.

Still, I let myself hope: *Maybe today will be different. Maybe we'll end it on a good note.*

That's when Bert came into the room, twirling his keys in one hand and grinning like none of the past week had happened.

"Wanna drive up to Lover's Point and catch the sunset this evening?"

I blinked.

Yes. God, yes.

A slow exhale left my lips. Time alone with him—no Bertha, no Olga, and no Bob hovering like a smug shadow—I needed that more than I realized.

And yet…something inside me still hurt.

We had talked about marriage before this trip. We had looked at rings. We had shared baby names and made plans. But now, after everything—after how effortlessly he had let me shrink beneath his family's cruelty—those conversations felt like dreams I no longer recognized.

Still, I thought, *Maybe this could be the moment I finally tell him.*

Later that afternoon, as we were getting ready, Bert grabbed a chilled bottle of champagne from the kitchen counter. His mother stood there, with her arms crossed, and eyes narrow.

"Dinner's in two hours," she said, with her tone clipped. "Where are you two going?"

Without skipping a beat, Bert shrugged and replied, "Heidi wants to go to Lover's Point."

I stopped cold.

My breath caught in my throat. He had asked me. It was *his* idea. And now here he was, tossing me under the bus like it meant nothing.

I turned to him, stunned. "Why would you say it was my idea?"

He laughed, brushing it off. "It's not a big deal."

And there it was again—my feelings, flicked aside like lint on a jacket. No acknowledgment. No apology. Just another invisible wound.

We drove in silence, the champagne bottle clinking softly in the seat beside us.

The road curved along the coast as the sky began its descent into something holy—brilliant hues of apricot melting into lavender, the ocean glittering like glass under the fading light. When we reached the bluff, we stepped out, and the wind whipped strands of hair across my face. For a heartbeat, I let myself imagine we were just two people in love, no baggage, no bruises. Just us and the horizon.

Bert leaned over and kissed me.

But I didn't lean back.

I took a breath, heavy and certain. "We need to talk."

His face stilled.

"I can't marry you," I said, the words trembling but true. "When you marry someone, you marry their family too... and I can't do that. Not after this week. Not with how they've treated me. And not with how silent you've been through all of it. When we get home, I think we need to break up."

I braced for the usual response—the defensiveness, the blame, the gaslighting that always seemed to follow.

But instead, he just looked at me.

"I'm sorry," he said finally. "I'll do better. Everything will be okay."

And what did I do?

I nodded. I let him hold my hand. I let myself believe him.

Even though every part of me—every cell, and every instinct—was begging me not to.

Because sometimes, the hope of being loved is louder than the truth.

Back in Colorado, life slipped right back into its familiar rhythm—our toxic pattern picking up exactly where we had left off, as if that brutal California Christmas had never happened. The sting of it lingered like a bruise just under the surface—fading, sure, but never forgotten. I carried it with me like a quiet ache I couldn't name.

A few months after our return, Bert came home with big news: he'd been offered a Station Manager position at a small radio station in Vail. His eyes sparkled when he told me—hopeful, ambitious, full of the kind of energy that made you want to believe in new beginnings. He asked if I wanted to move with him. He didn't say the word marriage, but it was there, in the pause between his sentences. I could feel it hanging in the air like a maybe.

And of course, I said yes.

Because by then, saying yes had become a reflex. I'd spent so much of my life folding myself into other people's dreams, packing up my world for the chance at something more—something lasting. I had a habit of mistaking sacrifice for love. Mistaking pain for passion. But I told myself this time would be different.

New town. New job. New version of us.

We moved to Vail. He settled into the radio station. I transferred to a local branch of the same bank I'd worked at before. And I'll admit it—getting away from my manager in Fort Collins felt like a win. For the first time in a while, things felt…calm.

I found my rhythm. I had my routines. I made friends. I still had Butters—my sweet, loyal orange cat who'd been with me since I was twenty. And most days, when I came home to the smell of pine and the stillness of the mountains, I felt something close to peace.

But beneath the surface, something was off.

Bert and I still fought—more often now, and more openly. Mostly about his flirting. "It's harmless," he'd say. But it didn't feel harmless. It felt pointed and sharp, like a game he didn't mind playing, even when he knew it hurt me. And while I never caught him outright, my gut whispered things I wasn't ready to hear.

He worked late and came home even later. Sometimes in the early morning hours, reeking of alcohol and feigning innocence. His drinking had escalated—heavily—but he stayed polished, composed. Still charming. Still functional. And so, I stayed quiet.

I convinced myself it wasn't my place to question him. That love meant patience. That I was lucky just to be chosen—even if it came in fragments. I told myself that all couples had rough patches, and that this slow ache in my chest was just part of growing up, of staying committed.

But deep down, I knew better.

The cracks in us were spreading, thin and dangerous. And I kept tiptoeing around them, pretending I didn't feel the floor giving way.

It was around this time Bert introduced me to Massey—his new manager at the station. She had just moved to town. She was petite, blonde, and effortlessly radiant. The kind of woman who didn't need to try to turn heads—she just did. She had presence, and confidence. And Bert was obsessed with her.

Every other sentence out of his mouth had her name in it.

"Massey said this…Massey wants that…Massey thinks we should…"

At first, I played it off. I told myself I was being dramatic. That it was just a professional thing. That I was overthinking.

Then came the barbecue.

She invited us to her place—something casual, a station hangout. I agreed, even though my stomach twisted the second we pulled into her driveway.

The second I walked through the door, I felt it.

Her eyes barely landed on me before drifting back to him. Their energy was unmistakable—quiet and charged. They moved around each other as if gravity had its own agenda. The way they spoke in low tones, stood too close, laughed at nothing. The way their hands brushed, lingered.

I felt myself disappearing.

I stood at the edge of it all—smiling, nodding, and holding a red plastic cup like a shield. Pretending I wasn't unraveling.

Her coldness wasn't imagined. It was deliberate. Dismissive. Like I'd already been weighed and deemed unworthy. Like I was in the way of something inevitable.

The car ride home was silent. The kind of silence that

feels thick and suffocating, as if it's pressing against your ribs.

I finally asked, "Is there something going on between you two?"

He laughed. But it wasn't kind or reassuring.

"Of course not," he said. "Don't be ridiculous."

And just like that, the conversation ended.

But I couldn't unsee what I saw. I couldn't unfeel what I felt.

From that night on, she lived in the background of my thoughts. Her name echoed in his stories. Her presence hovered between us, even when she wasn't there. I tried to ignore it. I tried to pretend it didn't matter. But I knew. In my bones, I knew.

And it hurt in that quiet, relentless way—the kind of ache that sets up camp behind your smile. I started shrinking again. Laughing less. Watching every interaction like I was waiting for the final blow.

I was ready to end it. I wanted to.

However, Bert had this way of knowing—like he could sense when I was about to leave. And right when I'd start pulling away, he'd reach for me. Soft at first, then sudden. Like reeling in a fish too exhausted to fight.

And I'd bite. Every time.

Because I was tired of starting over. Tired of not being enough. Tired of searching for something that felt like home in someone who only offered shelter when it was convenient.

And because a part of me still believed that love was supposed to hurt a little.

And just like clockwork, he proposed.

It was Valentine's Day. We'd both had long days at work. I still remember the heaviness in my chest as we walked into that little Italian restaurant he picked—a cozy spot with dim lighting and tiny red candles flickering on every table. My smile was soft but tired. Part of me just wanted pasta, wine, and silence. I wasn't expecting fireworks. I wasn't expecting anything.

But of course, he had a script.

The softened voice. The careful timing. The way he reached for my hand across the table, as if we hadn't been slowly drifting for months.

I should've seen it coming.

After dessert, just as I leaned back and considered asking for the check, he stood. Then dropped to one knee beside me.

Everything slowed.

The clink of forks. The buzz of conversation. That swell of romantic music I hadn't noticed until just then.

And then—he spoke. "Will you marry me?"

The question hung in the air like perfume, sweet and intoxicating. I froze. My breath caught. My mind scrambled to catch up. I didn't feel joy, or giddiness.

I felt panic and confusion. But then, there was a fragile flicker of hope that maybe—just maybe—this was a turning point.

I said yes.

The room erupted into applause—strangers clapping, cheering, and raising their glasses in celebration of a love they didn't know. A love they couldn't possibly see past the candlelight and champagne. I smiled. I kissed him.

And I let myself believe.

Hook, line, and sinker.

We picked a date—September. Seven months away. And just like that, I launched into full-on planning mode.

This was my jam. I'd always loved organizing events. The vision, the flow, the details. I threw myself into it like a woman on a mission—creating vision boards, color palettes, and vendor checklists. It gave me something to hold onto. A purpose. A future I could design from scratch.

I wanted our wedding to feel intentional, personal, and intimate—not a cookie-cutter celebration but something meaningful. Something that felt like us…or, at least, the version of us I was still clinging to.

Bert didn't want to be involved.

At first, I welcomed it—his indifference gave me freedom. However, as the days turned into weeks, it didn't feel like space. It felt like distance. He wouldn't try cakes, wouldn't look at venues, and didn't care about playlists or menus or flowers. Every time I asked for input, it was met with a shrug, or worse, an eye roll.

It was supposed to be our day. However, it already felt like I was walking down that aisle alone.

His mother offered to help. She offered money, vendors, and opinions. But I declined—politely, but firmly. I wanted the wedding to be ours. Funded by us. Free of strings. I built a budget—five thousand—and I stuck to it. It wasn't grand, but it was beautiful. Carefully crafted. Honest.

There were moments I'll always cherish. Dress shopping with my sister—my maid of honor—trying on gowns while we laughed until we cried. Hunting for the perfect bridesmaid gifts in boutique aisles. Sitting with my closest girlfriends over wine, imagining how the day would unfold.

Those moments felt like sunlight.

Until the letter came.

It was from Olga.

Handwritten. Self-righteous. Seething.

She demanded to be a bridesmaid. Not asked—demanded. As if being Bert's sister entitled her to stand beside me on the most intimate day of my life. Her tone was sharp and condescending. Anything less, she wrote, would be a "personal insult."

My stomach turned as I read it.

This wasn't a gesture of love. It was a power play.

I waited a day before responding. I was letting the emotion settle so I could answer carefully. I brought it to Bert first, hoping for support—for even a sliver of understanding.

"I want to be surrounded by women who've actually supported me," I said gently. "Women who've loved me through the hard stuff. Olga hasn't done that."

He didn't get it.

He said excluding her would create drama. That his entire family would take it personally. That I was overthinking it.

So, I offered a compromise. She could stand on his side—as a "grooms-woman." It honored her role without forcing her into mine.

And then, I did something I hadn't done often in that relationship: I held my ground.

I wrote back to her. I was clear, firm, and respectful. I told her exactly how I felt. I told her she was welcome—on her brother's side, where her loyalty belonged.

It was the first time I didn't shrink.

And I knew—I knew—it would cost me later.

But in that moment, I stood in my truth.

And that mattered.

Vail felt like something out of a storybook that week—pine trees dusted in white, crisp mountain air nipping at bare fingers, the hush of snowfall settling into every crevice of town like a whispered blessing. And right there, tucked beside the local bank at the far end of Main Street, stood the tiny white church where we'd be married.

Its steeple pointed modestly toward the sky, not boastful or grand, but humble, and sacred. I'd walked past it a dozen times before, always pausing to peer through its stained-glass windows, wondering what the light would look like as it spilled across the pews on my wedding day.

Now, it was happening.

That dream I'd carried since girlhood—lace veil, flickering candles, and snow gently falling outside—it had found a home here. A place where every detail was more than planned. It was prayed into being.

Our reception was set for Beaver Creek, a short drive away, nestled high on a mountaintop. Guests would arrive by ski lift, floating silently above the evergreens, with panoramic views stretched like silk across the sky. I imagined them stepping off the lift into champagne air, cheeks flushed from altitude and laughter, walking into a chalet glowing with warmth and music.

For those hesitant about heights, I had arranged vans to shuttle them safely to the top. I had left details unconsidered. I wanted ease. I wanted magic. I wanted to wrap every guest in a memory they'd never forget.

Most of our friends and family were flying in from out of town, so I reserved a block of rooms at a cozy, slope-side hotel. Welcome bags waited on every bed—filled with local treats, hand-written notes, itineraries tied in silk ribbon. It wasn't just a wedding. It was a gathering of hearts. And I was ready to hold them all.

Then came the storm.

The snow arrived fast and thick—fat flakes tumbling from the sky in a frenzied hush, blurring the edges of the mountains and swallowing the road signs whole. It didn't drift romantically. It dumped.

By noon the day before the wedding, the calls started coming in.

My planner's voice was tight. "The lift is down. It's not safe. The mountaintop chalet is inaccessible."

My breath hitched. I stared out the window of my

apartment, watching the snowfall turn the world white. Everything I had pictured—everything I had planned—was up there, out of reach.

"I'm so sorry," she added softly. "We'll find another space."

I nodded into the phone, unable to speak. My chest burned with grief, but I swallowed it. There wasn't time to break down. There were linens to reorder. Floorplans to redraw. A dream to somehow reimagine.

That afternoon, I followed her up to Beaver Creek, boots crunching against the packed snow as we wound through the village to a backup chalet nestled lower on the mountain. My expectations were low. My heart was heavy.

But then I stepped inside.

Stone fireplaces roared with firelight. Timber beams stretched overhead like cathedral arches. The scent of pine and firewood wrapped itself around me like a blanket. Glass walls framed the mountains in soft blue dusk, and for a moment, I forgot to be heartbroken.

It wasn't the mountaintop chalet. It wasn't the fairy tale I had dreamed down to the last twinkle light. But it was breathtaking. There was something about the way the warmth lived in the walls of that space—quiet, grounded, and real. Not the dream I'd clung to, but maybe…maybe something better.

The ache in my chest loosened. Not all the way. But enough to see clearly. Enough to believe that joy isn't always tied to a plan.

Sometimes, the most sacred moments arrive in places we never meant to go. And sometimes, the detour is the destination.

The morning of the wedding dawned bright and—eerily quiet. Not the kind of silence that soothes, but the kind that hums with something unspoken. Sunlight poured through the hotel window, warming the edge of the bed, catching on the curve of my wedding dress where it hung like a ghost waiting to be filled.

I stood barefoot in front of the mirror, veil draped over my shoulders, the cool fabric brushing my arms like a question I couldn't quite answer. My hands trembled as I adjusted the satin waistband. The woman staring back at me looked composed, radiant even. But just beneath the surface, everything was churning.

My heart pounded with more than anticipation. It pulsed with questions I'd been trying to drown out for weeks. Months.

Are you sure?

I blinked, then reached for my lipstick, as if color could anchor me. I dabbed it on carefully, my breath catching in my throat.

Are you really ready for this?

The question didn't scream—it whispered. Low and insistent. Like a child tugging at my sleeve. I swallowed hard and stepped into my shoes. I told myself this was just nerves. Cold feet. Every bride has them. But the truth felt heavier than that.

This wasn't just wedding-day jitters. This was grief. This was the quiet ache of a woman who knew, deep in her bones, that she was marrying someone who didn't make her feel safe. Someone who rarely chose her unless it was convenient. Someone who had let her stand alone too many times.

But I'd come too far to turn around now.

So, I buried the knowing beneath blush, beneath satin, beneath the thick weight of hope that maybe, just maybe, love could be enough. That maybe vows could change things. That maybe this time, the story would end differently.

The chapel bells rang, slicing through the stillness. And I walked down the aisle.

The tiny white church at the end of town felt like

something out of a snow globe—soft stained glass glowing against the morning sun, wooden pews filled with people who loved us, or at least loved the idea of us. I clutched my bouquet a little tighter and kept my eyes forward.

Bert stood at the altar, eyes misted, a practiced smile on his face. He looked like the man I had always wanted him to be. And for a heartbeat, I let myself believe he might become him.

The ceremony was beautiful. The vows emotional. We said all the right things—words about commitment and forgiveness, about walking through the hard stuff together. There were tears in the pews. People reached for each other's hands. It felt like everyone wanted to believe in us.

When the minister said, "You may kiss the bride," I let myself be kissed. I let the applause wash over me. I let myself pretend. We were husband and wife.

And for a moment, I believed that meant something solid. Something safe. Something sacred.

Then came the reception—and it was magic.

The alternative chalet, the one I had resisted so fiercely, unfolded like a scene from a dream. Firelight shimmered through the space, alive and welcoming. Everything above us felt lifted, expansive, almost sacred. Candles flickering on every table, casting halos of gold onto the glassware.

The food was perfection. The drinks flowed like celebration. The DJ played one joyful song after another, pulling even the shyest guests onto the dance floor. I danced with my sister. I twirled in my gown. I threw my head back and laughed like I didn't have a single scar.

Even the weather played along.

The day before had been a blizzard. But now it was eighty-two degrees and brilliant. The snow had melted into glistening run-off, sparkling under the sun. It was like the universe had leaned down and said, "This is your day." And for the first time in a long time, I believed it. The warmth felt like a benediction. Like the heavens had cracked open just for me.

I looked around at the people gathered there—their faces lit with love, laughter, champagne—and I thought, *This is what it feels like to be chosen.*

But even as I floated through the night on the music and the wine and the fairy tale of it all, something inside me stayed still.

A small, quiet knowing that hadn't left.

It stood in the corner like an old friend, watching me dance, watching me smile, watching me kiss my new husband in front of the people who mattered most.

It didn't shout.

It didn't plead.

It simply waited.

8

QUIET BETWEEN THE CRACKS

The morning after our wedding should have felt soft: holy, like the afterglow of something sacred. I had imagined waking up in that golden haze people talk about—the quiet kind of joy that hums beneath the skin. I thought maybe we'd hold hands a little longer, exchange sleepy smiles, whisper about the magic of the night before.

Instead, we were invited to breakfast at his parents' hotel suite.

I pictured something intimate. A small, warm gathering. Maybe a toast to our new life together. Maybe someone asking what our favorite part of the ceremony had been, or if the reception turned out the way we hoped. I imagined a room where I felt seen.

But when we walked in, it was like crashing someone else's party.

The suite buzzed with noise—laughter, the clink of silverware, mimosa glasses half-raised. At least fifteen of Bert's relatives were already there, sprawled out in chairs and on the couch, chatting like it was just another Sunday brunch. No one looked up. No one smiled. No one said,

"Congratulations." No one even acknowledged that I had entered the room.

I stood in the doorway for a beat too long, waiting for someone to see me. Waiting to be invited in.

Then his mom appeared.

Polished. Poised. Smiling like a hostess at her own private gala. She wrapped her arm around Bert's waist as if I wasn't even there and steered him into the kitchen. A mimosa in one hand. An egg sandwich in the other. Both passed to him like a king receiving tribute.

He smiled, took them, sat down and started eating.

He didn't look back to see if I had a plate. Didn't ask if I was okay. Didn't pull out a chair or pour me a drink. He just…forgot me.

It felt surreal. Like the pages of our story had been torn out and replaced with a version where I no longer existed. Just yesterday, we had stood in front of everyone we loved and vowed to take care of each other. And today, I was a ghost in a room filled with his name.

I pulled him aside, heart pounding, hands shaking. I whispered that I felt out of place. That I didn't feel welcome. That I was hurt. He shrugged. "If you want to go home, then leave," he said. "I'm staying."

Just like that. No fight. No apology. Not even a flicker of concern. So, I left.

No goodbyes. No polite nods or forced smiles. I slipped out the door as quietly as I had entered, like a shadow no one noticed was missing. I didn't know where I was going—my family had driven home that morning. I had no one.

I called my sister, hoping she might pick up. Hoping she could come back. Hoping someone would say, "You're not crazy. You're not alone."

No answer.

So, I drove home. Numb. Back to our apartment. Back to the silence.

The living room was filled with unopened wedding gifts—boxes wrapped in silver paper, bows still perfectly tied. They sat like quiet witnesses to a celebration that already felt like a lie.

I waited.

I called him hours later. No answer. Left a voicemail, my voice trembling, asking when he was coming home.

Still nothing.

As the silence stretched on, the numbness cracked open. And from it came something hotter. Rage. I tore into the wedding gifts—not with joy, but with fury. Tissue paper flying. Boxes gutted. As if the act of opening them could release something—pain, betrayal, grief. But all it released was emptiness. It made the room feel colder, and quieter.

Eventually, I put everything away. Folded the wrapping paper. Stacked the boxes. Neatly tucked away the evidence of a day that was supposed to change everything.

Then I curled up on the couch, wrapped in a blanket I couldn't feel, and rocked myself to sleep.

I don't know what time he finally came home.

The room was dark, and quiet, except for the hum of the refrigerator and the quiet throb in my stomach. I stayed still, pretending to sleep. But every nerve in my body was alive—listening.

The door opened.

He walked past me without a word.

The scent hit me first—alcohol and cigars, sharp and heavy. He didn't stop. He didn't check on me. He didn't speak. He just went straight to the bedroom and closed the door.

He slept alone.

At least I had Butters. My cat. My companion. His small, warm body pressed against mine, his purr steady against my ribs. In that moment, the unconditional love of a cat meant more than anything my new husband had to offer.

Butters didn't ask for anything. He didn't make me feel like I didn't exist. He just stayed.

The next morning came like a slap. The sunlight was too bright, and the silence too loud.

Bert didn't say a word. No apology. No explanation. No mention of the night before.

Just footsteps. Coffee brewing. Like it was any other Monday.

And just like that, the silence became routine. No big conversations. No heartfelt makeups. Just a quiet, mutual agreement to pretend none of it had happened.

I kept waiting for the shift. The honeymoon phase. The sacred "after" that people talked about.

But instead of growing closer, we grew quiet.

Two bodies sharing space. Not lives.

The ink on our marriage license had barely dried, but already the role of "wife" felt more symbolic than sacred. I signed my new name on checks and HR paperwork like it belonged to someone else—as if I was playing a part that didn't quite fit. And yet, I wore it. Like a costume. Like hope.

I kept waiting for something to shift. For Bert to soften. For tenderness to rise in the spaces where distance had lived. For that myth about how marriage changes people to become real in our living room.

But it never did.

Each day passed in quiet repetition—morning alarms, shared coffee, brief hellos and even briefer goodnights. We were a couple by title only, reciting our lines like stage actors trapped in a production we hadn't auditioned for. The life we had begun to build looked fine from the outside— neat, acceptable—but inside, it was hollow. Carefully arranged, but lifeless. I found myself longing for a connection that didn't feel choreographed.

So, when Bert came home one evening, breathless with news and possibility, I leaned in—hard.

"I got offered a co-anchor spot," he said, eyes lit like a boy who still believed in dreams. "It's a small market…in Napa."

I blinked. "California?"

He nodded. "It's a step. A good one."

The job paid just twenty thousand a year—barely enough for groceries, let alone rent—but I didn't hesitate. I'd always been the one holding the financial reins, and I never complained. I carried that weight the way I carried everything—with quiet grace and no scoreboard.

My response was simple. "Let's do it."

The bank I worked for had a branch in Napa, and when I asked about a transfer, it was granted within the week. I had worked my way up to New Accounts Specialist by then, earning—sixty-five thousand a year—more than enough to support us both, again.

But this wasn't about the money.

This was about chasing something bigger—his dream, yes, but maybe also mine. The dream of closeness. Of meaning. Of finally feeling like we were on the same team.

We boxed up our lives in silence and stretches of music—our mismatched dishes, our dusty photo albums, the wedding gifts we hadn't used yet. As we taped up the final box, I glanced around our apartment in Colorado, swallowing the lump that rose unexpectedly in my throat. This place had held more than furniture. It had held versions of me I was still trying to outgrow.

The goodbyes came fast and teary—hugs from friends who had become family, parting glances that lingered in my soul. Colorado was my home. My mountains. My memories. But I tucked them all into the rearview mirror, willing myself not to look back too long.

Butters had to be sedated for the trip. He curled in his carrier like a soft comma, breathing slow and shallow under the effects of the pill. I caught my reflection in the car window—jaw tight, eyes wide, masking my own kind of sedation. I, too, was quiet. Watchful. Drowsy with uncertainty.

The miles slipped past us like chapters in a book we hadn't decided how to finish. The roads curved and stretched until finally, we crossed into the lush vineyards and soft hills of Napa.

Our new place was a modest duplex—two bedrooms, two baths, nestled in a sleepy neighborhood with blooming rosebushes and neighbors who waved as they passed. It wasn't glamorous, but it felt…possible.

We hung art on the walls. We learned the layout of the grocery store. We tasted wine on Saturday afternoons and found new favorite restaurants. For the first time in what felt like forever, life didn't feel so heavy.

There was laughter—real laughter. There were light-hearted dinners and shared glances that didn't always carry weight. It was simple. Gentle. A version of happiness I hadn't known in years.

And for the first time since saying "I do," I let myself exhale.

Maybe we had made the right move after all.

The morning started with a strange unease—my stomach off, my limbs heavy, as if my body knew something I didn't. I moved through my routine in a daze, brushing my teeth, curling my hair, pouring coffee I couldn't stomach. At work, I tried to ignore the fog in my head and the nausea curling in my gut. But when I mentioned how I was feeling to a co-worker in passing, she tilted her head, raised a brow, and said it plain:

"Maybe you're pregnant?"

The words hit like a splash of cold water. I laughed it off, too quickly. But her eyes lingered. And something inside me shifted—quiet, but undeniable.

I hadn't been on birth control since before the wedding. We had talked about kids—someday—and I had stopped the pill, leaving the rest to fate. Maybe this was fate, whispering its answer in morning queasiness and spinning thoughts.

During my lunch break, I drove to the pharmacy. My fingers twitched as I picked up the pregnancy tests, hiding them beneath a pack of gum and a bottle of water like a teenager with a secret. Back at work, I locked myself in the upstairs bathroom, hands trembling as I opened the first test. The result came fast—one blue line, clear and certain.

Positive.

My heart paused. The air felt still.

Later that night, in the quiet of our bathroom, I took the other two tests. One by one, they lit up just the same.

Positive. Positive.

I sat down on the edge of the tub, plastic sticks scattered around me like tiny oracles. I wasn't afraid—not exactly. What I felt was reverence. A kind of holy hush. Like something ancient and beautiful had arrived, and I didn't yet know how to hold it.

That weekend, I waited until after dinner. We'd cleared the dishes, the room still warm with garlic and candlelight. I looked at Bert across the table and said it softly.

"We're pregnant."

His eyes went wide. He let out a small laugh, then stood and wrapped me in a hug. He kissed me. He kissed my belly. For a moment, I felt like we were glowing from the inside out. He was scared. So was I. But beneath it all, there was joy. Real joy.

This was it. Our beginning.

The first trimester was rough. Morning sickness clung to

me like fog, thick and constant. But Bert changed. He soft-ened. He stopped drinking—mostly. He held my hair back when I was sick. He rubbed my lower back at night and spoke to the baby with a tenderness I'd only dreamed of. I was glowing, everyone said. And I believed them.

But as my belly began to grow, the glow started to dim.

I had always been tall, lean, and confident in my body. But pregnancy reshaped me—my face, my arms, my thighs. Every mirror felt like a stranger. I tried to embrace it. I told myself it was normal, sacred, beautiful. But I could see it in Bert's eyes—how he looked past me now instead of at me. How his touch had slowly vanished. How the warmth had slipped out of his voice.

By the second trimester, he barely touched me at all.

And I noticed. Oh, I noticed.

A coworker, seven months pregnant, was glowing like a sunrise. Her husband dropped by the office, placed his hand on her belly, kissed her forehead, brought her favorite smoothie without her asking. I smiled and told her how lucky she was. Then, I cried alone in the breakroom.

At home, Bert came in later and later. I waited up. Asked him how his day was. Tried to share mine. Sometimes he'd grunt a reply. Sometimes nothing at all. There was no more baby talk. No more kisses. No more asking how I was feeling.

I felt like I was disappearing—day by day, inch by inch.

To keep from falling apart, I focused on work. I had just been promoted to Mortgage Sales Manager. The commute was long—forty-five minutes each way—but the raise helped, especially with a baby on the way. I was proud. I wanted to be proud.

But pride doesn't keep you warm at night.

Bert was slipping. I could feel it. That familiar distance creeping in again, like smoke under a door. I tried to reach him, to pull us back together, but I couldn't find the handle.

He was already on the other side.

• • •

It started small—innocent, almost. Bert would come home talking about work, his words orbiting one name over and over again.

"Frangelica said the funniest thing today…"

"Frangelica fixed the whole production schedule like it was nothing…"

"She's brilliant. Like, next-level smart."

Her name slid from his tongue so smoothly, it felt rehearsed. I laughed the first few times and tried not to flinch. But each mention carved a little deeper into my brain.

Then, I met her.

Petite. Polished. Red hair that tumbled down her back in loose, perfect waves. She shook my hand with a confidence that filled the room. Her body—slim and toned—was everything mine used to be. Before pregnancy. Before the swelling and stretch marks.

Before exhaustion made even brushing my hair feel like a win. She glowed in a way I no longer could.

She wasn't carrying a child. She was carrying light.

I wanted to believe it was all in my head. I had no proof. Just a growing ache in my gut and a silence in Bert that felt new. He pulled his phone away when I entered the room. He laughed too hard at things I didn't hear. He looked at me—but not really. Not like before. Not like he used to, when I was still magic in his eyes.

One night, waddling through the living room, my back screaming and feet ballooned, I reached for a glass of water. Bert looked up from the couch and said it—flat, emotionless.

"Wow. Your ass is huge."

I stopped mid-step.

My breath caught like it had slammed into a wall. "Are you serious right now?"

He didn't blink. "Yes. You have a fat ass."

Heat exploded in my chest—rage and heartbreak, all tangled up in a tight, breathless knot.

"I'm pregnant," I snapped. "I'm carrying your child."

He shrugged as if it meant nothing. "A fact is a fact."

That night, he slept on the couch. But the chasm between us stretched far wider than any sofa could measure. Something cracked inside me. Something that wouldn't heal with time.

Years later, I brought up that moment. Still raw. Still hoping he'd say he was sorry. That he hadn't meant it. That he remembered.

He just blinked. "That never happened."

Unbelievable…

The days that followed blurred into one long, slow unraveling. The commute, the pressure at work, Bert's coldness—it was too much. My body couldn't keep carrying it all. That morning, I sat in traffic with aching hips and swollen fingers, counting down the minutes to lunch. I had noticed a few specks of blood that morning in my underwear but brushed it off. Pregnancy was weird. It was probably nothing.

I made it through a few hours at my desk, then drove to my OB appointment, still chewing on emails and to-do lists. I casually mentioned the spotting to my doctor.

Her face changed instantly.

She moved gently, efficiently. Fetal monitor. Juice. Nurse. I lay back, staring at the ceiling as the belt tightened around my belly. The rhythmic whoosh of the monitor filled the room. My stomach vibrated with each pulse. Strange. But not painful.

Still, I felt fine. Just tired.

Then she said it. Calm. Controlled. Clinical.

"You're in preterm labor. You need to call your husband. You're going straight to the hospital."

The words didn't land all at once. They hovered in the air, then hit me like a freight train.

I had two months to go. His lungs weren't ready. None of us were ready.

Bert met me at the hospital with a bag. His expression was unreadable. They gave me an injection to stop the contractions. But it didn't work. My cervix was already opening. We were running out of time.

Then came the amniocentesis. A long, silver needle. A deep breath. A sharp plunge through my belly. My whole uterus revolted. I clutched the bedrail, with my teeth clenched, and tears hot in my eyes.

His lungs weren't ready.

They hooked me to magnesium, trying to hold back the inevitable. It slowed everything—my speech, my thoughts, and my limbs. When I called my family, I sounded drunk. My sister cried. I couldn't make the words come out right. I was floating somewhere far away, suspended in fear.

I stayed that way for a week. Tethered to monitors. Praying my baby would wait. Bargaining with God in the middle of the night. Whispering promises into the air like spells.

Eventually, the specialist came. They reviewed the charts, and said the words I didn't want to hear:

"There's nothing more we can do."

I was sent home on bedrest. No more work. No more plans. Just stillness. Just waiting.

Every day, I talked to my son. I told him we weren't ready yet. That he needed to stay. That I'd keep him safe as long as I could.

And somehow—miraculously—my body listened.

The days crept by on bedrest—long, quiet hours of swollen ankles, muted TV, and too much thinking. So, when my doctor finally gave me the all-clear to return to work, just two and a half weeks shy of my due date, I nearly cried with relief. I needed out. I needed people. I needed purpose. My world had become too small, and the silence was starting to scream.

That Monday morning, I rose with a kind of energy I hadn't felt in weeks. My back ached, but I brushed it off, savoring the feeling of mascara on my lashes and keys in my hand. I drove to the office, with the windows down and music on. For a moment, I felt almost normal again.

But by the time I pulled into the parking lot, something had shifted.

A low, steady tightening gripped my belly—rhythmic, pulsing, and real. My heart kicked up its pace. No. Not yet.

But my body had already decided.

I turned the car around and drove home, white-knuckled and breathing through each contraction like I'd practiced. As soon as I got inside, I called Bert.

"Hey…I think it's happening. Can you come get me?"

He said he'd leave work. Said he'd be right there.

Half an hour passed.

Then—forty-five minutes.

An hour.

The contractions were stronger now, pulling at me like tides. My breath came in shallow gasps.

"If you're not here in thirty minutes," I snapped, voice sharp with panic, "I'm calling an ambulance."

He got home with five minutes to spare.

The ride to the hospital was chaos. I was screaming at him to drive faster. He shouted back, flustered and overwhelmed. Every bump in the road felt like a knife in my spine. My hands dug into the seat, nails leaving crescents in the upholstery. It felt like the world had narrowed to one long, terrifying push forward.

We arrived in a blur.

Inside the delivery ward, the nurse handed me a gown. I told her I needed to use the bathroom first. As I sat on the toilet, pressure surged low in my pelvis. Then came the warm rush.

For a second, I thought I'd peed myself. But then I saw the clear fluid pooling at my feet.

My water had broken.

I managed to change, fingers fumbling with the gown's ties, and waddled back to the bed. The nurse checked me, her tone brisk and impatient.

"When did your water break?"

"Just now," I whispered, wincing at her sharpness.

Less than an hour later, I was holding him.

There are no words for the moment your child is placed on your chest—warm, slippery, and perfect. Dusty's tiny chest rose and fell against mine, and the sound of his breath was the most sacred thing I'd ever heard. He smelled like newness and magic and everything I didn't know I'd been waiting for.

I ran my finger down the curve of his back, memorizing every inch. His soft whimpering settled into sleep, and I swore—right there in that hospital bed—that I would protect this boy with everything in me. He would know love. He would know safety. He would know joy.

To my surprise, Bert rose to meet the moment.

He was there. He was present, and gentle.

When Dusty cried in the night, Bert got up without complaint. Sometimes he let me sleep, padding across the floor to rock our son in quiet circles while the rest of the world dreamed. When I struggled with breastfeeding—when my body couldn't give Dusty what he needed—Bert was beside me, bottle in hand, whispering, "We've got this."

And in those early weeks, we did.

We were tired and stretched thin, but we were a team.

For the first time in a long time, I let myself believe it.

Maybe—just maybe—we'd be okay.

•　　•　　•

Two weeks after bringing Dusty home, I was curled up on the couch, half-asleep, when my phone rang. Misty's name flashed on the screen. I answered with a smile, expecting sister chatter, maybe something about baby clothes or a check-in. But the second I heard her voice—shaky, too steady to be natural—my chest tightened.

"Heidi," she said, "Stan was sentenced."

The room seemed to tilt. My breath caught. I gripped the edge of the cushion like it could anchor me. "What do you mean, sentenced?"

As she spoke, her words landed like shards of glass. While I was on bedrest, while I was worrying about swollen ankles and preterm labor, Stan had been arrested. My sisters—Sharon, Suzi, and Stephanie—had come forward. They had carried their pain in silence for years. They were only babies when it started. Six. Four. Eight months old.

I pressed my hand against my chest, trying to hold my heart in place as it cracked wide open.

Misty's voice trembled as she told me how he had controlled them. Manipulated them. Hurt them at gunpoint. Even in high school. He had given them pagers—tools for summoning them home, no matter where they were. School. A sleepover. It didn't matter. They were his. And no one stopped him.

Stacey—Sharon's mom—had finally gotten them to safety. She called the police. Stan had been in jail for months. But no one had told me. Not a word. Not even when I called. Not even when I wondered why people had gone quiet. They were afraid the truth would send me into early labor.

I sat there, silent, the room spinning around me. My baby cooed softly from his bassinet, unaware of the storm ripping through my insides. I felt sick, betrayed, and furious. Why hadn't anyone told me? Why didn't someone stop him sooner?

And then came the guilt. Heavy. Paralyzing. I had known. Not in concrete terms, but in the way you know a house is burning before you see the flames. I'd seen things. Felt things. I had left at fourteen and never looked back—but I hadn't said a word. I told myself I didn't have proof. That I was just a kid. That no one would believe me.

But deep down…I knew.

And I did nothing.

Why hadn't anyone else said something? My mom. My grandparents. The people who lived under the same roof. How could they have not known?

I started sobbing—loud, uncontrollable sobs that made Dusty stir. Misty stayed on the line, whispering gently through my grief. "If he hurt you too…you can still write a letter. You can tell the judge your story."

After we hung up, I sat in silence, tears still tracking down my cheeks. My legs gave out as I tried to stand, and I sank into the nearest chair. I stared at the blank page in front of me, with a pen in hand, my grip trembling.

Then the flood came.

I wrote. Five pages. Maybe more. Each word scraped raw from the inside out. I didn't soften the edges. I didn't edit the memories. I wrote about the nights I couldn't sleep. About the fear that lived in my body long after I'd left. About the shame. The silence. The knowing.

I wrote for the little girl who had to flinch her way through childhood. For the teenager who was too scared to tell. For my sisters—who'd carried pain heavier than anyone should. And I begged the judge for justice. For mercy not for him, but for us.

Two weeks later, the phone rang again.

It was cold that March night. I remember because I stood

by the window while Misty spoke, her breath catching with every word. Stan had been sentenced—to forty-four years.

The judge said it was the worst case of child abuse he had ever seen.

I hung up, turned to Dusty sleeping peacefully in his crib, and wept. Not just for the horror of what had happened, but for the chance—maybe for the first time—to begin again. For something safer. For something better.

But relief didn't come clean. It arrived wrapped in grief.

Not for the man he was. But for the father he was supposed to be. I mourned the loss of something I never really had. A title he carried—but never earned. How do you grieve someone who was both your nightmare and your blood?

I cried for the girl who once just wanted a dad. And for the woman who now had to accept that even that fragile hope was gone forever.

Still, life didn't stop. Not for grief. Not for justice. Not for healing. There were bottles to warm. Diapers to change. A baby depending on me to keep going.

So, I did.

But the grief never left. It just folded itself into the corners of my life—quiet and heavy—waiting for the silence to settle.

The years that followed blurred together in a rhythm that felt both full and strangely hollow—bottles, bedtime stories, and three a.m. rocking-chair prayers. On the surface, we looked like a family finding its groove. From the outside, maybe even thriving. Smiling holiday cards, whispered lullabies, and framed milestones on the fridge.

To me, it felt like we were holding it together. Barely.

There were good days, even great ones. But the

arguments always circled back—like reruns we couldn't stop watching. His drinking. The late nights. His mother's disapproval. And what he called my "insecurities," which by then had started to wear a different name: Crazy. He said it often enough that I started to wonder if he was right.

But motherhood? That was my anchor. My truth. Dusty's gummy smiles, his sleepy weight curled against me, his tiny voice mispronouncing words with such confidence—it all grounded me. He made the world softer, even when everything else felt hard.

I poured myself into every part of it: messy art projects taped proudly to the wall, finger-sticky popsicles on summer walks, the tiny "I love yous" whispered before naps. I lived for it. I needed it.

Even my relationship with my mom began to flicker with something that looked like change. When she and her boyfriend flew out from Colorado for Dusty's baptism, I watched her cradle him in her arms like he was precious. And for a brief moment, I let myself believe she was trying. That maybe I wasn't the only one who wanted a second chance.

But the phone calls always ended the same. Just when I'd start to open up, to trust that maybe she could hold some of my heaviness, she'd interrupt with a curt "I have to go." And then she'd vanish again.

Eventually, I stopped trying.

Still, the fact that she came at all—to the baptism, to witness my son be blessed—meant something. A tiny offering. A sliver of effort. And I clung to that gesture with both hands. Sometimes, hope is quiet. And that day, it was wearing a pale blue dress and smiling at a baby she barely knew.

Time kept moving.

It was November, two years later, when I first felt it. Subtle at first—a wave of nausea that didn't pass, an ache that settled behind my ribs, the sharp pull in my chest when

Bert's cologne hit my nose wrong. My body was humming with memory, with knowing.

I stood at the bathroom sink one evening, staring at myself in the mirror. My hands moved instinctively, palms resting on the gentle swell of my lower belly, like they were remembering before my brain caught up.

I didn't wait. I grabbed my keys, heart pounding, and drove to Walgreens with my fingers clenched around the steering wheel and a prayer stuck in my throat. The cashier didn't say a word when I placed the test on the counter, but I could feel her eyes follow me as I left.

Minutes later, back home, I stood barefoot on the cool tile of the bathroom floor. One pink line, then two.

I blinked, breath caught between wonder and disbelief. Two lines. Baby number two.

A laugh broke from my lips—soft, trembling. Joy washed over me, unexpected and all-consuming. Against all the mess, the stress, the uncertainty…here was something pure. A life growing inside me. A new beginning.

When I told Bert, his reaction was layered. He smiled, kissed me gently, and held his hand over my belly—but there was a pause, a slowness behind his questions. "Are we ready for this? What if I can't love this baby like I love Dusty?"

I had those questions, too. But underneath the fear lived something stronger. Faith. A quiet knowing that love would multiply, not divide.

Bert started talking about the baby like he already knew her. A girl, he hoped. "Soft eyes like yours," he said. "She'll be a Daddy's girl."

But me? I couldn't echo that dream. A daughter terrified me.

I had seen too much of what the world did to girls. I had felt the sharp edges of female cruelty in middle school hallways and grown-up silences. I had watched my own mother disappear, emotionally checked out while I begged for closeness. I had been picked apart, dismissed, broken.

Worse, I had been abused. The kind of abuse a father is supposed to protect his daughter from.

How could I mother a girl when I was still trying to mother the broken child inside me?

So, each night, before drifting off to sleep, I whispered quiet prayers into the dark. My hands rested protectively over my belly, heart aching with guilt I couldn't explain.

Please, let it be a boy.

Not because I wouldn't love a daughter. But because I didn't know if I could survive seeing myself—my past—reflected in her eyes.

I wanted the familiar. The known. The safe.

I wanted another little boy to love.

This time, there were no sirens. No magnesium drips. No doctors whispering just outside the curtain with worry in their eyes.

My pregnancy with Toby, thankfully, was uncomplicated. Quiet. Measured. But that didn't mean it was light. The weight came differently this time—not in trauma, but in vigilance. After what happened with Dusty, I was flagged as high-risk from the start. More appointments. More questions. More eyes watching every detail like the past might repeat itself if we weren't careful.

And again, the same directive, echoing through every checkup like a drumbeat: *You have to reduce the stress in your life.*

Thank God I had already made a decision—a hard one, but the right one.

After Dusty's birth, I stepped away from the position I'd fought so hard to earn. No more forty-five-minute commutes or twelve-hour days. No more chasing quotas while trying to chase a toddler. I let go of the title—Sales Manager of Mortgages and Consumer Loans—and accepted a part-time role as a Senior New Account Specialist just five minutes from the condo we'd saved together to buy.

To some, it may have looked like a setback. To me, it felt like sanity.

The stress didn't vanish completely. I was still the main provider—bringing in—seventy-five thousand a year while Bert's small-market anchor job barely cracked twenty. He was up at three a.m. every morning, live by six, and home before noon. That's when we'd tag out, me heading into the office while he stepped into dad mode.

Our days became a quiet, worn rhythm. I'd wake Dusty, kiss his warm cheeks, get him dressed and fed. Mornings were packed: coloring at the kitchen table, baby giggles in the backyard, pediatric appointments, toddler haircuts, grocery runs, laundry tossed in between snack time and storybooks.

By twelve-thirty, I was clocked in.

When I returned in the evening, the scent of dinner welcomed me. Bert in the kitchen, bleary-eyed but trying. Family time. Bath time. Story time. That soft, sweet moment when I'd rub Dusty's back and feel his little fingers relax in mine as sleep carried him away.

Then Bert and I would fall into bed, too tired to talk. Too tired to fight. Just enough left to pull the covers up and try again the next day.

I carried a lot—but I *wanted* to carry it. I was determined. No daycares. No strangers raising my babies. That was my job. My sacred work. Even on the hard days, that belief kept me going.

And strangely, even the job—the demotion I'd once feared—turned out to be a gift. Five minutes from home. Manageable expectations. Space to breathe again. We weren't perfect, not even close, but we were surviving. And sometimes, that was enough.

Toby arrived the same way Dusty had—two weeks early.

It was a golden July morning in Napa. Sunlight stretched lazily across the sheets. The air already held the dense warmth of summer. I stirred, hand instinctively resting on my belly as a familiar ache curled through my spine and around to my front. The waves came in steady pulses, deep and sure.

I didn't need confirmation. I knew.

This was it.

I sat on the edge of the bed, my heart thudding with a rush of anticipation and tenderness. Today, I would meet him. My second son. My belly trembled under my palm, and my eyes filled with tears. That miracle was about to be in my arms.

We'd known it was a boy for months. During the ultrasound, the technician had smiled gently. "Would you like to know the gender?" she asked, the probe gliding over my skin. Bert and I exchanged a glance and nodded. "It's a boy," she said.

My heart soared.

Bert smiled, too—but his eyes hesitated. Just for a second. He had hoped for a girl. He'd said as much in late-night conversations, with his voice softened by the dark. There was something in him that longed for the sweetness he imagined only a daughter could bring.

Each time, I'd gently remind him, "If it's a boy, you'll love him just the same. All that matters is a healthy baby."

And every time, he nodded.

But I saw the flicker. The quiet shadow behind his smile.

There's a silent grief in wanting something you'll never hold.

Still, as the hours rolled forward and the contractions

deepened, all I felt was joy. I was ready. My heart was wide open. I had made space inside myself for this new little life—this new chapter. And when the time came, I would welcome Toby with every ounce of love I had left to give.

There was so much to be grateful for. A second baby on the way. A home of our own. Some kind of rhythm that resembled stability, even if it was stitched together with threadbare hope.

When labor came, it arrived like a wave that knew exactly where it was going. No confusion. No questions. My body remembered this part.

This time, I got the epidural. Sweet relief poured in, turning the pain into manageable pressure. I could breathe. I could *be* there—fully present—for every moment of Toby's birth. There was no fear clouding my vision, no magnesium fog to wade through. Just me, grounded in the now, waiting to meet the child who had already stolen a piece of my heart.

But Toby had his own timeline.

The nurse had checked me only ten minutes earlier, giving a casual smile as she stepped out. But when she returned and lifted the sheet again, her eyes went wide. "You're fully dilated," she gasped, snapping into motion as she grabbed the intercom. "Page the doctor again—emergency status!"

The hallway outside our room exploded into motion—heels clicking, carts rolling, voices rising. I could smell the sharp tang of antiseptic as the air shifted.

The doctor burst into the room moments later, pulling gloves over trembling hands, voice short and urgent: "Don't push! Hold on just a second!"

But there was no holding back.

My body had already decided. With one instinctive, unstoppable surge, Toby launched into the world like a football spiraling through the air—straight into the doctor's hands. There was no countdown. No composed final push. Just momentum and magic.

And just like that, he was here. Toby. My wonderful— boy with searching eyes and a spirit that already felt wide open to the world. The room, the chaos, the fluorescent light—all of it melted away the second they placed him in my arms.

I traced the curve of his cheek with the back of my finger. Counted his fingers. Felt the rhythm of his breath against my chest. Everything in me softened.

I felt at peace. Not the loud kind. The kind that steals in quietly. A stillness that says, *You made it. He's here. You're both okay.*

And in that moment, life felt full—whole in a way I hadn't dared hope for. But joy and grief often ride the same tide.

As I stepped into one of the most sacred chapters of my life, another was slowly, silently closing. My grandfather's body was failing. He had fought for years—survived triple bypass surgery and fought his way back more times than anyone thought possible. But now, his heart was giving out. One system after another flickered, dimmed, and finally failed. The machines hummed, doing what his body could no longer manage.

And even as I rocked Toby in the early hours—skin to skin, heartbeat to heartbeat—I could feel the edges of good- bye pulling in.

The call came when the afternoon sun had just begun its slow descent, casting long shadows across the kitchen floor. I saw Lena's name light up my phone, and my stomach dropped before I even answered.

Her voice was trembling—thin and far away, like it had

to travel through some other world to reach me. "He's on life support," she said, barely louder than a whisper. I gripped the counter, the breath knocked from my chest.

This wasn't just anyone. This was *him*. The one man who had never left. The one who had quietly, steadily filled the role of "father" when no one else could. He didn't need a title—he had earned it a thousand different ways.

My grandfather.

He was kindness wrapped in calloused hands. Quiet in his wisdom. Strong without making a show of it. A master of everything he touched—if it was broken, he could fix it. If it didn't exist, he could build it. His humor was dry and sneaky, always catching you off guard in the best way. And his laugh was the kind that filled a room and stuck around long after the sound faded.

Growing up, weekends with him and my grandma meant deep cleaning from top to bottom. No shortcuts. No missed corners. Baseboards. Doorknobs. Even the water heater gleamed. Their house was sacred in its order—clean, calm, and predictable. I loved it.

One day, I had just finished scrubbing the kitchen when he walked in with a glint in his eye. He slipped on a pair of white plastic gloves—our version of a spotlight—and with exaggerated drama, ran one finger along the top of the doorframe.

Clean.

We both cracked up, with full belly laughter, the kind that shakes the walls. I had watched him for so many years, I knew where the dust liked to hide. That was our moment—our shared language.

After that, it became our thing. I'd pull a pair of white gloves from my pocket anytime I visited, and like clockwork, we'd collapse into laughter like it was the first time. That joke never got old.

Neither did he.

His eyes were the softest sky blue—so kind, and so open. There was never judgment in them: only warmth and love. And now, they were closing for the last time.

"They're taking him off tonight," Lena said softly, breaking my spiral. Her words landed like glass shattering on tile.

"No," I gasped. "I'll fly out—I'll be there tomorrow."

But she hesitated. Then, through her own tears, she said, "You wouldn't want to see him like this. I've seen him…and it's devastating."

Silence stretched between us. My heart begged to fight, to scream, to protest. But somewhere deeper, I understood. I knew she was right. I didn't want to remember him like that—frail, fading, hooked up to machines.

We hung up, and I stood alone in my kitchen, the world too quiet around me. I pressed my hands to the counter and whispered through tears to the one man who had ever made me feel safe. "I love you. I'll always love you. If you're tired…it's okay. You can go home now."

Later, Lena told me that when they removed the machines, he took one last breath—and just…slipped away.

No struggle. No fight.

Just peace.

Just like him.

Toby's first birthday was warm and golden, the kind of day that makes you believe—for just a moment—that maybe everything's going to be okay. Balloons bobbed in the backyard breeze. Laughter rang from the mouths of children chasing each other around the grass. I watched from behind the lens, with my heart full, as Toby and Dusty stood side by side—two little boys, growing up together, framed by sunlight and sweetness.

Later, when we developed the photo, something caught

my eye. Behind them, soft and translucent, was the faint outline of a figure.

Not a smudge. Not a trick of the light.

A presence.

Grandpa.

I didn't need anyone to tell me. I *knew*. He was there. With us. Watching over his great-grandsons, laughing quietly to himself the way he always did—eyes crinkled at the corners, spirit warm as ever.

Years later, I'd get confirmation—small, sacred validations that the prayers I whispered through tears had reached him, that love like his doesn't end. It shifts. It shows up in unexpected places. It lingers in birthday snapshots and quiet moments when you need it most.

Still, life kept moving forward, softly, but insistently. Grief didn't ask permission to linger. Bottles still needed warming. Tiny socks still needed folding. The ache folded itself into the rhythm of my days—tucked into story time and bath time, hidden behind the smiles I wore like armor.

Bert and I slipped back into our routine, the familiar dance of parenting two small boys. The soundtrack of our lives was one of lullabies and binkies, cartoon theme songs and the crackling of grilled cheese in a pan. There was laughter. There was love. There was everything you'd expect from a young family trying to do their best.

But underneath that surface—beneath the baby giggles and late-night feedings—a quieter current pulled at me. One no one else could see.

Our marriage was unraveling.

It didn't happen all at once. It was slow, and subtle, like water slipping through a crack in the foundation.

I don't think he noticed. He seemed fine. He always seemed fine.

But I noticed. I felt it in my bones.

Years of being brushed off, belittled, labeled "too

emotional," "too sensitive," or "too much," had left bruises no one could see. Some nights, I'd sit in the glow of a night-light, one arm cradling a nursing baby, the other wiping away tears I didn't understand. I asked myself the same question over and over again:

What's wrong with me?

If I just loved him harder…if I loved him *better*…would it change anything?

The answers never came. Instead, came the doubts. Maybe I *was* too sensitive. Maybe I *was* crazy. But underneath all that questioning, another voice whispered: *You're walking on eggshells.*

Every day, I shrank a little more—made myself smaller, quieter, and easier to digest. I hid my feelings behind smiles, swallowed pain like pills, and told myself it was just a phase. But I wasn't happy. And I hadn't been for a long, long time.

I asked him more than once, "Are you happy?" He'd shrug, say, "Yeah," and move on as though the question meant nothing. But it meant everything to me.

Anytime I tried to peel back the layers of my pain, to show him the raw and bleeding parts of me, he'd twist my words and turn them against me.

"You're overreacting."

"You're too sensitive."

"You're crazy."

Was I?

I clung to the idea of therapy, as though it might save us, like a life raft I wasn't sure he'd ever reach for. I brought it up, gently at first. Then more urgently. But every time, he brushed it off. Therapy's for the weak," he said. "We're fine."

He was fine. And that was all that seemed to matter.

So, I did what I'd always done. I packed up my pain, sealed it tight, and tucked it away behind folded laundry and packed lunches. I had a remarkable ability to keep going—to mother, to function, and to smile. But I was glass. Strong, yes. But brittle.

And I was cracking.

Each dismissal etched a hairline fracture. Each rolled eye or cruel word chipped a little more from the inside out. I could feel it—the spiderweb of damage growing across my heart. Like a windshield, cracked from a single stone, slowly splintering outward until one day…

It shatters.

No one else could see it yet.

But I could feel it.

I was breaking.

It was not long after Toby turned one that that familiar ache crept back in—the quiet, insistent longing that lived in a mother's heart. It wasn't loud. It didn't beg. It whispered, softly and tenderly.

I tried to ignore it at first, tried to tell myself I was imagining it. But every time I watched Dusty and Toby play, every time their laughter echoed through the hallway, something stirred. A gentle pull. A vision I couldn't shake— of another set of bare feet pounding across the floor, another giggle in the mix, another sticky hand reaching for mine.

It wasn't about fixing my marriage. I had no illusions about that.

It was about me.

About creating the kind of home I had always dreamed of. A place filled with unconditional love—not something you had to earn or beg for. Just love that simply *was*.

Still, I knew better. Another baby wouldn't mend what was already fractured between Bert and me. I wasn't naïve. But part of me ached to feel that sacred bond again—the one that bloomed the moment I first held Dusty, the one that deepened as I rocked Toby to sleep, that pure connection that told me *this* was what I was made for.

One evening, while the boys were down and the house had settled into its quiet hum, I found myself saying it out loud. Have you thought about maybe…having one more?"

Bert didn't pause. Didn't consider. His response was immediate, sharp as glass. "No. Absolutely not." The finality of it hit like a slammed door.

I nodded and said nothing more. I didn't push. Didn't plead. I simply swallowed the ache, as I had done so many times before, and let the silence settle between us.

I was already on birth control. I had been since shortly after Toby's birth. Each morning, I took it without thought—just another part of the routine. Brush teeth. Swallow pill. Swallow truth.

There would be no more babies. I accepted it. But resignation isn't the same as peace. The longing didn't leave. It simply curled up inside me, quiet and persistent.

Then, two months later, something odd landed in our laps—Bert and I received jury duty summons. The same day, the same courthouse, and the same panel.

We laughed at the strangeness of it, joked about the odds. Fate, we said. Playing games again.

Sunday night, we called the jury line together, phones pressed to our ears, side by side on the couch. Both our numbers were called.

Monday morning, we left the boys with a sitter and drove to the courthouse—two adults, alone for the first time in what felt like forever. We sat side by side in the jury pool room, flipping through old magazines, stealing glances at each other, and exchanging quiet conversation. There was no chaos. No kids crying or work calls buzzing. Just us.

When we were dismissed for lunch, it felt like a strange kind of gift—time we hadn't planned for.

Bert grinned, a mischievous glint in his eye. "Wanna sneak off to a motel?" he teased.

I surprised myself by saying yes.

We found a cheap room nearby, and for one brief, impulsive afternoon, we were just two people, not parents nor spouses with wounds between them—just two people who once loved each other deeply. Later, when we learned we were both excused from duty, we lingered, half-laughing in disbelief. A strange bubble of lightness was wrapped around us that day. It felt good. It felt easy.

And then life continued, the way it always does. Two months passed. And then my body shifted.

First, the soreness. Then the waves of nausea. Familiar signs. Ancient instincts.

No. It couldn't be.

I was on the pill.

But something in me already knew.

Still, I bought a test. Just to silence the whisper. But the whisper was right.

Two pink lines. I was pregnant.

I stared at the result, with my heart pounding, a mix of wonder and dread pooling in my chest.

Bert's voice echoed in my memory—*Absolutely not.* This wasn't what he wanted. Before telling him, I made a doctor's appointment. I needed confirmation. I needed to understand how this could happen.

The doctor was kind, her voice calm as she explained. "Were you on antibiotics recently?"

I blinked. "Yes. The flu. Just before jury duty."

She nodded. "That can affect the pill's effectiveness."

My mind raced. The motel. That strange, serendipitous afternoon. We hadn't used protection. We didn't think we needed to.

Armed with the truth and still shaking, I sat Bert down. His face fell. It was not anger—just shock, and disbelief. The air between us was thick with the weight of the unexpected.

I tried to ease it. Reached for a thread of hope.

"Maybe this one's a girl."

That softened him, just a little. A ghost of a smile tugged at his lips.

We joked about baseball—three kids made a quarter of the team. Slowly, the tension lifted, and he started to meet me in that space of possibility.

But for me, it was never just chance. It felt divine. What were the odds? Same jury panel. Same day. Same room. A moment of reconnection, of vulnerability, exactly when it needed to happen.

I believed, with all of me, that this child—this surprise, this quiet miracle—was meant to be.

This pregnancy felt different.

I felt different.

I wasn't stumbling through the unknown this time. I knew the rhythm—the way my body would soften and swell, how the faint flutters would slowly become tiny kicks that thudded against my ribs like Morse code. And instead of fighting the changes, I welcomed them. I wrapped myself in them.

Each curve, each pound, each new stretch mark was sacred—a reminder that life was growing inside me.

I gave myself permission to rest. To eat what I craved without shame. To soak in warm bubble baths at the end of long days, belly rising like a quiet moon above the waterline, hands gliding gently across the curve of my stomach. For once, I didn't just endure the process—I let myself enjoy it.

Maybe I needed to. Because with every inch my body grew, Bert pulled further away. It started small—an averted gaze, a lingering pause before undressing. Then came the unspoken critiques—the way his eyes skimmed past me, the stiffness in his body when we shared a bed, the cold that settled between us like an unwelcome draft. He didn't have to say it. His silence said everything.

However, this time, it didn't cut as deep.

Because somewhere along the way, I had learned the truth: his rejection wasn't mine to carry. It wasn't about me. It never had been.

I was healthy. The baby was healthy. And that was enough.

Even without dieting, I gained exactly thirty pounds—the textbook, expected amount. Still, I knew the pressure that would follow. I always worked hard to return to my pre-pregnancy weight. Not for me. For peace. For the sake of dodging the jokes, the side-eyes, and the comments masked as concern or sarcasm.

As the months passed, each night I curled into bed, hands resting on the swell of my belly, whispering a quiet, steady prayer: *Please, let it be a boy.*

The day of the ultrasound arrived like a held breath finally released.

I lay on the exam table, heart fluttering, gratitude pulsing through every cell of my body. The sound of the baby's heartbeat filled the room, rhythmic and strong, and I felt tears rise. That sound never stopped feeling like a miracle.

The technician smiled gently. "Would you like to know the sex?"

We both nodded.

She turned the monitor slightly and said, "Congratulations. It's a boy."

"Yes!" I gasped, a grin breaking across my face as I shot my hand up in celebration. I high fived her, laughing through tears, joy spilling out of me like light. But when she turned toward Bert with the same smile, hand raised to include him in the moment, he glared at her.

Then he stood, cold and furious, and stormed out of the room—slamming the door behind him.

Humiliation flushed hot beneath my skin. I lay there, stunned, eyes fixed on the ceiling tiles, wishing I could disappear. The technician tried to mask her discomfort, but I could feel it—thick and awkward between us.

We argued the entire ride home.

"I was so embarrassed," I snapped, my voice sharp with hurt. "You humiliated me."

He didn't flinch. Didn't apologize. Instead, he turned to me and spat, "This is your fault."

I stared at him, stunned, nausea rising in my throat. "You think I *chose* this? That I made the baby a boy just to spite you?"

He said nothing.

My hands trembled on my lap. "Actually," I said quietly, voice tight, "scientifically, the father determines the baby's sex. So technically…you're the one shooting boys."

Still, nothing.

He brooded the rest of the night, silent and stewing. We went to bed without a word. Again.

The next morning, the ache in my gut hadn't faded. So, I found an article—one that explained the XY chromosomes, how the father's DNA is the deciding factor. I emailed it to him at work. No subject line. Just the truth.

He never responded.

And in that silence, something settled in my chest. A knowing.

The joy. The resentment. The shame. The hope. The ache.

I was carrying it all.

And it was all mine to hold.

• • •

Motherhood didn't come with instructions. And neither did the invisible boundaries I kept tripping over—those unspoken lines between what I felt, what I knew, and what everyone else thought I should be doing.

I was still learning to trust myself. To tune out the noise. To hush the well—meaning suggestions, the passive-aggressive remarks, the advice laced in judgment. Somewhere beneath all that was a voice—a small, steady whisper that said, "You're the mother. You know." That voice was mine. And I was learning to listen.

Living in the same state as Bert's family gave them proximity, but thankfully, not access. California stretched long between Santa Barbara and Napa, and those hundreds of miles became more than geography. They were breathing room: a moat, wide and necessary.

Had they lived any closer, I don't think I would have survived it. Their opinions, their expectations, their presence—it would've swallowed me whole.

And Bert? He was a mama's boy in every sense. Not in the sweet, affectionate way. No, this was something else. Something deeper. The umbilical cord had never been cut. It was just invisible now—woven into every decision he made.

It wasn't just that he loved her. Love would have been fine. What hurt was the weight her words carried—heavier than mine. I could tell him something I'd learned, something that sparked something in me—and he'd barely look up from his phone. But if his mom mentioned the same thing the next day, suddenly it was inspired. "Did you know…" he'd say, quoting her like scripture.

I would sit there, quietly, swallowing the lump in my throat, wondering if he even heard me the first time. My voice hung in the air like forgotten perfume—soft, fading, unnoticed.

I wanted to believe it wasn't personal. That he didn't realize he was dismissing me. But over time, it became impossible to ignore. I was living in the background of my own marriage, cast as a supporting character in a story I had built from the ground up.

Then, one day, there was a call.

I was folding a mountain of laundry when I heard the familiar excitement in Bert's voice. "Olga's getting married," he said, grinning. "At the Country Club. In two weeks in Santa Barbara."

My heart paused. Two weeks.

"I'll be full term," I said, carefully, setting down a tiny sock. "You know we can't go."

But he had already promised her. I'll take Dusty and Toby with me," he said casually. "I'll be back in four days."

I stared at him. "What if I go into labor?"

"I'll drive straight through," he shrugged, like it was a minor inconvenience.

I blinked, trying to absorb what was happening. He knew my history. He knew both of our boys had come early. He knew I was high risk—and yet, this wedding, this venue, this dream of Olga's...it was untouchable.

I tried again. "Can they move the location?"

He looked at me as if I had just asked them to cancel Christmas. "Olga has always dreamed of getting married there."

And there it was. Her dream was sacred. My safety was negotiable. The line had been drawn. And I wasn't on their side.

The stress wrapped itself around my belly like a tightening rope. Three weeks before my due date, I doubled over in pain. At the ER, the doctor clicked through the ultrasound, frowning slightly. "Mild contractions," he said.

"Triggered by a kidney stone, probably brought on by stress." He glanced at me. "You under any?"

I lied. "No."

We were sent home, but I couldn't lie flat. I slept upright for two nights, propped by pillows, with my body aching, and my mind racing. I was exhausted—physically, emotionally, spiritually.

The night before he left, I gave it one last try. "Please don't go," I whispered. "I need you here. I'm scared."

He looked me in the eyes. "I'm going." And that was it.

The next morning, I stood in the doorway as he buckled the boys into the car. My heart thudded in my chest as the taillights disappeared. The silence he left behind was deafening.

I sat on the edge of the bed, rubbing my stomach, trying to calm the rising panic. Then, without fully thinking it through, I grabbed the phone.

I called a locksmith.

I changed the locks.

I wasn't going to let him walk back into this house as if everything was okay.

Because it wasn't.

But I hadn't thought it through. He had our children.

Four days later, I heard the tires in the driveway. The key turned—then jammed. A pause. Knocking.

I stayed on the couch, arms folded, letting the silence answer for me.

My phone rang. I didn't move.

Then I heard it—

"Mommy?" Dusty's voice. And everything inside me shattered.

I rose, my feet slow and heavy beneath me, and unlocked the door.

He stepped inside, angry. "Why the hell did you change the locks?"

I stood in the kitchen, one hand on my belly. "Because I felt abandoned," I said. "You chose them over me. Again."

He rolled his eyes. "You wasted money. On locks." That stung: the coldness, and the focus on dollars.

Not the fear I'd lived with. Not the nights I sat up alone. Not the thought of giving birth without him.

I bit my tongue. I wanted to scream: *I make most of the damn money*. But I didn't.

I swallowed it down, like I always did.

And then he said it. "I told you so."

I blinked. "What?"

"I told you the baby wouldn't come while I was gone."

Like he'd won something. Like the risk he had taken with my body, with our baby, didn't matter—because his gamble had paid off.

But he missed the point. He always did. It was never about the baby coming. It was about the fact that he left. That he always left.

Two weeks later, right on time, our son Ryan came into the world—bright-eyed, beautiful, and full of fire.

And in my own quiet way, so did I.

The pain that morning wasn't labor—not yet. It was something else.

Something deep. Something off.

Not the familiar rhythm of contractions I'd come to know, but a heavy, unsettled ache—like my body was bracing for something it hadn't yet named.

The house was still when I woke. No birdsong, no boys thundering down the hallway: just the hush before a storm. I lay there for a moment, with my hands resting on my belly, trying to decode the strange static humming under my skin. I needed the bathroom. That was nothing new. But when I returned and tried to settle back under the covers, my body wouldn't comply.

A sharp tug bloomed low in my pelvis, not sharp enough to scream but strong enough to demand attention. I shifted. Then I shifted again. Sitting hurt. Lying down hurt more.

I swung my legs over the edge of the bed, rubbed the sleep from my eyes, and stood. A low wave crested through me—steady, uncomfortable, but controlled. I breathed through it. This was labor. I knew it. But it wasn't rushing in with the crashing urgency I'd felt before.

In the bathroom mirror, my face looked calm, almost expressionless, like it hadn't gotten the message yet. But inside, I was buzzing. Something was different this time.

I stepped into the shower, let the water run hot across my back. It helped. I stood there longer than I needed to, letting the steam rise around me like fog before a battlefield.

Downstairs, I could hear the familiar clatter of breakfast—Bert's voice, and the boys giggling between bites of cereal. The sense of normality felt like a lifeline. I wasn't ready to say it out loud yet: "I'm in labor." Saying it would make it real.

I walked into the kitchen. Bert looked up and smiled. He was already cracking eggs. "You hungry?" he asked, as if it was any other morning.

He handed me a plate—eggs and toast, golden and warm—and I sat. I tried to eat, and to act normal. Then pain—sharp and sudden—shot through me like lightning. My fork clattered against the plate as I stood quickly, one hand gripping the back of the chair.

"It's time," I said.

There was no drama. No panic. Just a quiet seriousness in my voice that made Bert stop mid-bite.

We called a friend to come for the boys. I paced the living room, pausing every few minutes as another contraction hit, each one a little stronger, and a little closer.

The drive to the hospital was brutal. Every bump in the road felt like a jab from the inside out. Getting into the car was a feat of determination—I braced my hands on the doorframe and forced myself down into the seat, the belt stretching tight across my belly.

Tears slipped down my face, silent and warm. Not from fear, exactly. Just…everything.

"Drive fast," I whispered. Bert nodded. He didn't need to be told twice.

At the hospital, a nurse appeared with a wheelchair as if it was a prize on a game show.

"I need to stand," I told her, panting through another wave. "Standing helps."

"You have to sit to be checked in," she replied, her tone kind but unbending.

I lowered myself into the chair, gripping the sides as if I was descending into fire. A searing jolt of pain cut through me as I sat, and I clenched my jaw to keep from crying out.

Once checked in, they wheeled me toward labor and delivery, the hallway stretching endlessly in front of me. Every turn jarred something inside me, and I clutched the armrests tighter.

Inside the room, I stood next to the bed, bracing myself on the mattress. Another contraction hit, this one deeper—like my entire body was folding in on itself. Then, warmth. Sudden. Rushing down my legs.

"My water just broke," I said breathlessly.

The nurse was already gloving up. "Let's get you on the bed. I need to check you."

"I want to deliver standing," I managed, barely audible through the pressure and discomfort. "It helps with the pain."

She shook her head. "The doctors are with a set of twins right now. If you want this baby out, you need to lie down."

It wasn't a suggestion.

I hesitated. But the pain was barreling down now, relentless and hot, and I knew there was no time.

I laid down. Pain rolled over me like a fierce tide, crashing again and again with no mercy, no pause. It felt like my body was tearing open from the inside, and for a moment, I truly thought I might die. The pressure, the fire, the rawness—it was all-consuming agony—I had never known pain like that.

But even through the haze, all I could focus on was bringing Ryan into the world. I didn't wait to be told—I pushed.

The next contraction hit like a freight train. I screamed out loud. The pressure was overwhelming, tearing through me like wildfire.

I pushed, again.

Once.

Twice.

On the third, he came.

His cry filled the room, sharp and beautiful, and I crumbled beneath the sound of it. They laid him on my chest, and I wrapped my arms around his tiny, squirming body. He smelled like life itself. My tears soaked his hair.

He was here: safe, and perfect.

Another nurse took him gently, cooing as she carried him to the newborn table. I watched, but my arms felt like they still held him. My chest still echoed with his warmth.

A soft voice brought me back. "Okay, now I need you to push again so we can deliver the placenta." I nodded, still hovering somewhere between worlds. I pushed.

Nothing. "Try again," she said gently. I did. Still nothing. She reached for the cord and gave it a little tug.

Pain exploded through me. Not labor pain—something worse. Wrong. She tugged again. The pain intensified, bright and awful.

Then the room changed. The nurse's tone shifted, her

posture tightened. She called for the doctor, her voice low but urgent.

When he entered, the silence between them said everything. He came over, didn't say a word. Just pulled on the cord. I screamed.

Again.

And then—he was holding it in his hand. It was detached. The placenta was still inside. But the cord was gone.

He reached inside me. I cried out. He tried again. And again. I begged him to stop. My whole body trembled with pain I didn't know how to survive.

Finally, he stopped.

"Call anesthesia," he said.

Someone tucked a dissolvable tablet under my tongue. "This will help," the anesthesiologist said kindly. It didn't.

The doctor looked at me—my body shaking, my voice gone—and nodded. "We're taking her to the OR." I was bleeding out.

Monitors were disconnected. The bed unlocked. The team moved fast.

As they began rolling me away, I turned to Bert. Gripped his hand.

"Don't leave the baby," I said, every word carved from instinct. "Stay with Ryan. No matter what."

I didn't know why it mattered so much. I just knew it did.

The doors to the OR opened. It wasn't what I expected—no dramatic lights or orchestrated chaos. Just a tight, silver room. Cold. Detached.

The anesthesiologist placed a mask over my face. "Take a deep breath. Count backward from one hundred."

The oxygen hit my lungs like ice.

And one thought rang out through the noise:

Don't go to sleep. Stay awake.

9

HOME

The next thing I knew, I was waking—not with the heaviness of returning from sleep, but with the lightness of remembering something I never truly forgot. I wasn't in a body, yet I was still me. Whole. Awake. And I wasn't alone.

I was home.

Around me shimmered the presence of beings so radiant, so familiar, it brought tears to the deepest part of who I was. Angels. Loved ones I hadn't seen in years—lifetimes, maybe. Jesus. Mother Mary. And God. But not as people. Not with faces or hands. They were light and sound and vibration—living frequencies that pulsed around me in colors and warmth I could feel in my soul.

They didn't need to speak. I didn't need to see. I sensed them with something far beyond human senses. A knowing. Their energy surrounded me like a hum—sacred and alive—moving not just around me, but through me.

And it wasn't just presence. It was love.

A love so vast, so unfiltered, it blanketed every part of me. It didn't rush. It didn't shout. It wrapped itself around me slowly, completely. Like sunlight on bare skin. Like being held after a long journey. It filled the spaces inside me I hadn't realized were empty.

Their love didn't ask anything of me. It simply was.

It was everywhere. Woven into the air, the light, and even the silence. I wasn't observing it. I was inside it. Bathed in it. Known by it.

And then, from within me, came a truth I didn't learn—I remembered it: we are all connected.

Not just emotionally. Not metaphorically. We are truly, infinitely, vibrationally one. There is no distance between us, and no loneliness that cannot be bridged. That belief of separation—it's a story we tell ourselves down there. But here, in this space, I could feel the fabric of unity in every direction.

This was belonging.

The Divine Beings moved around me—not in circles or lines, but in harmony. Each one distinct, yet inseparable. Their energies pulsed and shimmered, not colliding, but merging like chords of a perfect symphony. It was music I didn't hear with ears. It was color I didn't see with eyes. Light and sound and feeling—woven through each other like golden threads in an endless tapestry.

They danced.

And I danced with them. My energy was a note in their chorus, a brushstroke in their living light. I had my own frequency. My own color. And it mattered. I could feel myself woven into something bigger, something infinite. Not lost in it, but essential to it.

I didn't have fear. I couldn't. It didn't exist there. Neither did doubt. Or pain. The things that had shaped so much of my human experience had no place in that space. Here, there was only love.

And that love—it moved. It breathed. It laughed. It sparkled.

The light around us glowed white-gold, not harsh or blinding, but soft and effervescent, like champagne kissed by morning sun. It shimmered with joy. It felt like comfort—like the softest blanket warmed by decades of sun and memory.

I was held in it. Completely.

Not as someone who had arrived. But as someone who had returned.

This wasn't new. This was remembrance.

The Divine Beings—separate in identity, yet unified in purpose—loved me without question, without hesitation. Their love didn't overwhelm me. It steadied me. It reminded me of who I truly was.

We moved together, our energies weaving in and out of one another in fluid, harmonious motion. Each soul carried its own distinct signature—a rhythm, a frequency, a presence. Including me. I was one of them. Always had been. And in that moment, I remembered.

I had never not belonged.

There was no fear. No ache. No sadness.

Just love. So much love.

Endless. Gentle. Alive.

The light wasn't just around me—it was within me, pulsing softly like a second heartbeat. It radiated in hues of white gold, the most beautiful I'd ever seen, glowing with a gentle brilliance that shimmered like sunlight dancing across water. But it wasn't blinding or distant. It was close, intimate, and alive.

It didn't just illuminate—it embraced.

It wrapped me in warmth that wasn't heat, but something deeper. Like being swaddled in the softest cashmere, sun-drenched and weightless, wrapped in the quiet hush of something sacred. I sank into it, exhaling fully and freely, as if for the first time. Every breath brought relief, a lightness that reached the places in me no human touch ever could.

And in that moment, I felt it all.

Immense happiness. Deep peace. A contentment that had no beginning and no end. A love so profound, it moved through me with ease, touching every forgotten corner of my being. I had longed for this—perhaps my whole life—and now, here it was. Surrounding me. Becoming me.

There was no judgment here. No cruelty. No shame. No fear. No anxiety. No depression. No hate. Only love—pure, unconditional, absolute.

The deeper I moved into that space, the harder it became to describe. Words simply couldn't follow me there. Language...fell away. What I was experiencing wasn't just a thought, wasn't even a feeling. It was a knowing.

I didn't just *understand* unconditional love—I *became* it.

It pulsed through my essence, flowed like light through glass, soft and steady. It didn't ask to be earned or proven. It simply was. It had always been.

And I remembered—clearly, powerfully—that I had always been loved. Fully. Without condition. Without exception.

Then something shifted—not outside me, but around the idea of time itself. Everything was happening at once, and yet each moment stood apart, full and complete. It's hard to explain. Human minds crave sequence—this, then that. But here, time didn't behave. It folded. Stretched. Spiraled. There was no ticking clock, no next step. Just now. Always now.

I was shown that time—at least the way we live it on Earth—is man-made. A construct. A way to make sense of days and years and memory. But here? Time didn't exist in lines. It existed like breath. Expansive. Everywhere. Always.

There was no beginning. No end.

Only presence.

Only love.

I was also shown something that shook me—not with

fear, but with a depth of knowing that settled into my bones like truth coming home. All religions, I was shown, are true. Every single one. Not in their dogma or rituals, but in their origin. Their roots all reach back to the same sacred Source.

But something happened along the way. The original truth—the pure essence of Love—was bent and broken, reshaped by human hands with human agendas: greed, power, control, fear, and hate. And those distortions left behind a trail of suffering.

Because I was raised Christian, Jesus and Mother Mary were the ones who came to me. Their presence was familiar and comforting. But I understood—instantly, unquestionably—that if I had been raised Buddhist, it would have been Buddha who stepped forward. Spirit shows up in the form we most easily recognize. It speaks the language of our hearts, not our doctrines.

Even as a child, I had sensed something off in the church pews. The harshness disguised as love. The judgment wrapped in scripture. The hollow echoes of hypocrisy I couldn't name yet but felt in my gut. And I walked away, quietly, carrying that unease with me.

This experience, this divine clarity, was not just a confirmation—it was a validation. It gave words to everything my heart had always whispered but never dared to say out loud. I no longer believe in organized religion, but I hold sacred space for those who do. Because I saw it clearly: every soul walks its own path home. And every path is holy.

I was also shown the truth about hell—not as a punishment, not as a place of fire and torment, but as something far more profound. I saw the balance of it all. Light and dark. Good and evil. Yin and yang. Opposites, not enemies. Necessary counterweights. The framework of free will.

There was no external judge, no cosmic courtroom. We are not punished by some faraway god. We live the consequences of our own choices. Every day, in every moment, we decide: will we walk through this life in love—or in fear, anger, and hate?

The real hell is not a destination—it's a creation. It's the life we build when we betray our truth, when we choose control over compassion, bitterness over healing. It isn't a place we're sent to. It's what we create when we stop choosing love.

And yet, even in that, there is hope. Because every moment is a chance to choose differently, to return, and to remember. To come home.

I was shown the life review—not my own, but the process itself. And what I saw dismantled everything I thought I knew about judgment, redemption, and what happens when we cross over.

There was no gavel. No scolding. No condemning throne in the sky.

When a soul returns home, they are not met with judgment. Not from God. Not from angels. Not even from themselves. They are met with understanding.

I watched as a soul stood in quiet stillness, surrounded by light, and their life began to unfold—not as a movie on a screen, but as living memory. Every word spoken, every choice made, every moment once lived was relived. But this time, through the hearts of others.

When they gave kindness, they felt the warmth it created. When they caused harm, they felt the ache they left behind. Not as punishment, but as perspective. They didn't just see what they had done—they became the ripple it created.

There was no guilt heaped upon them. No shame. Only the sacred weight of compassion. A soft unraveling of all the ways their choices had mattered.

Some life reviews were lighter. Others, heavier. There were souls who had caused deep harm—wounds that stretched across lifetimes. And still, they weren't cast out.

They weren't damned. They were surrounded by angels, wrapped in light, and gently—patiently—healed.

Nothing was wasted. No one was lost. No soul discarded.

I saw, too, that we are not limited to one lifetime. We live many. Across realms and dimensions. At once, and not at once. Before entering any one life, we gather in love—with our Guides, our Guardian Angels, our Soul Family. We sit together, surrounded by divine presence, and we plan.

The small details and the big ones. What we're ready to learn. What we hope to heal. What we want to remember. We choose our challenges. Our losses. Our lessons. Not as punishment—but as purpose.

And though the path is mapped, the journey is never forced. We still have free will. Always. We decide how we will walk it.

Will we fight it, blame it, and resist every crack in the road? Or will we breathe, lean in, and trust what it's shaping in us?

Either way, we grow.

And then I saw—clearer than anything—I had chosen mine.

All of it.

The pain. The betrayal. The heartbreak. The beauty.

Not because I was weak, but because I was ready.

Because my soul had whispered, "Let me rise." No words passed between us. There was no need.

Everything moved through thought—pure, seamless, and immediate. Communication wasn't spoken. It flowed. Complete understandings rose into my awareness like breath meeting lungs. I didn't have to ask questions. The answers were already there, waiting for me, arriving the moment curiosity stirred in my soul.

One thought would begin to flicker, and before it could take shape, a response would unfold—clear, kind, and whole. It was like dancing with truth itself. There was no reaching, and no grasping. Only receiving.

And then, like chords of sacred music playing through the fabric of my being, three messages pulsed through me. Not with volume, not with demand, but with a Love so vast it settled into the marrow of who I was.

You are unconditionally loved.

Everything is always how it's supposed to be.

Everything will always be alright.

They didn't echo—they anchored. I didn't just hear them. I became them. These truths weren't offered as comfort. They were reality. They existed beyond reassurance. Beyond belief. They simply were.

I absorbed them with a knowledge that went deeper than thought—past intellect, past emotion, into something timeless and whole. I knew, with unshakable certainty, that if I chose not to return to my body, my children…my husband…my family and friends…they would be okay.

Truly okay.

Not merely surviving, not barely holding on—but cradled in the same Love that now held me. Surrounded by it. Guided by it. The same Love I now remembered we all come from and return to.

And in that moment of knowing, everything opened. Not just my story—but everyone's. I saw it, all of it—like golden threads interwoven into an infinite tapestry. The patterns of our lives, the connections between us, the choices, and the meanings. Past, present, future—they all folded into one breath, one heartbeat.

It was all energy. And that energy…was Love.

Not the kind we try to earn. Not the kind we fear we'll lose. But something far purer. Undiluted. Unending. The kind that simply is.

And that Love—gentle, radiant, all-encompassing—that Love is God.

I wanted to stay.

Every part of me—every particle of my soul—ached to remain in that light, wrapped in that Love. I wasn't ready to leave. I didn't want to leave. But it wasn't my choice.

Without warning, everything shifted.

In an instant, the warmth disappeared. The golden glow dissolved. The peace I had been bathed in, the Love I had become, was ripped from me.

And then—impact.

I slammed back into my body like falling from a great height, crashing into flesh and bone with a jolt so jarring it stole my breath before I could even draw it.

"Wake up! Open your eyes!"

The voice cut through the fog—sharp, urgent, and too loud for the silence I had just come from. A doctor. Yelling. Barking commands I didn't want to obey. His hands on me, shaking me back into this world.

I blinked against the fluorescent light overhead, which was cold and clinical. The contrast was unbearable. The stillness was gone. The light was gone. The love was—gone.

In its place there were cold sheets, sterile air, and the crushing weight of being alive. Everything felt heavy. My chest. My limbs. My heart. Grief settled into me like concrete. I was furious. Not at death—but at life. At the doctor. At the sound of his voice pulling me back when I had finally remembered what it felt like to be whole.

I didn't care that he had saved me.

I didn't want saving.

All I wanted was to go back.

Back home.

10

INTEGRATING

"The journey to self-love is not about fixing yourself;
it's about remembering that you were never broken."
— Anonymous

The next morning, in the soft hush of the recovery room, I lay propped against a stiff hospital pillow, the air still thick with antiseptic and aftermath. My limbs felt heavy, my thoughts slow, swimming in the haze of medication and shock. But I couldn't hold it in. I turned my head, slow and deliberate, toward my husband.

"I need to tell you something," I whispered, my throat dry, my voice trembling with both awe and hesitation.

I told him.

I told him about the light, the love, the presence of angels—how I had left my body, how I had been held in a space too sacred for words. Each syllable tumbled out, fragile and raw, carrying the weight of something I didn't fully understand but knew was real.

His expression changed before I had even finished.

A flash of discomfort twisted his features. He shifted in his chair, eyes darting toward the floor as if hoping to escape the truth in my voice. "You're crazy," he muttered, lips tightening. "It had to have been a dream." The words struck me like a slap. Not loud. Not cruel. Just…final.

I felt the door inside me close: quietly, without ceremony. I nodded, but I didn't speak again. Not about that.

Not to him. Not to anyone.

The memory folded in on itself, tucked away like a delicate letter sealed and hidden in the deepest part of me. I knew then—I wouldn't talk about it again. Not for a long time.

Later that morning, just as I started to drift back into that fragile in-between of rest and reality, a man stepped into my hospital room.

He didn't wear scrubs or a stethoscope. No kind smile or clipboard cluttered with baby stats. He wore a suit and tie, polished shoes, and a crisp name badge that caught the light. His presence felt off. Too formal. Too sterile.

He asked, flatly, "Do you remember anything?"

I froze. The question landed with a thud inside me, and I turned toward Bert, hoping for reassurance. But he gave a subtle shake of his head—barely perceptible, but unmistakable.

I looked back at the man.

"No," I said.

He handed me the clipboard without hesitation. A pen appeared in my hand. I signed without reading, without thinking. He left as abruptly as he came.

The room felt colder after that.

I'd given birth before. Twice. But nothing like this had ever happened. No dark suits. No strange questions. No mystery paperwork shoved into my hands.

Something had happened.

I could feel it in my chest, in the marrow of my bones. Something I wasn't supposed to remember. Nearly ten years later, that feeling—the unsettled weight of it—finally pushed me to act. I requested my medical records. I wasn't even sure what I was looking for. Only that I had to know.

The truth waited for me in black ink on white paper. My heart had stopped, in the operating room. Complications due to heart disease, the report claimed—an echo from my teenage diagnosis of Mitral Valve Prolapse. A condition where the valve leaflets collapse back into the heart like a broken parachute.

But my soul knew better.

I had been shown the truth during the experience. It wasn't the MVP. It was the anesthesia. I had an allergic reaction, clear as day in that sacred space beyond. My body couldn't tolerate it, and my heart surrendered.

And yet, no one had told me. Not in the hospital. Not during follow-up. Not ever.

Only then did the puzzle pieces click—the man in the suit, the clipboard, the urgency to sign. It hadn't been a dream. And I hadn't imagined it. They just didn't want me to remember.

But I did.

And once that realization rooted itself inside me, it cracked something wide open—light spilling through the fracture.

I would never see the world the same way again.

For the first few weeks after my near-death experience, all I wanted was to go home. Not to my house, not to the four walls filled with dishes and diapers and obligations. I longed for the *other* home—the one made of light, the one where peace wasn't earned, borrowed, or chased, but simply *was*.

That ache came with a quiet shame. I had three beautiful babies. They needed me. And yet...I wanted to leave. I wanted to return to the place where love didn't hurt, and where joy didn't come with a price.

The contrast between the worlds was unbearable.

Here, everything felt loud—too loud. Sharp. Heavy. The weight of gravity pressed against me in ways it never had before. The hospital lights buzzed overhead. The beeping machines droned on. The smell of bleach and breast milk mingled in the air. Everything was too *much*, and not enough.

I moved through the days like a ghost—arms full of baby, voice soft with gratitude, face arranged in something close to contentment. But inside, I was unraveling. I had tasted something divine. I had *remembered* who I was.

And now I was back in a world that had forgotten.

That place—*Home*—was beyond comprehension. There was no judgment. No sorrow. No shame. Only joy, creativity, peace…and Love. The real kind. The kind my soul had been starving for in silence.

Before my near-death experience, life had worn me out. One exhausting season after another. And somewhere between the sleepless nights and the heartbreaks I never fully healed from, I stopped reaching.

I stopped praying.

I stopped hoping.

What was the point of calling out, when nothing ever answered?

I was drifting. Lost, alone, and hollow.

But in that space beyond time—when my breath stopped, and my soul left my body—I saw the truth. I *knew* it. Even in my most abandoned moments, I had never been alone. I had been held. Witnessed. Wrapped in a love so vast, so all-knowing, it made every unspoken ache inside me exhale.

I had been loved beyond measure.

And that knowledge didn't leave me—not completely.

Even through the grief of returning, even through the static of life pressing back in, something stayed.

It was hope.

Not the kind you force yourself to believe when the world is crumbling. Not the kind that fades in the dark. This hope was different. It lived in my bones. It hummed beneath the weight of sadness, whispering, *You're not alone. You've never been alone.*

I came back carrying that truth.

And it changed everything.

Something deep inside me had shifted—quietly, but irrevocably. It wasn't a single revelation but a slow, steady unfolding. A remembering. I hadn't just glimpsed something holy—I had come home to a part of myself I'd forgotten existed.

And I couldn't unsee it.

So, I began peeling back the layers—gently and curiously. Who was I beneath the weight of roles I'd carried for everyone else? Beneath the expectations, the self-sacrifice, and the silence?

What do I like? What do I want? What do I need?

And maybe most importantly: *What would it mean to love myself?*

I had spent so many years trying to earn love—holding everything together with quiet endurance, wearing my strength like armor. I thought worth had to be proven. I thought peace had to be paid for.

But now, I was beginning to remember the truth. I was worthy. Of love. Of rest. Of joy. Not later. Not someday. Now. And the more I embraced that truth, the more I began to change.

But not everyone welcomed that change.

Some people—friends I thought were forever, family I had leaned on—started to pull away. My healing made them uneasy. My boundaries looked like betrayal. My voice, once so small and careful, suddenly sounded loud in their ears.

And I had to let them go.

At the same time, life didn't go easy on me. There were still storms. There were still heartbreaks. There was loss that came like waves, knocking the breath from my lungs. But through it all, something in me stayed rooted. A deeper knowing, anchored in that place beyond pain, reminded me: *You've seen the truth. Don't forget.*

I couldn't.

For years, I had carried the financial weight of our family as if it was mine alone to bear. I stretched every dollar, made magic out of nothing—birthday cakes, holiday dinners, scraped together field trip money. I made sure the boys had what they needed, even if it meant I went without.

But something in me snapped.

One night, I looked at Bert across the room and said, *"Something has to change."*

He needed a job that could carry more weight. Something that offered stability. Options. A way for us to live closer to family—either in Colorado, where my roots were, or central California, where his were. I didn't just want support. I needed it.

Because I wanted more for our sons. Not material things. Not trophies or trips. I wanted them to feel like they belonged.

Growing up, I had always felt like a guest in my own family—hovering at the edge, never quite sure if I was wanted or merely endured. I didn't want that for my boys. I wanted cousins tumbling over each other in backyards. I wanted Sunday dinners filled with burnt rolls, second helpings, and noisy love. Even if it was messy—even if the family was dysfunctional—I wanted them to know where they came from.

I wanted them to feel seen.

I was desperate to rewrite the narrative. *Their* narrative. To give them what I had only ever dreamed of: connection. A tribe. A net to catch them when life knocked them off balance.

Two years after my near-death experience, the door finally opened.

Bert was offered a position at a college in Santa Barbara.

So, we packed up our lives—again—and moved.

It wasn't seamless. It wasn't simple.

But it another step closer to the woman I was always meant to be.

In the quiet corners of my soul, where truth whispers when the world falls silent, I already knew. Moving to Santa Barbara would break us.

I didn't want to admit it—not even to myself. I clung to hope like a fraying rope, pretending the unraveling wasn't already in motion. But the truth had been blooming in the shadows for a long time, pressing against my chest like something trying to break free.

It was in the way his family looked *through* me, not *at* me. In the clipped tones, the polite dismissals, the way I was tolerated but never embraced. I was the outsider in every room, the wrong piece in a puzzle I had never asked to be part of. And Bert said nothing and did nothing. He had just stood there while their coldness wrapped around me like frost. Not once did he reach for my hand. Not once did he say, *This is my wife. You will treat her with respect.*

He never had my back.

Everyone else came first—his mother's opinions, his sister's needs, his friends' demands, even the strangers who tugged at his time. I was always last. An afterthought. The one expected to understand, to endure, to carry on.

And then there was the drinking.

Not the kind that crashes cars or slurs words. No, his was more subtle. Controlled. Denied. But still there, creeping into the cracks of our marriage like water into stone. Just enough to excuse, never enough to ignore. I saw what it did to him. To us. How it blurred the lines of loyalty. How it opened the door to women who lingered a little too long, smiled a little too wide. Nothing overt. Nothing concrete. Just whispers. Gut feelings. Suspicion without proof. But still…it was all there.

So, yes, deep down, I knew. Santa Barbara would be the final thread pulled loose. But I didn't say a word, because I was exhausted. Drowning beneath the weight of it all—motherhood, marriage, bills, expectations, the ache of carrying everything alone in a life I had helped build, but could no longer breathe in. I needed help. Desperately. And that admission came with its own kind of shame.

So, I stayed silent.

I nodded when the job offer came. I packed the boxes. I smiled for the boys. I let us move closer to his family, even though every part of me knew I'd be the one paying the price.

If I had known then what I know now, I would've fought harder. I would've planted my flag in Colorado soil, close to my roots, close to people who saw me. I would've said *no*—not because I didn't need help, but because I did. Real help. Not help that came with cold shoulders and conditional love.

Because what followed wasn't just hard.

It was erasure.

The slow, quiet death of who I was.

The move to Santa Barbara felt like being caught in a storm with no shelter in sight.

Between juggling work, listing the condo, wrangling the boys, and packing what felt like an entire life into cardboard boxes—I was drowning. Chaos became my new normal. Each day spun faster than the last, a relentless blur of to-do lists, tantrums, and decisions made under pressure.

And in the middle of it all—his parents.

They had offered to help with the down-payment on a new home, a gesture that, on the surface, felt like grace. A miracle, even. Santa Barbara real estate wasn't just expensive—it was impossible. Their offer cracked open a door that would've otherwise stayed bolted shut.

However, like everything with them, the gift arrived tethered to invisible strings.

Soon, they weren't just helping. They were orchestrating.

His mom took the reins of the house hunt as if she was auditioning for a reality show. Every week, a new list of properties showed up in our inbox—her curated selections, filtered through her lens of what was "suitable" and "appropriate." They weren't suggestions. They were instructions.

We didn't have time to argue. We were in Napa, they were in Santa Barbara and driving back and forth wasn't an option—not with the boys, not with our budget, and not with our sanity already hanging by a thread. We were preparing to buy a house we had never even walked through.

It made my stomach churn.

I stared at online listings, flipping through glossy images, as if they could reassure me. I told myself it would be fine. That a house was just walls and roof, and that we could make it a home. Even so, my unease lingered like static.

Eventually, we made an offer on one of the homes she pushed forward. It was accepted. And a week before our scheduled move, I finally stepped through the front door.

It was beautiful.

Sunlight poured through the windows, pooling across warm tile floors. The kitchen opened into the living room, inviting conversation. Four bedrooms. Two baths. A garage. The yard stretched wide and green like an invitation. The neighborhood was nestled into a quiet pocket of the city, with a shared pool tucked around the corner.

Relief flooded me. Maybe this wouldn't be a disaster after all.

We settled in with ease. For the first time in years, I could breathe a little deeper. The house held space for all of us. The boys tore across the backyard with bare feet and wild laughter. Butters raced after them, tail high, slipping in and out through the doggy door like a king in his domain.

They were still so little—seven, four, and two—and the house cradled their childhood like cupped hands. The two youngest shared a bedroom big enough to hang a swing from the ceiling. The oldest had his own space next door. The third room became an office, where stacks of paper would eventually compete with late-night screen glow. Bert and I had the master suite—our own bathroom, our own retreat.

I poured myself into making that house feel like home. Decorating became a comfort, something I could control when everything else felt slippery. I never liked staged perfection. I leaned into the messy magic of real life. Our furniture welcomed paws and spills. The coffee table could take feet and forgotten snacks. Toys lived underfoot. Unfinished crafts peeked from corners.

The boys had these oversized floor pillows shaped like baseballs and footballs. On weekends, we'd pile on top of them, tangled in blankets, watching movies and eating popcorn. Those were sweet moments: honest, and full of life.

But underneath it all—beneath the laughter and the softness—something didn't sit right. Even as I folded blankets and hung curtains, even as the scent of dinner filled the air and the boys' voices echoed through the hallway, a quiet dissonance hummed through me.

It never really felt like mine.

I couldn't explain it then, not even to myself. But I look back now and see it clearly—the tension. The silence between Bert and me that never raised its voice but still said everything. The kind of silence that wraps around you like fog, the kind that tells you the ground you're standing on might not hold.

Maybe I always knew.

That house was never my forever home.

I transferred with the bank into a part-time role as a New Accounts Representative at a branch tucked right into our neighborhood. It felt like a gentle landing after the chaos of moving. Bert had just started his new position as the Media Relations Manager at a university in Santa Barbara, settling into a routine with a calm I hadn't seen in him in years.

He got paid sixty thousand a year.

And for the first time in what felt like forever, I could exhale. The strain I'd carried for so long—quietly, but relentlessly—began to lift. I didn't have to be the sole provider anymore. The bills didn't rest entirely on my shoulders. There was still pressure, sure, but not the crushing kind.

However, just as I was beginning to find my feet again, something started shifting at the bank. It was subtle at first—a change in tone, in meetings, in how we were spoken to. I had been with that bank for a decade. When I started, the mission was clear: people mattered. Customer service wasn't just a goal—it was the culture. We were trained to listen, to understand, and to build trust. It wasn't about numbers; it was about relationships.

But the industry was changing.

Quotas became the new gospel. The pressure to perform, to sell, and to hit metrics—weighed on all of us like an invisible yoke. If you didn't meet your numbers, you were written up. Three write-ups, and you were gone, with no conversation, and no grace.

And that pressure warped everything.

I watched coworkers start cutting corners. A savings account pitched as "required" to qualify for a free checking account. Credit pulled without consent. Credit cards opened without request. Debit cards ordered and mailed before the client even knew they existed.

I still remember the look on a woman's face as she held up a brand-new debit card she never asked for.

"I didn't open this," she said, confusion creasing her brow.

I took the card gently from her hand, trying to mask the pit growing in my stomach. I apologized. I fixed what I could. But the damage was done. And somewhere, the person who opened the account got credit for another "success."

It wasn't a fluke. It was happening everywhere.

The worst part was that it was being rewarded.

I tried to talk myself into staying. I needed the job. The hours worked with the kids' schedules. The paycheck helped. But every time I sat behind that desk, something in me recoiled. This wasn't who I was. This wasn't what I had signed up for.

Eventually, I stopped fighting the truth.

I walked away.

I found a part-time position as a mortgage processor at a local bank. The pace was different. The environment was quieter. The expectations felt human again. It wasn't just a career move—it was a reclamation, of my values, my peace, and my integrity.

With Bert working full-time and me on a part-time schedule, plus help from his parents, we didn't have to put the boys in daycare—a blessing I didn't take lightly. Being home with them mattered deeply to me. But the price for that arrangement came steep, wrapped in daily tension and the steady erosion of my spirit.

His parents' proximity felt suffocating. Their presence was constant, and their coldness toward me didn't soften, not even with their grandsons giggling in their laps. If anything, their judgment seemed to sharpen. Every parenting decision I made was met with scrutiny, their voices edging in where they didn't belong. They tried to parent my children as if I didn't exist.

And Bert always took their side.

Every disagreement, every moment I needed him to stand with me, he turned toward them instead. I began to feel like a ghost in my own home—there, but unseen, and unheard. The distance between us stretched wide and silent, filling with the weight of things unsaid. I reached for him over and over, suggesting counseling, voicing my unhappiness, begging him to see me.

"Well, I'm happy," he would say flatly, as if that settled it.

I felt like a pressure cooker, all heat and silence, moments from exploding.

Every summer, Bert's family made their pilgrimage to Bridgeport, California—days of camping, fishing, and boating. It was a tradition that threaded back to his childhood, full of mountain views and cool lake air. That year, for the first time, I was invited.

Something in me flickered with hope. Maybe this was it—maybe I was finally being accepted. I grew up in the mountains, hiking and camping. I imagined long walks through pine trees, the boys playing near the water, and nights under stars. Maybe this time would be different.

We were to camp in a tent while his parents and their

longtime friends stayed in cabins. On the way, we stopped overnight in Friant. There was a casino there. I fed and wrangled the boys alone in the hotel room while Bert disappeared for hours, gambling with his parents.

By the time we arrived at the camping resort the next evening, I was exhausted. We pitched our tent on the far edge of the resort, away from the cabins, and I was grateful for that small mercy. The two older boys stayed in the cabin with their grandparents. Bert, baby Ryan, and I tucked into the tent for the night.

I had just started to drift off when I heard it.

Crunch. Crunch. Slow, deliberate footsteps cracking over twigs.

I held my breath, every muscle tight with fear.

Then came the snort—low, guttural, and close. My blood ran cold.

A bear.

Panic welled up in my chest. Ryan squirmed in my arms, fussing. Teething, probably. I prayed he wouldn't cry. I didn't know if sound would scare the bear away or draw it closer. I lay frozen, whispering silent pleas to God while the weight of fear settled heavy on my chest.

Bert stirred beside me. I whispered, "What do we do?"

"Stay still. Don't make a sound," he murmured.

We lay like that, stiff and breathless, until the sounds faded into the woods. At sunrise, we unzipped the tent and stepped out into morning light that felt anything but warm.

Paw prints circled our tent. Deep imprints near the cooler. Scratches near the car. They'd tried to get in.

"There's no way I'm sleeping out here again," I said, my voice shaking.

When we told his parents, they laughed. They shrugged it off and called me dramatic. Bert said nothing.

They wouldn't let us stay in the cabin. "No room," they said.

Ryan cried all day. He was hot, flushed, and inconsolable. Bert's mom raised her brow and asked what was wrong with my parenting. "Why can't you settle your child?" she said, more accusation than concern. I wanted to scream. I knew it was more than teething. He was sick. I could feel it in my gut.

I begged to get a hotel in town. Bert refused.

We moved the tent to another corner of the campground, farther from the cabins, farther from help. That night, the bears returned—louder, and bolder. Ryan cried and cried, his little body burning with fever. I shook Bert awake, panic bubbling over.

He ran to the car, slammed the doors, and started the engine to scare them off.

We left the campground that night and didn't look back.

Later, he told his family that I had begged him to go to the hotel. He needed a story that made him look noble.

The rest of the trip, I was the punchline. The city girl scared of wildlife. The overreacting mother. The one who couldn't "tough it out." They mocked me to my face, and Bert just let them.

When we finally got home, I took Ryan straight to the doctor. He had a severe ear infection.

He'd been in pain for days. And I had known—of course I had known—but I'd been too afraid to speak up, too worn down to fight the tide of their dismissal one more time.

If I had to choose between another night with a bear outside my tent and another night of pretending everything was fine with Bert—I'd take the bear every time. A bear is dangerous, yes. But it doesn't look you in the eye and pretend to love you while it tears you apart.

Bert's love was quiet control. Smiles laced with contempt. A slow unraveling of who I was. And somewhere in the corners of that relationship, I lost the last flicker of the woman I'd been fighting to become.

• • •

Bert and his family weren't just difficult—they were calculated and polished in their cruelty. They knew where the bruises lived and pressed into them with a smile, always careful not to leave a visible mark. It was psychological warfare dressed as propriety: death by a thousand dismissals.

And I was starving—for kindness, for softness, for someone to see me and not turn away.

That's when I found MySpace. A new frontier. A strange little corner of the internet where I could disappear into anonymity while quietly begging to be seen. It offered both freedom and illusion. And I was desperate for both.

I created a profile, carefully curated. Never my face— just glimpses. A dress cinched at the waist. Heels against sunlit hardwood. My legs stretched out on a blanket in the yard. Sunlight casting shadows across my skin like poetry. Always faceless. Always a mystery. And people noticed.

The likes, the comments, the curiosity—they poured in. For the first time in years, I felt beautiful. Desired. Wanted. Strangers called me radiant. Men flirted. Women praised my aesthetic. But more than the pictures, it was the words that kept me there.

I started posting poetry—snippets of aching, longing, and hope. Pieces of myself I had buried beneath diapers, dishes, and silent dinners. And people responded. They said my words moved them. That I had a gift. That I made them feel something.

And for the first time in a long time, so did I.

MySpace became a sanctuary. A secret room in the house of my life that no one else had a key to. I'd log in after the boys were in bed, after the kitchen was cleaned, and Bert retreated to the television. I'd slip into the computer room and vanish—into words, into music, and into the glow of a screen that felt warmer than the bed I shared.

That's when the messages started.

Men. Curious, kind, and attentive. They weren't hitting on me—not at first. They were simply present. They listened. Asked questions. Said things like, "You're fascinating," and "I feel like I know you."

Then, one man stood out.

He lived in Santa Barbara, just like me. His messages were thoughtful, funny, and patient. He made no demands. Just showed up—in my inbox, in my thoughts.

He knew I was married, that I was unhappy, and that I wasn't looking for an affair. But he didn't disappear. I told him no when he asked to meet. Again, and again. And still, he stayed. He became my confidant, my sounding board, the person I turned to when I was angry or anxious or simply needed to feel something other than numb.

He made me laugh. He saw me. And I stopped feeling guilty.

One Sunday afternoon, I agreed to meet him.

A coffee shop tucked in the corner of town. Neutral. Harmless. But my heart was pounding as if I was walking into a storm. Butterflies tangled with dread. I knew this was a line—not physical, but emotional—and once I crossed it, I couldn't go back.

We sat outside, with the sun warm on our faces, and the conversation flowed as if we'd known each other for years. No awkward silences. No masks. Just breath and honesty and easy laughter.

For two hours, I forgot who I was supposed to be.

When I got home, guilt hit me like a tidal wave.

I walked through the front door, and the weight of my choices pressed against my chest like a confession. I hadn't touched him. But I had betrayed something. Something sacred.

I never saw him again in person. But we stayed connected. MySpace messages became lifelines. He was still my escape, my secret harbor.

My dirty little secret.

Until he wasn't.

It was around this time that I was laid off. The call came on a Tuesday.

My manager's voice was tight and rehearsed. "The entire mortgage division is being outsourced," she said. "Effective immediately."

Just like that, the department was gone. Not phased out. Not restructured. Gone. One day we were processing loans, fielding calls, making plans for the next quarter. The next, our desks were being cleared and our emails disabled. It happened so fast, it didn't feel real. I sat there for a full minute after the call ended, blinking at the screen like it might flicker back to life with better news.

But it didn't.

I felt the floor tilt beneath me—my stability had been ripped out from under my feet. My breath caught, and for a second, panic fluttered in my chest. I wasn't ready. I hadn't seen it coming.

I stared at the boxes. At the office around me that no longer felt like mine.

And then I stood up.

I've always been good at that—standing up. Brushing off the dust. Finding my next move before the fear could fully settle in. And thankfully, we had a buffer. Bert's paycheck came in like clockwork, and we'd managed to build a modest savings account. We weren't in crisis. Not yet.

Still, the lay-off left a bruise. Not because of money, but because of what it meant. I had worked hard. I'd been loyal.

And none of that mattered in the end. My position was nothing more than a line item on a spreadsheet.

Within two weeks, I was back in the game. A private lender hired me as a part-time mortgage processor and pre-underwriter. It was a small office, with flexible hours, and no drama.

The work was steady, there was room to breathe and space to learn. I was sharpening skills that would serve me for years to come, even if I didn't realize it yet.

What I also didn't know then was that this was just the beginning—lay-off number one in a string of four over my career. Each one would leave its own scar. Each one would challenge my resilience in new ways. But this first one cut the deepest.

It was the moment I learned that effort doesn't always equal security. That you can pour yourself into something for years and still be let go without warning. That kind of disillusionment changes you.

But with the loss came something I hadn't expected: stillness.

For the first time in years, I had space in my days. Breathing room. Quiet.

And in that quiet, something began to stir.

Not just professionally—but personally.

Old connections. Forgotten voices. Unfinished conversations.

Things I thought I'd left behind began rising to the surface.

Janice had been my best friend for nearly a decade—my opposite in every way, and yet, my sister in spirit. We met in Napa, back when I was still learning the rhythm of married life and motherhood. She was a teller at the bank, with a quick wit and a bold laugh that filled every corner of the room. From day one, we clicked.

Janice lived for luxury: the designer handbags, the stilettos, and the sleek convertible parked just right in her driveway. She had a taste for flash and flair, for everything top shelf. By contrast, I leaned toward comfort. If it was functional and got the job done, that was enough for me. Still, I adored her. I admired her unapologetic boldness, even when her work skirts pushed the limits of dress code, or her heels clicked too confidently down the polished bank floors.

We were yin and yang. And it worked.

When Bert and I left Napa for Santa Barbara, hugging her goodbye was one of the hardest parts. We promised to keep in touch—and we did. Not every week, not even every month, but when we talked, time melted. The bond never loosened.

So, when Janice called in tears, her voice cracking through the phone as she spoke about the unraveling of her marriage, I didn't hesitate. "Come here," I said. "Just for the weekend. Get away. Clear your head."

The timing was perfect. There was a Dodgers game that weekend—Janice's and Bert's favorite team. The boys were staying with his parents. I pictured laughter, fresh air, maybe a little clarity for her. I just wanted to be there for my friend.

We picked her up from the airport and headed straight to the stadium. The sun was still high, warm against our faces. We drank—casually, not recklessly—but enough to blur the edges of the day. Somewhere between the fourth inning and the seventh, I noticed it.

The way Janice leaned into Bert when she laughed. The way he laughed back, his eyes lingering a second too long. It started small—just under the surface—but it rippled through me like a tremor. I tried to shake it off. Maybe I was being paranoid. Maybe the drinks were making me over-sensitive. But the ride home confirmed what my gut already knew.

The flirting didn't stop. It intensified. Their energy crackled in the tight space of the car. By the time we pulled into our driveway, my skin was buzzing with unease. I didn't say a word. I just grabbed my keys, slid behind the wheel, and drove two blocks to the park. I knew I shouldn't be driving—I'd had too much—but I couldn't stay in that house. Not with them.

I curled up in the front seat of my car, the upholstery cold against my cheek. I stared out the windshield as the streetlight flickered overhead. My heart was pounding. My stomach twisted. I slept, restlessly, under a sky that felt too quiet.

At dawn, I called him.

My voice was thin. "Did you and Janice have sex?"

Silence.

Then—"Yes."

The word cut clean through me. I gasped. The air fled my lungs. Rage erupted in a roar.

"Get that bitch out of my house," I spat into the phone. "She'd better be gone when I get there."

I didn't go straight home. I drove aimlessly for hours, letting the road carry me wherever it pleased. Eventually, I found myself in the parking lot of a hotel off the highway. I sat there for a long time, staring at the dashboard, with my mind racing. I felt wrecked. Betrayed. Hollow.

My phone buzzed with calls and texts-messages I refused to read. I silenced it and checked into the hotel with shaking hands.

That night, I collapsed into bed, tears soaking the pillow. I wept until I couldn't anymore. Then, I stared at the ceiling, empty. By morning, something inside me had shifted. Not peace. Not forgiveness. But a flicker. A breath of space.

Maybe this was it. Maybe this was the moment to leave. To stop pretending, and to stop dying inside.

My phone lit up again. A text from Janice: *I'm sorry.* There was also a voicemail from Bert. One from her. Both apologizing, both empty.

I stayed one more night, to give myself that time to breathe.

On Sunday, I called Bert. I told him I'd be home that evening, and he should pick up the boys. I told him Janice needed to be gone.

Then, as the sun sank low over the highway, I made a second call, to her.

I don't even remember what I said. Just that I asked the one question that wouldn't leave me alone. "Why?"

Her voice was flat. "You've been unhappy. I thought I was helping."

I ended the call.

When I walked through the front door that evening, the air felt stale. The house looked the same, but everything inside me had changed. I hugged the boys. I put away my overnight bag and sat down with Bert.

"I want a divorce."

He blinked. Surprised. "What about counseling?"

I hesitated. My soul was tired. But my mind wouldn't settle. The boys. They were still so young—eight, five, and three. What would happen to them if we split? What would happen if we stayed?

I didn't want them growing up thinking this was love: that silence, resentment, and betrayal were normal.

So, I said yes.

To counseling.

We gave it a shot.

A few counseling sessions, here and there. Sitting stiffly

on that beige loveseat, facing a stranger with a clipboard and a practiced nod. We answered the questions. We did the work—or, at least, went through the motions of what that work was supposed to look like. But in truth, I had already left the marriage.

Not physically, not yet. But emotionally? I was gone. My heart had packed its bags months before I ever stepped out the door. And if I'm being honest, I don't think Bert's heart had ever fully moved in.

To fix what had broken between us would have required something neither of us had left: years of gut-wrenching honesty, fierce accountability, and the kind of personal growth that starts with a mirror and ends in therapy. We'd have to dig into childhood wounds, face trauma we'd long since buried. We'd have had to peel back layers of hurt we'd convinced ourselves didn't need healing.

I was willing.

But Bert wasn't.

After a couple of months of dragging ourselves to sessions and tiptoeing around the real issues, we came to a quiet, shared understanding.

It was over.

There was no dramatic finale. No slamming of doors. No plates flying across the kitchen. Just the subtle sound of something slipping—finally—out of our hands.

And still, even in that soft surrender, I hadn't expected the next part.

Bert wasted no time. He began his campaign immediately, planting his version of the truth like weeds in every ear that would listen. Because the story had to be told. And it had to paint him in the right light.

He couldn't be the one who failed, or the one to blame.

That's not how narcissists work. They don't grieve. They strategize. They twist, reshape, and retell until the version that survives makes them the hero—or at the very least, the victim.

I was the villain in his tale. The destroyer of a carefully curated image. The one who shattered the illusion he had so meticulously polished for the outside world.

His anger at me didn't just simmer—it burned, white hot. And he made sure it spread.

What no one knew—but what he made sure everyone eventually knew—was that I had been staying up late during those final months. I had been logging into MySpace after the boys were in bed. I was posting poems, talking to strangers, and flirting. Sitting alone in a dimly lit room, hunched over a keyboard, aching to feel alive. To be seen. Bert had noticed the late nights. His suspicions swelled like a tide. One evening, while I was out, he came home early and sat at the computer. He didn't ask. Didn't wait. He went through my search history, opened my account, and scrolled through my messages.

But he didn't confront me.

He created a fake profile.

He watched. He waited.

He studied my words, read my poems, and examined the comments. He saw that I was flirting, vulnerable, and open. That was his jackpot. His proof.

He never said a word.

Because he didn't want clarity. He wanted ammunition.

From that moment on, he had what he needed to justify the story he'd already started telling. "She cheated."

He repeated it like gospel. He whispered it into the ears of coworkers, friends, acquaintances—even people who barely knew us.

By the time I left the house for good, the soil had been thoroughly seeded. My reputation, already wilting under years of isolation and judgment, was now poisoned with rumor.

And as he spun his version of events, he was already filling my place.

Women began appearing.

Then, one afternoon, he walked through the front door with one.

"Heidi," he said casually, "this is Beth—my friend from high school. Just showing her around." There she stood, framed in the entryway as if she belonged there, her eyes scanning the room, scanning me, with smug curiosity. Her smile was tight. Her tone, clipped. Every word that fell from her lips was laced with condescension.

I stood frozen, the air thick with something sharp and unspoken.

She looked at me as if I was the guest. Like *I* was the one trespassing in my own home.

Since I was a little girl, I've had a gift—if you can call it that. I could read a room before a word was spoken. Especially when the energy turned. Especially when it turned on me. It was how I survived. How I learned to dodge the blows that didn't always come with fists. The cold glances. The shifting tones. The heavy silences. I felt them before they ever reached the surface.

Beth's energy announced itself the second she stepped into a room. It was loud, draining and mean.

By then, everything under that roof felt suffocating. The walls themselves seemed to be holding their breath, waiting for the next blow-up, the next wound. The air was dense, thick with bitterness and unspoken accusations. I felt like I was walking barefoot across shattered glass, every step a silent plea not to bleed again.

The divorce process dragged on like an embedded, aching splinter. Every day in that house pressed harder against my chest. I could hardly breathe. I needed out.

We'd agreed to mediation. For the boys. To avoid dragging them through the courtroom mud. I didn't want them to be pawns. I didn't want their childhood memories colored with court dates and custody battles.

But deep down, I knew—if it went to court, I wouldn't stand a chance.

Santa Barbara might look like a city on a map, but it operated like a village. Everyone knew someone who knew someone.

Bert's family were rooted deep in the soil. His father was the oldest of fourteen, his family name laced through the community like ivy. Third-generation Santa Barbarians. Their story was already being told, passed along like gospel.

And mine? It didn't matter. I was already the outsider.

Still, I clung to one hope.

One day, the boys would grow up.

One day, they'd see with their own eyes.

And maybe—just maybe—they'd understand.

But hope didn't make the present any less brutal. Mediation wasn't the neutral ground it promised to be.

From the start, I felt outnumbered and outranked.

Because when we walked into that room on a warm spring afternoon, Bert wasn't alone. His parents came with him.

They said it was because they had contributed to the down-payment on the house. I knew the truth was that they came to make sure I left with as little as possible.

I had never gone through a divorce before. Never sat across from a mediator.

I had no lawyer. No family support. No one to say, "You can object." No one to say, "This isn't right."

The mediator didn't help. She didn't suggest their presence might be coercive. She didn't raise a single concern. Sometimes I wonder if she had already picked a side.

And it wasn't mine.

There is so much I would do differently now. But that day, I took my seat across the table—just me, against three of them. I folded my hands in my lap and tried to steady my breath, my voice, and my spine.

Bert's parents wasted no time. They wanted the house. They were willing to "buy me out" —but only after deducting what they had once labeled a gift. Now, conveniently, it was a loan.

The house had been worth a million when we bought it. Not a mansion—just a standard tract home. But it sat in a good neighborhood, in a district with strong schools. A place where the boys could grow up with some sense of normalcy.

I had already decided to let Bert keep it. Not because he deserved it—but because the boys did. I didn't want them uprooted. New schools. New bedrooms. New friends. That kind of instability scars.

I would know.

So, I gave it all up.

Even as I sat there, watching them negotiate what was once my life like it was a business deal—I stayed quiet. I didn't push back. I swallowed the bitter taste of injustice because I believed the boys deserved peace more than I deserved equity.

I told myself I could live in an apartment. I told myself safety was more important than ownership, that as long as we had walls and a roof, we'd be okay.

But God, did I sacrifice.

The divorce was finalized in 2007—right as the housing market crumbled beneath our feet. That million-dollar home we'd once bragged about was suddenly appraised at six hundred-fifty thousand. I sat across the table from Bert and his parents, the air thick with smugness and strategy. They didn't just want the house—they wanted it for a steal.

Their offer to buy me out was as a measly sixty grand. I stared at the figure on the paper, my chest tightening. I should've walked away with no less than one-hundred thousand.

But logic and fairness didn't matter. I was outnumbered, outmaneuvered, and out of hope.

"If you don't accept this," Bert's mother warned, her tone cool and practiced, "we'll take it to court." I knew what that meant. I wouldn't win. Not in that town. Not against that family.

And in the back of my mind, the boys' faces rose like anchors. A court battle would tear through their lives. I couldn't do that to them. I couldn't live with that.

So, I signed.

When I walked out of that office, the sun hit my face like a spotlight, too bright for how small I felt. My legs moved, but my body felt heavy—numb. I got in the car, gripped the steering wheel with shaking hands, and sobbed the entire way home.

The only thread keeping me from unraveling completely was the alimony and child support. We'd been married for eleven years, which meant I qualified for spousal support. The child-support software calculated that I would receive eight hundred dollars a month, and it broke down the payments in a way I didn't expect—two hundred-fifty of it counted as taxable income.

It wasn't much. But in that moment, it was lifeline enough.

Still, no check—no number—could quiet the storm churning inside me. So, I turned to the one thing that always had.

Running.

I laced up my shoes and hit the pavement, the slap of rubber against concrete syncing with the beat of my heart and the ache in my chest. Running was where I sorted through the mess—where I could lose myself and, somehow, come back more whole.

During the divorce, I trained for the Nike Women's Marathon. Each run became a sacred ritual—grief, frustration, fear all leaking out through every labored breath, and every aching step. I didn't just run—I prayed. I cried. I fought.

And when it was over—when the ink on the papers had dried and the dust had settled—I showed up. I ran that marathon. Five and a half hours later, I crossed the finish line, with legs like jelly, and my chest heaving. A volunteer slipped the medal over my head, and for the first time in months, maybe years, I felt powerful.

Exhausted and sore, but invincible.

That finish line didn't just mark 26.2 miles—it marked a turning point. If I could survive a marathon, I could survive this next chapter. I was strong. I was resilient. I was just getting started.

I went on to run another full marathon and more half marathons than I could count. Every race became a form of therapy—a place to reclaim myself. On those long runs, I wasn't a divorcée or a single mom. I was steady. I was powerful. I was whole.

But no matter how many miles I logged or medals I earned, they couldn't give me what I craved most.

A home of my own. Somewhere to land. Somewhere to breathe. Somewhere that belonged only to me and the boys.

That was all I wanted.

After months of sifting through listings, crossing fingers, and facing one rejection after another, I found it—a two-bedroom, one-and-a-half-bath condo perched on the Mesa. It overlooked the ocean. The breeze carried salt and quiet. And the first time I stepped inside, I felt it settle in my chest: *This feels safe.*

And at that point in my life, safety meant everything.

However, getting there hadn't been easy.

The search had become a grueling lesson in judgment. Application after application, I was turned down. Landlords scanned my information and smiled politely—until they saw the part where I checked "divorced" and "three dependents." Their smiles tightened. Their decisions never changed.

Never mind that my FICO score was a solid 720. Never

mind that I had sixty thousand sitting in my bank account. Never mind that I'd just secured a full-time position and a higher income. On paper, I was a dream tenant. But to them, I was just a single mom. A risk. A story they thought they already knew.

And in that small town—where Bert's name cracked doors wide open—mine only seemed to close them.

Their whispers wrapped themselves around me, thick as fog. I could feel their quiet judgments pressed against every wall I tried to lean on. The shadow of Bert and his parents stretched long, reaching even into the places I hadn't stepped yet.

Still, I stayed. Because the boys were here. Because leaving them was never on the table. Not then. Not ever. So, when I scheduled a walk-through of the condo, I did something that made my stomach twist—I called Bert.

I asked him to come with me.

It bruised my pride more than I cared to admit, but I needed a favor. I needed him to vouch for me. Some naïve, desperate part of me hoped that if the owner met him—if he gave some sort of nod of approval—I might stand a better chance.

It worked.

Can you believe that? In 2007, I had to drag my ex-husband along just to qualify for a place to live. A place *I* would be paying for. But that sting of humiliation, sharp as it was, came with a quiet win. I got the keys. I had a place.

That first night, the boys and I didn't have much furniture, but we didn't care. We spread the softest blanket we owned across the living room floor, curled into one another like puppies, and turned on *Finding Nemo*.

The soft glow from the TV danced across their faces, lighting up their tired eyes and wide smiles. I lay there with them, their little limbs tangled around mine, and for the first time in a long, long while—I exhaled.

We spent the weekend unpacking, turning those blank white walls into something that felt like ours. The boys got the bigger bedroom. We set it up dorm-style—bunk beds for the older two, each with their own tiny desk. Ryan's toy box sat in the corner, already overflowing with stuffed animals and plastic heroes.

It was cramped. It was imperfect. But it was home. And we were together.

That was everything.

Adjusting to the custody schedule looked simple on paper—fifty-fifty. Half the week with me, half with Bert. Fair, structured, balanced.

However, nothing about that first drop-off felt fair.

I sat in the car outside Bert's house, with my hands gripping the steering wheel, the boys' backpacks still indented into the seats behind me. I watched them walk up the driveway, their little shoulders sagging under the weight of too much. I waved, swallowed the lump in my throat, and waited until they disappeared inside.

Then I broke.

Tears streamed down my face, the ache of their absence hollowing me out from the inside. Letting them go—even for a few days—felt unnatural, like a piece of me was being peeled away.

I can only imagine what it was like for them—shuffling between houses, juggling different sets of rules, carrying backpacks stuffed with more than just books and stuffed animals. They carried uncertainty, confusion, and quiet heartbreak.

At least they had school. At least their friends stayed the same. That sliver of consistency became everything.

I never slept well when they weren't home. The house felt too quiet. Too still. Even now, all these years later, my body rests easier when they're under my roof.

The next few years blurred into a rhythm that was more

survival than routine. Work. School. Sports. Homework. Dinners. Bath time. Chores. Repeat. It wasn't glamorous, but it was ours.

Early on, Bert and I agreed that the boys should participate in sports and activities. But "agreed" might've been generous. The reality? They did what *he* wanted.

T-ball as soon as they could hold a glove. Then soccer, basketball, roller hockey—and eventually ice hockey when the city put in a rink.

Bert craved structure, achievement, status. And control. Always control.

He wanted them to play instruments, too. It was another point of tension. I didn't believe in forcing them into things they didn't love. I wanted them to explore, to find their voices, to figure out who they were outside of expectations. They weren't extensions of us. They weren't Bert. They weren't me. They weren't their grandparents. They were *them*.

However, Bert didn't see it that way.

He ruled his house with volume and fear. His voice—a booming thunder—commanded silence. Orders barked, hands shoved and yelling that could rattle the walls. He taught the boys how to pour beer from his kegerator—a mini beer-tap fridge—acting like it was some kind of father-son rite of passage.

In between homework and games, they scrubbed floors and took out trash, chore after chore after chore. I just wanted them to be kids. Yes, they needed responsibility. But they also needed to laugh, to rest, and to play without fear of getting it wrong.

When Bert started enrolling them in overlapping sports—sometimes three at once—it didn't just consume the boys' schedules. It took over mine.

My phone lit up constantly.

Pick up Dusty at 5:00. Drop off Toby at 6:15. My parents will get Ryan from the rink. Text after text. Email after email. My life became a rotating door of drop-offs, pick-ups, and dictated logistics.

Eventually, I sat the boys down. Do you *want* to do all these sports?" I asked gently. "Do any of them actually make you happy?"

They looked at each other, then at me. "Not really."

One sport each. That's all they wanted. Just one they actually enjoyed. But that wasn't enough for Bert. He kept signing them up anyway, turning every season into another battleground. And the more he controlled them, the more he controlled me.

My stress became a silent hum I carried everywhere.

Ryan, my youngest, finally found something he was excited about—football. He talked about it with a spark in his eyes, bouncing with energy each time practice came up. I supported him fully.

Bert didn't. He said it was too dangerous. His parents agreed. Concussions. Injuries. "It's not worth the risk," they insisted. But I saw how much it meant to Ryan. I signed the permission slip anyway.

He played one season.

Then the comments started chipping away at him.

He came to me one afternoon, with his shoulders slumped. "I don't want to do it anymore," he whispered. And just like that, something he loved was lost.

Later, Ryan asked to try acting. I could see the light in him again—his curiosity, and his eagerness to perform.

Bert said no. Again. "It's a waste of time," he scoffed. So, I enrolled him myself. I paid for the classes and drove him to every session.

He thrived.

At the end-of-season showcase, I sat in the front row, my heart bursting as I watched him take the stage. He shone. He found himself. When the lights came up, he scanned the audience.

No dad. No grandparents. Just me.

He smiled, and I smiled back—proud, unwavering.

I was enough.

But that didn't make the absence hurt any less.

Then the floor fell out. I was laid off. Again.

The mortgage brokerage I'd worked at for years had been bought out. New ownership. New rules. No warning. Just a severance check and a goodbye.

Three months' worth.

On paper, it looked manageable. But life doesn't happen on paper.

Meanwhile, the mediation agreement Bert and I had in place—meant to protect structure and balance—was unraveling due to years and years of Bert's dominance and manipulation.

What started as shared parenting turned into a chess-board. And Bert wasn't playing fair. Every time I tried to set a boundary, he shoved back hard. Every revision I proposed, he twisted. Every clause, he contested.

He wasn't trying to co-parent. He was trying to win. And once again, the battleground wasn't paper.

It was the boys.

We ended up where I'd hoped we'd never go.

Court.

Bert's parents didn't just lend support—they launched a legal offensive.

They hired one of the top divorce attorneys in the county for him. The kind of lawyer with a reputation that made people's stomachs flip before hearings had even begun. Ruthless, polished, and precise.

Meanwhile, I was flipping through my checkbook and stretching numbers that refused to bend. I found someone I could afford—barely. She was kind. Competent. Steady. But in the courtroom, it wasn't a fair fight. The playing field wasn't just uneven. It was a landslide.

I cashed out my retirement. Just like that—years of saving, sacrificed for a chance to stand my ground.

The glow of security from the divorce settlement vanished, swallowed whole by hourly fees, court filings, and the price of protecting my boys.

The battle dragged on for a year.

A full year of hearings and filings, each one peeling back layers I didn't even know I had left. The original agreement was paper-thin. It hadn't accounted for the details that now defined our lives—school decisions, holidays, even the basic right to care for my own children when Bert left town. Everything had to be renegotiated.

I'd walk into that courtroom with my head high and leave each time feeling hollowed out. The wood-paneled walls, the echo of arguments that weren't mine to start, and the sterile weight of judgment—it all pressed against my chest.

In those moments, I wasn't just defending my parenting. I was defending my worth.

At night, I'd lie in bed staring at the ceiling, doing math in my head. Wondering how many days I had until the account hit zero. Wondering how many pieces of myself I could afford to give away before there was nothing left to barter.

I was tired. It wasn't the kind of tired sleep could fix. It was the kind that wraps itself around your bones.

The last of the divorce money went toward groceries. A power bill. Shoes the boys had outgrown again. And when that ran out, I dipped into my retirement. Again.

Every dollar I'd carefully set aside over the years—gone. Just like the job that once made me feel steady.

I hadn't wanted to take him back to court. I had clung to the hope that things might settle. That he might stop using the boys as pawns.

But he didn't want peace. He wanted control. And I had no choice.

This time, he didn't even pretend to compromise. Why would he? The custody schedule was working in his favor. Through sports, pick-ups, logistics, and relentless communication, he was still pulling the strings—and he knew it.

Somewhere amid that chaos, I made a change. A footwear company in town offered me a credit analyst position. It wasn't finance, not in the traditional sense, but after three lay-offs and the emotional fallout of each one, I needed something new. Something that didn't feel like the ground might shift out from under me.

It came with a pay cut. A big one.

I had been paid thirty dollars an hour, which dropped to eighteen. I filed paperwork to have the child support recalculated. It seemed reasonable, and necessary.

What I didn't expect was how fast things would change. Within the year, I climbed the ranks—entry-level to senior analyst. I was supervising a team of five. The raise came quickly. Back to thirty an hour. Then bonuses.

By year's end, I was earning seventy-five thousand.

And with that, the court reran the numbers.

The outcome punched the air from my lungs. My support dropped from eight hundred dollars a month to two hundred-thirty dollars—including alimony. It felt like a gut punch.

Bert and his parents celebrated it like a trophy: another win for their side.

But I knew better. They might've taken the money, but I took something greater. Time with the boys was no longer his to manipulate.

And for me, that was everything.

However, victory came with a cost.

The legal fees didn't stop just because the hearings did. For years after, they continued to chip away at the life I was trying so hard to rebuild. Credit cards hit their limits. My savings dried up. My retirement was gone, spent trying to keep the lights on. By the time it all caught up with me, I was living month to month—one paycheck away from unraveling.

Rent due. Groceries rationed. Breath held.

But still standing.

The porch light buzzed faintly above me as I turned the key and stepped up to the door. The boys were at their dad's that night, and the house was still, the kind of quiet that usually felt like a small gift.

I reached for the handle—then paused.

A folded piece of paper flapped slightly in the breeze, taped right to the center of the door. I peeled it off without thinking, more curious than concerned. Maybe a neighborhood notice. Maybe a delivery slip. I didn't expect it to matter.

But before I even stepped inside, I read the first line.

It mattered.

Rent increase: $1,900 to $2,100, effective the next month.

I stood frozen in the entryway, the letter crinkling in my shaking hands. My eyes scanned the words again, hoping I'd misread. That maybe the number would somehow change.

It didn't.

I dropped onto the couch, with the letter still clenched between my fingers, and my heart pounding so hard I could feel it in my throat.

An extra two hundred dollars a month I didn't have.

The walls closed in around me.

I was already stretched to the edge—every paycheck mapped to the cent. No cushion. No safety net. No partner to split the load. No family to swoop in and say, *Don't worry, we've got you.*

Just me.

The weight of it all crushed down at once.

Before I could stop it, the tears came—hot, messy, unstoppable. Not the kind of crying that trickles politely, but the kind that steals your breath. The kind that drives you to your knees on the cold kitchen floor, fists clenched against tile, prayers spilling from your lips between gasps.

"God, please," I whispered. "Please, help me. Show me what to do. I can't do this alone."

And then—I heard it.

Not in my head, but around me. Outside me.

You are unconditionally loved.

Everything is always how it's supposed to be.

Everything will always be alright.

The words wrapped around me like warm air after a storm.

It wasn't a memory from my near-death experience. It wasn't a hopeful echo. It was *now*. Clear. Steady. Real.

I sat in that stillness, letting the truth of it wash over my broken edges.

Then I stood.

I wiped my face. I changed into pajamas. I climbed into bed.

And I slept.

When morning came, something had shifted.

The weight wasn't gone—but the fire was lit.

I was going to find a new place. Smaller, maybe. Different, definitely. But it would be *ours*. The thought of my boys living full-time with their dad while I lived out of a car flickered through my mind—and burned it clean.

No.
Not this mama.
Not yet.
I was scared.
But I was still standing.

11

MY FAMILY DYNAMICS

Even as a little girl, before I had the words to name it, I knew my family wasn't like other families.

We weren't just dysfunctional—we were woven together by trauma, each thread pulling tighter around the next. Hurt layered over hurt, abuse buried beneath generations of unspoken pain. The silence wasn't a glitch in our system. It *was* the system.

My father's side was a ghost story I only partially knew.

I remember meeting his parents and my great-grandparents when I was little. There were cousins, a few strained introductions, but no warmth. No effort to connect. No curiosity. They drifted out of my life like smoke through a cracked-open window. No explanation, and no goodbye. They were just gone.

The only thing anyone ever said about my father's mother was that she was *crazy*. That one word was supposed to explain it all.

But over time, that story stopped fitting. The older I got, the more I understood. I believe now that she was abused. Her so-called *madness* wasn't madness at all—it was grief. It was trauma. It was unhealed pain wrapped in silence and labeled for convenience.

Calling someone *crazy* is easier than confronting the truth. Easier than facing the cruelty. Easier than admitting that the very people who should protect you are the ones doing the damage.

And while my father was a convicted child molester who terrorized our family for years, the hardest person to forgive has always been my mother. That truth scrapes against every part of me, even now. But she was supposed to be my safe place. The soft landing. The protector. The one who saw me, heard me, held me.

Instead, I was barely tolerated.

I was dismissed and emotionally abandoned.

That kind of betrayal doesn't fade into the past. It leaves a wound that never quite closes. It leaks silently, unpredictably, even when you think you've stitched it shut. On my mother's side, the silence wore a different mask.

They didn't deny what happened. They buried it under shame.

Everyone knew what Stan had done. They just didn't talk about it. Not because it wasn't real, but because *family business stayed behind closed doors*. You didn't air your dirty laundry. You shoved it into closets, locked the doors, and prayed the stink didn't seep through the floorboards.

Even in that family, where secrets grew like mold, there were gifts.

My grandmother had psychic abilities. So did my mother.

I wouldn't learn about that part of myself until my late thirties—but when I did, something shifted. Puzzle pieces began clicking into place. All those years of feeling *too* much, sensing what others couldn't, knowing things I couldn't explain—I wasn't broken.

I was gifted.

I just didn't know how to live with it in a world that didn't understand. As I dug deeper into my healing—through therapy, through brutal self-reflection, through the slow peeling back of layered pain—I started to find language for the things that once haunted me.

My pain had context.

My gifts had a name.

My siblings and I each wore our trauma differently.

Misty's body carried it—chronic illness that clung to her like a second skin.

Lena couldn't bear touch, keeping her hands and her heart busy with work so she didn't have to feel.

Hunter numbed it all with drugs, vanishing into the criminal justice system, drifting in and out like a man untethered.

And I disappeared into people-pleasing. I made myself small, soft, agreeable—whatever I thought others needed. I became the version of myself that wouldn't be rejected.

I had no voice, no self-love, and no identity.

I was a ghost in my own story.

When the world got too loud, I retreated into the only comfort I had ever known.

I sucked my thumb. As a child, and well into my twenties. It was private. It was my version of survival.

I'd catch myself doing it in the dark, behind closed doors, without even realizing. My thumb would find its way to my mouth when I was exhausted or overwhelmed. And in those moments, the noise of the world would dim.

Everything would go quiet.

I remember as a toddler, my mother tried to break the habit. She smeared hot sauce—red pepper, maybe—onto my thumb. I cried.

But I kept going.

(And ironically, I love spicy food to this day.)

I finally stopped when Dusty was born. I couldn't bear

the thought of him growing up watching his mother self-soothe like that. So, I made myself quit. But it was harder than I imagined—like giving up a lifeline.

I replaced it with another.

Now, when stress threatens to pull me under, I rub my eyebrows.

Even now—years later—when the weight gets too heavy, my fingers reach for that familiar motion.

A thread of survival I've never fully cut.

We survived. Not gracefully, not cleanly—but we made it through.

Each of us emerged in our own fractured way, stitched together by instinct and pain.

We're not perfect. God, we are far from it. But considering where we came from, the fact that we're still standing means something.

I don't fault my siblings for the paths they've taken. I see the pain beneath their choices. I know the weight they carry.

However, they don't always extend that same grace to me.

Their judgment isn't loud or cruel—it's quiet. I feel it in the pauses, in the sideways glances, and in the things they don't say. It is a silent verdict that hangs between us.

We show up when we have to—smiles that don't quite reach our eyes, and conversations that skim the surface like skipping stones. But the distance is there.

Sometimes I wonder if I've lost my family more than once.

Other times, I wonder if I ever truly had them at all.

It's taken years—through therapy, through grief, through the sacred clarity of my near-death experience—for me to understand something simple but radical:

Boundaries are sacred.

They're not punishments.

They're not walls.

They're doors.

And I get to decide who walks through.

Family doesn't get a free pass to violate my peace. If someone, blood or not, continues to cross the lines I've drawn, they lose the privilege of staying in my life.

That's not cruelty. That's self-respect.

I choose peace.

I choose love.

I choose harmony—not the fake kind that comes from avoiding conflict, but the real kind that comes from honoring the truth.

It's important you understand this piece of my story—this complicated family tapestry I was born into—because getting to this place of peace wasn't easy. It took years to forgive, not just the people who hurt me, but myself.

For staying silent.

For carrying shame that was never mine.

There's a particular kind of ache that comes from living your life apologizing for wounds you didn't cause. From confusing survival with weakness. From believing you were broken when you were really just bruised.

Day by day, moment by moment, I began to integrate the quiet wisdom of my near-death experience.

You are unconditionally loved.

Everything is always how it's supposed to be.

Everything will always be alright.

I learned to trust the deeper rhythms of life.

I learned to listen inward.

So, when the custody battle with my ex exploded into chaos—when my job disappeared, my savings were drained, and I found myself holding my breath between paychecks—it didn't surprise me when my mother began reaching out.

•   •   •

The calls came quietly at first.

Always on the days when I felt like I was hanging by a thread. Days when the boys were with their dad, and the silence in the house was thick and pressing. I'd be sitting on the couch or standing at the kitchen sink, and the phone would ring—her name lighting up the screen.

It was as if she knew. With her psychic abilities, maybe she really *did*.

I'd answer with hesitation, my voice clipped and careful: "Hey."

"How are you?" she'd ask, softly.

"Fine." One-word answers. Guarded.

I didn't trust it. I didn't trust *her*. But still, she called. And something about her had shifted.

She listened—not out of obligation or curiosity. Not to fix me or dismiss me.

She just *listened*. She didn't interrupt. She didn't shame. She stayed.

And in that stillness, something long-frozen inside me began to thaw—not all at once—but slowly, and cautiously. The cracks that had once made me feel broken began to feel like open doors.

She had always been crafty. A creative alchemist of sorts—turning broken glass, scraps of fabric, and forgotten junk into beauty. There was something wild and gypsy-like about her spirit. Something restless but radiant.

And her art became a language between us.

The first birthday package arrived with a card taped to the outside and ribbon curling at the edges. Inside were hand-made gifts for the boys—simple, sweet, and full of intention.

It was the first time I'd ever received something like that from her.

Then came Christmas. Another box. More thoughtful pieces, each one a quiet offering of something we'd never had: connection.

When I started a side business making baby bibs to make ends meet, she wanted in.

"I can help," she said.

So, I did the shopping—picking out hand towels in soft blues and greens, mailing them to her in Colorado. Weeks later, they'd return transformed—sewn neatly, packaged carefully, ready to sell.

Then she taught herself to embroider. Suddenly, the bibs arrived stitched with kittens and daisies, puppies and pastel flowers.

Every time, I offered to pay her. Every time, she refused.

"You need it more than I do," she said, her voice gentle.

By then, she was in a committed relationship with a man she'd met in Montrose, Colorado. He adored her—made her laugh, made her feel safe.

He asked her more than once to move in. After six divorces, she hesitated. But eventually, she said yes.

They made a home together—warm, quiet, and full of light. She spent her mornings in the garden, pruning her roses with tender care. Roses had always been her favorite.

She retired and took a part-time job at the local craft shop, selling her artwork alongside the bibs we made. Her laugh became softer. Her spirit was lighter.

She had inherited my grandfather's striking blue eyes—eyes we used to tease her about, calling her "Misty-Blue-Eyes."

Even now, I can still picture them—sky blue, wide, and deep. The kind of blue that makes you believe the world is still capable of magic.

Finally, she was building a life that felt like her own.

And just as she began to soften into it—just as the foundation between us started to feel steady…she was gone.

•　　•　　•

It was a cold January Sunday when the phone rang.

I was in the kitchen, with the boys nearby, and the scent of dinner still lingering in the air. I glanced at the caller ID and froze.

Dean.

My mom's longtime boyfriend.

The moment I answered, I heard it.

The weight in his voice. The pause that dragged a little too long. The kind of silence that holds something sacred—and shattering.

"Your mom had a stroke," he said softly. "You need to get here as soon as possible. The doctors say she has anywhere from two days to two weeks."

Time slowed. My heart dropped—no, *plummeted*—into my stomach. My mind scrambled, refusing to absorb the words.

"No…no. People survive strokes all the time," I stammered. "She's strong. She'll recover. She *always* bounces back. She's not…"

His voice cracked, hard and raw. "Stop. The stroke was too big," he said. "There's nothing they can do. Please, book a flight."

A pause, then—barely audible—"Would you call your siblings? I don't have the strength."

I closed my eyes. Swallowed the scream that was caught in my throat. "Yes," I whispered. "Of course."

The line went silent.

The phone slipped from my hand as my knees buckled.

I hit the floor.

The sob that rose out of me was animal—raw, guttural, unfamiliar. It cracked the air open. I curled into myself, gasping, shaking, and broken wide.

This wasn't possible. My mom. Strong. Stubborn. Healthy as a horse. She was supposed to outlive me. I had *always* believed that.

The boys ran in, their faces pale with fear.

"Mom?" Dusty knelt beside me. "What happened?"

I pulled them close, holding their arms, their cheeks, anything I could reach. I had to say it out loud, and I didn't know how. "Grandma Rose had a stroke," I managed, my voice a rasp of air. "She's not going to make it."

They collapsed into me.

We held each other in a pile of trembling limbs and wet cheeks. One tangled, desperate embrace. I don't know how long we stayed like that. Time no longer moved the same. Eventually, I peeled myself off the floor.

I had calls to make.

Each one cut deeper than the last.

With every sibling I reached, I had to repeat it: *She had a stroke. There's nothing they can do. You need to get there.*

Each repetition felt like ripping a fresh wound open. By the end, I wasn't sure how I was still upright. But somehow, I was.

I booked the first flight to Montrose for the next morning. When the plane touched down in Colorado, the cold hit me like a wall. The sky hung low and heavy, gray with snow, the air sharp enough to sting my lungs. Typical January weather, but that day it didn't feel seasonal—it felt personal, as if the world itself was grieving alongside me.

I stepped outside, called a cab, and sank into the backseat, watching snowflakes blur against the window as we sped toward the hospital. I didn't speak. I didn't blink. I just held my breath and braced for what I already knew I couldn't handle.

When I walked into her room in the hospice wing, the quiet was immediate. No beeping machines. No IV poles. No flickering monitors. Just a dimly lit room. A soft hum of fluorescent lights. The hush of heartbreak. And the sound of her breathing.

It rattled in her chest—wet, uneven, and gurgling. The sound of a body letting go. It shattered something in me.

Misty was there, and so were my niece Isabella, and Dean, my mom's partner. They stood near the window, with their eyes puffy, faces pale, and their silence filled with everything none of us could say.

Lena and her husband arrived shortly after. Hunter came in behind them, with his shoulders hunched, and gaze cast low.

Isabella looked especially shaken. She was studying to be a nurse at the time, but nothing in her textbooks had pre-pared her for *this*—for watching someone she loved slip away by the hour.

I pulled Dean aside. "What happened?" I asked, my voice a whisper, barely able to push out the words. "What led to this?"

He exhaled slowly, the grief thick in his chest. "The day before," he said, "she had a headache. Told me she didn't feel right."

He had offered to take her to urgent care. She had waived him off.

"She hated doctors," he said, shaking his head. "You know how tough she was." That night, she'd curled up on the couch to watch *Survivor*—her favorite show. But the headache lingered.

"She said she was going to take a shower and lie down," he continued. "I watched her walk from the bedroom to the bathroom. She had her nightgown in her hand." Then, just minutes later, he heard it. Vomiting, followed by a thud.

He rushed in.

She was lying on the cold tile floor—naked, unconscious, her face bruised, her body crumpled in her own vomit.

Dean swallowed hard. "I covered her with a robe. Called the ambulance. Tried to wake her, but…"

He paused, eyes glistening.

"One eye was swollen shut. Her face was so bruised. Black, purple…she must've hit the sink on the way down."

I couldn't speak.

The image gripped me by the throat—my mother, proud and private, alone on the bathroom floor, her strength stolen in a single, brutal moment.

I tried to blink it away. I couldn't.

I didn't want to.

I just wanted her back.

I turned to Dean again. "Did they try to drain the bleed?"

Before he could answer, Isabella cut in, her voice sharp with urgency. "They couldn't," she said quickly. "It was too massive."

I heard her. But I didn't *accept* it.

This was my mother. *My* mother.

I needed to hear it from someone who had walked this path with other families. Someone who had held this kind of finality before.

Not a first-year RN student.

Not even my niece.

When the doctor entered the room, I didn't hesitate. "Did you try to drain the bleed?" I asked. "Is there *anything* you can do?"

His expression softened, but his voice was steady.

"No," he said gently. "It wouldn't help."

My stomach dropped.

"No," I repeated, louder now. "There has to be something."

He reached for the scan.

Held it up.

Pointed.

The image looked like a storm had swept through her brain—dark shadows swallowing everything in their path. A map of destruction.

Behind me, Isabella muttered under her breath. "See? I told you."

Her words sliced through the air, landing hard. I flinched.

Maybe she felt dismissed. Maybe she *was* hurt I hadn't taken her seriously. Maybe she had every right to feel that way.

In that moment, this wasn't about her. This was about trying to survive the unthinkable.

And the unthinkable was there in front of me.

On that scan.

In that hospital bed.

In the sound of my mother's breath—fading.

I had this overwhelming pull—this ache—to touch her.

Not out of obligation or ritual, but from some primal place that needed to *feel* she was still here.

I walked slowly to her bedside, barely breathing, and reached for her hand.

It was warm, soft and familiar. The warmth of it grounded me. I wrapped my fingers gently around hers and closed my eyes, clinging to the silent hope that some part of her—some flicker buried deep within that still body—could feel me there.

I bowed my head and began to pray. Not the kind of polished prayer you speak in a church pew. This one came from the pit of my soul.

"Please, God…please let her open her eyes. Just once. Just long enough for me to see those magnificent, misty-blue eyes again."

I was begging for a miracle.

That first day, I couldn't let go. Her hand in mine was my anchor, the only thing tethering me to a reality I wasn't ready to face. Misty gently touched my shoulder. "Eat something," she whispered. "Take a shower."

I nodded, but my limbs didn't move.

What if she slipped away while I was gone?

Before stepping away, I leaned in close and whispered one more plea. "Please, God…just let me be by her side when it's her time to go home."

I slipped into the bathroom, every movement slow,

hesitant. My breath caught as I cracked open the door to peek back into the room.

She was still with us.

Dean had taken my place beside her, his quiet presence steady and calm. I crossed the room and sank into the chair on the opposite side.

My vigil continued.

Because I wasn't ready to let go.

Not yet.

That first night, I didn't sleep.

I tried, curled in the corner, exhaustion gripping every muscle—but my mind wouldn't stop. I lay awake in a fog of disbelief.

She's really dying. My complicated, fierce, newly softened mother was slipping away. And I couldn't stop it.

Each time my eyes began to flutter closed, someone tapped me.

Shook me.

"Dean wants that chair," they said.

Again.

And again.

And again.

I moved without protest—at first. But by midday of the second day, I was unraveling.

Everyone was frayed.

No one had slept. Emotions buzzed like static in the stale air. But somehow, I was the only one being shuffled around like luggage.

The only one being woken. It felt deliberate.

Isabella stormed over and shook me. "Move," she snapped.

I didn't answer.

I was done being handled like an afterthought. No one else was being treated that way—just me.

It made me feel like that invisible child. The one who

didn't matter. The one who'd been made small for so long that she'd *become* small, just to survive. But not anymore.

They didn't know who I had become. They hadn't seen the climb back from the edge. I had died. Literally. And I had come back.

I had learned self-love. I had boundaries.

I was not their doormat anymore.

When Isabella "told" on me to Hunter, like we were twelve years old, and he came storming into the room—face tight, voice raised—I didn't flinch. "Get off your ass and move," he growled.

I met his eyes without blinking.

"No—*FUCK YOU.*"

(I know I could've handled it better. I know. But in that moment, I was seeing red.)

Hunter exploded. "You're so selfish. Go fuck yourself!"

Isabella chimed in from behind him, her voice slick with sarcasm. "Nice."

And that was it.

I snapped.

"Leave me the hell alone!" I shouted. "Dean is a grown man. If he wants this chair, he can ask me himself!"

I turned to Dean, voice calmer now, leveled. "Do you want this seat?"

He shook his head. "No."

There were plenty of chairs. This was never about furniture.

This was about control. Roles. Old expectations.

And I was done playing my part.

I looked back at them—at the weight of years between us—and said, "Then get out of my face."

It was loud.

It was messy.

And yes, there were two hospice volunteers in the room. They looked uncomfortable. Shame crept up my spine like a slow burn. I turned to them, voice trembling. "I'm sorry," I said.

One of them placed a warm hand on my shoulder. Her face was kind. "We see this a lot," she said. "It's the stress. We understand."

And her words helped. But only a little. Because deep down, I knew the truth. *She* had heard us.

Even if she couldn't speak. Even if she couldn't move.

My mom was still there.

And we'd filled her room with fighting.

And that broke my heart all over again.

I couldn't take the tension in the room a second longer.

Without a word, I reached for my suitcase, my fingers stiff with frustration, and wheeled it slowly behind me as I stepped into the hallway. The air outside the room felt thick—heavy with grief, and with everything unspoken. I didn't know where I was going. I just knew I couldn't stay.

My chest tightened with each step. My jaw ached from clenching it. The weight of that room—the charged glances, the hurtful words, the old family roles I refused to wear anymore—it scraped across every raw place inside me.

I wandered the corridors, passing buzzing fluorescents and posters curling at the corners. My footsteps echoed softly, their rhythm oddly soothing in the quiet of the hospital's after-hours lull.

Eventually, I stumbled across a waiting room tucked away in a forgotten corner of the building. It was dim and silent, as if the world had pressed pause. A worn sofa sat along the back wall, slouched from years of use. It looked like it had been waiting just for me. I sank into it, my entire body sagging under the weight of the day.

The ache wasn't just physical. It was in my spirit, in my soul. It was exhaustion that reached the marrow.

The soft hum of hospital machines drifted through the walls, but inside me, there was only silence—deep, aching silence.

I closed my eyes and folded my hands, whispering prayers into the quiet.

"God…I'm sorry," I murmured. "I didn't mean to lash out. I didn't mean to lose my temper. Please forgive me for the way I spoke to Hunter…to Isabella. Give me grace. Give them grace. Give us all peace."

My words trembled as I continued.

"If it's truly her time, please…carry her gently. Let her go softly. Don't let her be afraid. Don't let her be alone."

My voice cracked.

"Let her be held."

I didn't know if she'd still be there in the morning.

So, I let go. I placed it all—my anger, my sadness, my fractured family, my mother's fate—into the hands of the Divine.

And then, as sleep began to pull me under, something shifted. A vision appeared, clear and undeniable. A hand— massive, luminous, and pulsing with light—reached down from the heavens toward me. It wasn't just a symbol. It was a presence.

God.

There were no words. No sound.

Just knowing.

A peace so full it hummed in my chest.

In that moment, I knew.

She would still be with us in the morning.

And somehow, some way…everything would be okay.

Then the scene changed.

Wildflowers.

An entire mountainside blanketed in them—purple, yellow, orange, and red—dancing in the breeze like tiny prayers. The colors shimmered with life. The air was cool and sweet with earth and sunlight and something sacred.

It was breathtaking.

Holy.

Wrapped in that vision, I finally released everything I'd been clinging to.

And I slept.

Deeply.

Peacefully.

Until morning.

The sun was filtering through the narrow window when Lena found me. Her voice was soft, and careful. "She's still with us," she said. "And she'd want you there."

I nodded. We didn't need to say anything more.

I rose slowly, wheeled my suitcase behind me, and followed her back down the corridor. When I stepped into the room, the shift was immediate.

The energy had changed. The sharpness from the night before had dissolved into something softer.

Maybe it was the long night. Maybe it was reflection. Or maybe we had all finally realized how close we were to the end.

Whatever it was, no one snapped. No one shouted.

There was only stillness, reverence, and the slow, sacred rhythm of waiting. Not much changed as the hours slipped by. The room was thick with stillness, each second stretched long and slow. Rose's body continued to surrender. Her breaths grew shallow, each inhale catching in her chest, the gurgling louder now—more pronounced. It was the sound of release. The sound of a body loosening its hold on life.

I sat quietly beside her, fingers wrapped around hers, clinging to the fragments of warmth still lingering beneath her skin. Her hand—cooler now—was still unmistakably hers. I held it tighter, willing it to stay, to remember the pulse of living.

My gaze drifted toward the small side table. A book lay there, its cover soft from wear—one of those gentle hospice guides meant for grieving families. I reached for it, needing something, anything, to anchor me.

Flipping it open, I landed on a random page. And froze.

There, printed across the glossy spread, was a photograph—a mountain slope bursting with wildflowers. Purple, yellow, red, and orange. The exact same vision I'd seen the night before. The same field. The same palette of living color.

Tears pooled, blurred the page. My breath caught. The room around me stilled. I could feel it again—that sacred hush, the unmistakable hum of something greater.

I wasn't imagining it.

We weren't alone.

God was here. The Angels were here. And deep within, a stirring.

A calling.

It pressed gently against my spirit—Hospice. I didn't know how, or when, or in what form…but I knew I was meant to walk alongside the dying. Not just for her. For others. For something more.

Later that afternoon, the air had grown heavier, as the weight of the day pressed on our shoulders. I slipped quietly from the room and stepped into the hall.

The fluorescent lights buzzed overhead, their cold hum echoing down the sterile corridor. I found an empty chair just outside her door, lowered myself into it, and dialed work.

My voice was low, measured, and mechanical. I kept it brief. I told them I was still here, that she hadn't passed yet.

When I hung up, I leaned back against the wall and let out a long, trembling breath. My eyes fluttered closed. I was so tired.

That's when I heard the footsteps. Quick. Uneven. Urgent.

Lena's husband rounded the corner. His face was pale, panicked.

"You need to come," he said, breathless. "She's going."

My heart dropped.

I was on my feet before he finished the sentence. I burst into the room—and time stopped.

There she was.

Rose. My beautiful, stubborn, fiercely tender mother.

Her arms were lifted toward the sky, fingertips stretching upward with purpose and grace.

Her eyes were opened.

Misty-blue. Brilliant. Awake.

Alive.

She looked up—beyond the ceiling, beyond this world—then lay back down with the gentleness of a leaf drifting to the ground.

One last inhale.

Then nothing.

Silence.

But it wasn't empty.

The room swelled with presence—so thick it felt like love itself had taken form. A hum filled the air, invisible but undeniable. And then I saw it. A shimmer, a lifting—her spirit, rising. A shift in the energy above her body, like light bending. Like a whisper of wind no one else could feel.

Then a hand.

Radiant. Vast. Reaching down from the heavens.

The hand of God.

And she went.

Just like that.

Peace draped over the room like a sacred veil. Not a single word passed between us. None were needed.

Because I knew.

She had gone home.

And I had been allowed to witness it. Not just the

passing, but the crossing. The sacred unraveling of life from body.

I hadn't just said goodbye. I had seen the divine.

And in the stillness, one truth echoed louder than the rest:

I had asked for one last look. And The Divine had given it to me.

Her misty-blue eyes—wide open, radiant, reaching for Heaven.

God granted a few miracles that day.

One unfolded in the time it took me to step into the hallway and make a simple phone call. I'd only been gone a few minutes—just long enough to check in with work, to steady myself with something ordinary—but in that quiet sliver of time, something holy stirred in the room I had left behind.

My mother and Lena hadn't been close in years. Their rift wasn't loud or obvious, but it ran deep—a silent wound that never quite scabbed over.

It started after my grandfather died.

Rose—my mother—had always assumed she would carry out her parents' final wishes. She was their only child, and she had been named Executor of their estate—a role she had accepted with quiet dignity.

But after he passed, everything shifted.

Grief clouded my grandmother's judgment, and somewhere in the fog of mourning and generational thinking, she changed the will. Without warning. Without conversation.

She named Lena and her husband as co-executors.

My mom wasn't told. She wasn't asked. She found out like an outsider—after the ink had dried.

The justification was that a man needed to be in charge.

That's how she was raised. That was the way of her world. But for my mother, it wasn't just about paperwork. It was about trust.

It cut her in that soft, hidden place where duty and love blur together. Where children become caretakers. Where honor becomes identity.

And when Lena and her husband accepted the role without pause—without even a phone call to check in—it broke something that had been holding them together. The hurt settled between them, quiet and cold, and neither of them ever spoke of it again.

Until that day.

While I was in the hall, talking through the line of a cell phone, Lena sat quietly beside Rose's bed. The room hummed with the sacred rhythm of almost—goodbye. My mother's breaths came slow and shallow, her hand limp beneath Lena's.

And then, something shifted.

Later, Lena told me it was as if something moved through her—a gentle presence, nudging her past the wall of silence she had built.

She reached for my mom's hand and held it.

"I'm so sorry," she whispered, her voice breaking. "We should never have accepted the executorship. It hurt you. I see that now. I'm sorry for all of it."

The words hung there for a moment, suspended in the quiet.

But they didn't just land.

They were received.

My mom didn't speak—couldn't—but something softened in her. A visible shift.

Her fingers twitched, just slightly, around Lena's. Her jaw relaxed. The lines on her forehead eased.

Forgiveness passed between them like light slipping through a cracked door.

And then—she let go.

That was the moment her spirit began to lift.

The Divine has a way of orchestrating things beyond what we can understand.

Rose—who had endured so much, who had waited so long for that moment of healing—held on just long enough to be seen. To be honored.

She waited for peace.

And she waited for me.

Because the moment I stepped back into the room, with my breath caught in my chest, she opened her eyes.

Those soft, brilliant blue eyes.

She gave each of us a gift before she left.

To Lena, a closing of the circle.

To me, the miracle of one last glance.

To all of us—grace, forgiveness, love, and peace.

There were more miracles that day than I can count.

And I carry every one of them with me.

Looking back now, I truly believe my mom knew.

Not in a way she ever said aloud, but in the quiet, intuitive way she had of sensing the deeper currents beneath life's surface.

A few months before she passed, a small package arrived in the mail—one of those padded envelopes with her familiar handwriting scrawled across the front.

Inside was a ruby and gold ring. It was elegant and warm, just like her. Tucked beside it was a folded note. Her penmanship was instantly familiar—curvy, thoughtful, and unmistakably hers.

"I wanted to make sure you had something of mine," she wrote. "Something real. Something lasting."

I remember staring at the ring in my palm, confused. She

was only seventy. She was strong and healthy. Our family members lived well into their nineties. Death wasn't knocking. At least, I didn't think it was.

I called her immediately. "Mom," I said, trying to keep my voice light, "the ring is beautiful...but what's going on?"

She laughed softly, brushing it off. "It's just important to me that you have it," she said. "Just in case anything ever happens."

She didn't say more.

And I didn't push.

But her words clung to me. That gentle, knowing tone. Like her spirit had already begun preparing for what her body hadn't yet revealed.

After she passed, Misty and I went to her house to begin the painful task of sorting through her things.

We moved slowly, as if everything we touched might break open the grief we were barely holding together. Each drawer we opened, each cabinet we peeked into, felt like peeling back a layer of her life.

In her bedroom, I reached for the jewelry box beside her bed. The tiny gold clasp clicked open, revealing the gentle chaos of earrings and old brooches tangled together.

And beneath it all—two folded letters. Each one was addressed in her soft script: *To My Children.*

My breath caught.

Hands trembling, I opened the first one. It wasn't a farewell. It was a list: *her favorite things.*

Number one: Listening to my daughters laugh.

Number two: My grandbabies' laughter.

Number three: The smell of grass after it rains.

Tears blurred the ink.

I could barely breathe.

The list continued—quiet joys, soft moments, little details that made up the soul of her. It read like a love letter to life.

The second letter was a poem. Its message simple but powerful:

Don't mourn me.

Celebrate me.

Carry me in your laughter, not your sorrow.

I handed the letters to Misty, and the dam broke.

We sat on her bed, tears streaming, clutching those pages like scripture—fragile and sacred and everything.

Later, we asked Dean if he'd known about the letters.

He shook his head slowly, his voice soft. "No. I had no idea."

He wasn't sure if she had left a will either.

So, Misty and I searched—through drawers, cabinets, folders stuffed with papers—but never found one.

What we did find was a small life insurance policy.

I took the lead on finalizing the claim. Dean was grateful. He said the policy would cover the cremation, a simple service, and an urn.

"If you want anything more than that," he added gently, "you'll have to pay for it yourselves."

So, I did.

I bought mini urns for my siblings. I ordered flowers. I had prayer cards printed, photos enlarged and framed. I didn't ask anyone else to contribute.

They each said money was tight. I didn't press.

Misty and I were asked to lead the service. Together, we wrote the eulogy—our hands moving slowly across the page, our hearts aching with every line.

At the podium, we stood shoulder to shoulder, voices trembling as we spoke her story. Then I read the letters.

There wasn't a dry eye in the room.

I could barely make it through, my voice cracking under the weight of it. But it felt sacred. Like she was there, between the syllables, holding us all.

I stayed in Colorado for a week after the service.

There were bills to transfer, accounts to close, household things Dean didn't know how to manage.

I taught him how to use the washer and dryer.

He watched the buttons like they might explode, his grief making every small task feel enormous.

He was lost without her.

We all were.

On the last night of my trip, the panic crept in—quietly at first—a subtle tightness in my chest, and a whisper in the back of my mind.

Reality was setting in.

Paying for the service, the flights, the urns, the flowers—it had drained everything.

My savings account? Empty.

Emotionally spent. Physically exhausted. Financially tapped.

I sat on the edge of the guest bed, *her* guest bed, feeling the weight of it all press down on me like a second skin. I hesitated, then found Dean in the living room, sipping a cup of tea, his face unreadable.

"Would you be willing to help with some of the costs?" I asked, carefully. "I...I covered everything, but I'm really struggling now."

He didn't flinch. Didn't blink. He just looked me dead in the eye and said, "Absolutely not. Your mom wouldn't have wanted to help you."

The words punched straight through my chest.

My throat tightened. My vision blurred. I couldn't speak.

I nodded once—silently—and turned away. I didn't argue. I just went to bed.

That night, I curled into her sheets—her bed, her space, her scent still lingering faintly in the pillows. The room held her energy like a whisper, soft and sacred. She and Dean had always had separate bedrooms, and tonight, this one belonged to me.

I lay there, heart splintered open, eyes fixed on the ceiling as prayers slipped through my lips. I prayed through the hurt and betrayal.

Through the ache of being reminded—again—that I had never been the daughter they embraced.

"Please," I whispered, "if you're still with me...show me."

Sleep came slow and heavy. But when it did, it carried something with it. A few hours later, I shot upright. A thought—no, not a thought. A message. Clear. Calm.

Certain.

Check the little wrapped package on the bookcase. The voice was quiet, but resolute.

I slipped out of bed and padded barefoot across the dark room. Misty and I had already gone through everything. Every drawer. Every shelf.

But still—I reached for the tiny tissue-wrapped bundle on the bookcase. My hands trembled as I peeled it open. Inside was twenty-five hundred dollars in crisp, folded bills.

The exact amount I had spent.

My knees buckled. I sank to the floor, the tears coming fast and hot.

It was her. I knew it. A mother's love wrapped in silence, tucked away like a secret blessing. A final miracle.

I see you. I'm proud of you. You are not alone.

Peace flooded me. Gentle. Complete.

• • •

On the flight back to California, I stared out the window, the clouds below like frozen waves.

I wasn't ready to return. I wasn't ready for a world without her.

For so long, our relationship had been rocky—layers of hurt and distance woven between us. But in recent years, something had shifted.

We'd started to soften. There were phone calls that didn't end abruptly. Laughter that felt real. Conversations that opened tiny doors in the walls we had spent decades building.

She was starting to show up—not just as a mother in title, but in presence: in spirit. And just as we began to rebuild what had been broken for so long…she was gone. The grief hit like a rogue wave: unpredictable and crushing.

I knew she was home now—wrapped in light, free from pain, with her spirit whole again. I pictured her laughing with her dad, young and radiant, held in divine arms.

But even that beautiful vision didn't dull the sharp edge of her absence. Because grief doesn't live in logic or faith. It lives in the ache of silence. In the reach for a voice that no longer answers.

In the empty seat beside you.

And it wasn't just her I lost.

Somewhere high above the Rockies, as the plane cut through the sky, I felt it—the end of something deeper. Her death had unraveled whatever fragile threads had once tethered our family together.

I didn't know if I'd ever see my siblings again. Not really. Not as family.

A chapter closed.

And with that, a part of me faded too.

The part that still longed to belong.

The part shaped by her voice, her touch, her absence, and presence.

The part of me that once held our family's story...now drifting, unanchored.

12

A NEW BEGINNING IN SOLVANG

Back in California, the dust hadn't even settled. And already, the next mountain stood in front of me.

We couldn't stay in the condo much longer. With the rent increase, my budget—already stretched to its limits—was now splitting at the seams. We needed a new plan. A new place.

Something affordable. Something steady. Somewhere we could breathe.

One afternoon, after dropping the boys at school, I sat at the kitchen table alone. The silence in the condo was unfamiliar—too clean and too hollow. I stared out the window for a long minute before pulling open the drawer beneath the counter.

There it was.

That thick, outdated phone book. Yellowed, ignored.

A relic from another time.

I don't know why I'd kept it.

I flipped past the business ads and dinner coupons, finally landing on the apartment listings in the Yellow Pages. My fingers scanned the thin columns, name after name, as if I was skimming braille for a hidden message. Most listings were scratched out in my head before I even finished reading them—too far, too expensive, and too impossible.

Santa Barbara was out.

I couldn't keep pretending I could make it work there. Not with Bert and his family watching from the shadows, not with prices climbing like wildfire. But the county…the county was big.

I turned my sights north. My finger stopped on a name: *Solvang Gardens Apartments.*

Solvang.

I blinked at the word, half-ready to move on—but something in me paused.

That name. That town. I'd heard of it, driven through it once. Quaint. Quiet. Tucked into the hills like something from a storybook. It was thirty-five miles from Santa Barbara. Still in the county. Still within the bounds of the custody agreement.

I pulled out my laptop and looked it up. Wooden signs. Danish bakeries. Horse-drawn carriages. It looked like peace.

I drafted a message, hands slightly trembling from a mix of hope and doubt.

Hi, my name is Heidi…

I told them I had a steady job. Three kind, respectful boys. I didn't oversell, didn't sugarcoat. I just told the truth.

I hit send.

Not ten minutes later, that voice inside me—the one I'd come to trust—whispered:

Call. So, I did.

The man who answered introduced himself as Bill, the property manager. His voice came through the line like a blanket—steady, calm, full of warmth.

"I just read your email," he said. "And as it happens, one of our units just became available." He paused. "Would you and your boys like to come see it this weekend?"

I nearly dropped the phone.

"Yes," I breathed. "We'd love to."

That night, I gathered the boys around the kitchen table. I told them gently.

About the rent, the need for change, and the new opportunity. I promised them the things that mattered would stay the same—same school, same friends, and the same schedule with Dad.

Just a longer commute and a new zip code.

They didn't cheer. They didn't complain. They just listened. They had seen enough to understand. So, they nodded, looking quiet and thoughtful.

I reached across the table and held their hands.

That weekend, we drove north.

The road curved through golden hills, as the sky stretched wide like a canvas above us. Every mile peeled away the tension. Every bend in the road felt like a turning point.

Solvang was even more charming than I remembered.

Windmills spun lazily beside bakeries. Wooden storefronts lined the streets. Tourists strolled with ice cream cones and cameras. It didn't just look like a storybook—it felt like a sanctuary. The apartment was modest, nothing flashy. But it was clean. And it was safe.

A downstairs corner unit with two bedrooms, two bathrooms, and washer-dryer hookups.

I didn't dare dream that big, but there it was. From the patio, you could see the hills, soft and green under the winter light. I pictured the boys sipping cocoa out there on foggy mornings. I pictured us healing.

Bill met us outside the door. He had kind eyes. The kind that saw past paperwork and credit scores. "If you want it," he said, "it's yours."

No credit check. No deposit. No games.

Just trust.

I signed the lease on the spot.

As we drove back to Santa Barbara, I waited for the worry to come. But it didn't. What came instead was peace.

It settled into my chest like an old friend, and I knew—I *knew*—I was exactly where I was meant to be.

The message from my near-death experience echoed inside me once again:

You are unconditionally loved.

Everything is exactly as it's supposed to be.

Everything will be okay.

And this time, I didn't just believe it.

I felt it.

Packing up seven years of memories wasn't just a chore—it was a slow unraveling. The boys and I moved through the condo like ghosts, taping boxes, wrapping dishes, packing up beanbags we'd once curled up in for movie nights. Each drawer we emptied, each cabinet we opened, tugged loose a memory we weren't quite ready to let go of. But we packed anyway. Because we had to.

The U-Haul sat out front like a deadline. Its metal ramp clanked beneath our feet as we loaded it, piece by piece, our laughter echoing off the walls just enough to sting.

By the time I turned in the keys, my bank account was bare. The move to Solvang had emptied what little I had left. No savings. No cushion. No backup. Just grit, love, and a truck full of hope.

The new apartment was smaller, quieter, but it belonged to us. The boys took the master bedroom again—dorm-style. Twin beds, video game consoles, and the same blankets that smelled like home. Their laughter was softer here, like even they understood we were beginning again. It wasn't perfect, but it was ours. And for a moment, that was enough.

Still, no amount of fresh paint or open windows could hide the reality.

The debt followed me.

Notices arrived like clockwork—bold letters, red ink, unpaid balances stacking like accusations on the kitchen counter. I worked. I hustled. But the numbers refused to budge.

Eventually, I hit the wall.

More than twenty years in banking, mortgages, credit analysis—I knew exactly what bankruptcy meant. I'd watched it block home loans, and crush dreams. I never thought I'd be the one filling out the forms.

Filing felt like swallowing glass. But it wasn't about ego anymore. It was about survival. Rent before credit. Food before interest. My kids before a FICO score.

On the day of the hearing, I walked into the courtroom with my shoulders back and my stomach in knots. The place was cold, fluorescent, and sterile. I sat in the back, with my knees jittering, trying not to cry.

When they called my name, I stood.

The questions came sharp and fast. No warmth. No context. No one asked what it cost me to get here—emotionally, spiritually. No one asked about the sleepless nights or the fear in my son's eyes when I said, "Not this week, baby."

Just numbers.

Just debt.

Just facts.

I left the building feeling stripped. Exposed. But also— something else.

Unburdened.

Something shifted. I stopped judging. I stopped whispering "How could they?" when someone filed for bankruptcy.

Now I knew. I knew how heavy it was to choose between groceries and the electric bill. I knew the panic of watching your card being declined at checkout while your child stood beside you.

Bankruptcy didn't ruin me.

It woke me up.

I was still a mother. Still a provider. Still a woman trying to rebuild from the ashes. And now—finally—I could breathe.

I wasn't waking up in the middle of the night anymore, drenched in panic.

I wasn't drowning.

For the first time in a long time—I was living.

The boys and I had settled into a rhythm—steady, quiet, and full of just enough structure to feel safe. Weekdays hummed along with school runs and dinners, their laughter echoing through our small apartment like a balm. But it was at the weekends—those stretches of stillness when they were with their dad—that something inside me began to stir.

Not loneliness. Not emptiness. Just space.

Space wide enough to feel curiosity. Gentle enough to let something long buried begin to rise. So, I followed the pull.

Late at night, after the dishes were done and the house had gone still, I sat at my laptop and searched—keywords, message boards, local community sites. I scrolled past yoga retreats I couldn't afford and paused on the ones that felt like home: Angel Therapy. Crystal Resonance. Sound Healing. Animal Communication. Energy Work.

If it whispered to my soul, I showed up.

Some classes were held in living rooms with flickering candles and thrift-store beanbags. Others took place in libraries, back rooms of wellness stores, or Zoom screens glowing in the dark. I didn't care where it was—I just needed to be there. I didn't know what I was looking for, not exactly. But every time I stepped into a new space, my heart whispered the same word:

Home.

I began meditating—before sunrise, while the boys slept; in the carpool line, windows cracked to let the wind in; at night, cradled in a silence I once feared but now welcomed. And slowly, something inside me began to change.

Then came the moment that cracked everything wide open.

I had closed my eyes for a meditation I'd done a hundred times before. But this time was different. I saw it. Not a dream. Not a hope.

Energy.

It moved like sunlight through water—fluid, bright, and alive. I could see it enter my body and flow through me like a current, shifting and changing colors. Gold for emotional healing. Blue for the nervous system. Green for the body's aches and wounds. Sometimes it swirled outside my body like a dance. Sometimes it dove deep, straight into bone and memory.

I opened my eyes, breath held.

I knew then—I was being called to something more.

I signed up for Reiki training and studied with reverence, as if I was remembering something ancient. Eventually, I became a Master Reiki Healer. From that sacred knowing, ACE Holistic Healing was born. A quiet little practice built on trust, energy, and grace.

I worked with clients in person and remotely, blending Reiki, Angel Therapy, and Crystal Resonance into each session. I listened deeply. Held space gently. I offered every soul the tenderness I had once begged for.

And, of course, I practiced on the boys, too.

They didn't always understand it, but they could feel it.

And somehow, I think they knew their mama was finally beginning to remember who she really was.

One of my earliest sessions was with Dusty.

He was about twelve at the time—sweet, wiry, with big curious eyes and a fidgety body that never quite settled unless food or "Minecraft" was involved. He didn't really know what Reiki was, but when I told him it meant he could lie still on a yoga mat for a while and not do homework, he was all in.

We set up in the living room, with sunlight spilling across the floor like a soft invitation. I rolled out the mat, dimmed the lights, and turned on the gentle hum of singing bowls playing through a Bluetooth speaker. He laid back, with his arms at his sides, looking more like he was preparing for a nap than an energy session.

I moved quietly, grounding myself, then knelt beside him and began the session—hands hovering gently over his belly, tuning into the warm, subtle currents of his energy.

And then it happened.

A loud, unapologetic fart broke the silence. Dusty's eyes popped open, wide with surprise. Then came the second one—longer, louder. By the third, he was grinning. The fourth sent him into full-blown belly laughter, his body shaking on the mat like a popcorn kernel in oil.

I held my focus—barely. A single eyebrow twitched. My lips pressed into a firm line. Inside, I was cracking up. But outwardly, I stayed composed, centered, and professional.

"Mom," he wheezed between laughs, "why am I so gassy?"

I gave him a warm smile. "Your body's releasing energy, sweetheart. That's how it let go."

He blinked at me like I'd just told him a secret of the universe. "Huh," he said, nodding solemnly, like a tiny monk.

Then came the real kicker: "But how did you not laugh?"

I shrugged, fighting the grin now stretching across my face. "It was hard, believe me. But I had to be a professional." That broke us both. We sat there in the middle of the living room, doubled over in laughter, the sacred and the silly braided together in the most unexpected harmony.

That session reminded me that healing isn't always some heavy, shadowed pilgrimage through pain. Sometimes, healing sounds like uncontrollable giggles and smells like leftover takeout. Sometimes it happens on a yoga mat, under a ceiling fan, in the middle of a weekday afternoon.

And sometimes, it happens through joy.

Pure, ridiculous, holy joy.

I ran ACE Holistic Healing for several years, quietly and steadily, offering Reiki and intuitive healing to anyone who felt drawn to my little sacred space. People came with everything—grief, anxiety, physical pain, heartache—and left feeling lighter, brighter, and different.

But the truth is, as much as I helped them, those years were healing *me*.

With every session, my hands grew steadier. My trust in myself deepened. The intuitive nudges I used to question started to feel like second nature. My sensitivity—which I'd once tried to hide—began to feel like a gift. Not a liability. Not a flaw.

Then one day, while scrolling through a community calendar, I saw it: *Understanding the Empath*. The title practically glowed. I signed up on the spot, with my heart pounding like it knew this would change everything.

And it did.

I sat in a circle of strangers, the soft hum of a diffuser in the background, and for the first time in my life, I heard language that fit me.

I wasn't "too sensitive."

I wasn't "dramatic."

I wasn't "overreacting."

I was an empath.

And I wasn't alone.

Tears welled in my eyes as the instructor described the exact ways I moved through the world—how I could feel the temperature of a room shift before a single word was spoken, how I absorbed emotions like a sponge, how crowded spaces sometimes left me raw.

It wasn't brokenness. It was a superpower. A soft, sacred knowing.

Being an empath meant I could see the ache behind someone's smile. I could sit with pain without needing to fix it. I could love deeply, hold space, and offer tenderness in a world that too often rewarded cruelty.

But there was a shadow side too. Empaths attract narcissists like flowers attract bees. And suddenly, the puzzle of my life began snapping into place.

I was raised by two.

I married one.

And I'd filled my life with "friends" who smiled wide but left me drained, discarded, or doubting my worth. I had called it love. Loyalty. Devotion. But really—it was manipulation wearing a friendly mask.

The shift began when I turned inward. I lit candles and cried in meditation. I pulled tarot cards and met my younger self in journal pages. I stopped looking for external validation and started whispering, *I see you* to the girl I used to be.

And I continued with the hardest work of all: boundaries.

Setting them felt brutal. Like betrayal. The guilt tangled itself around my spine and whispered, *You're hurting them.*

But I kept going. Because underneath the guilt was something truer: *You're finally protecting yourself.*

Each time I said *no*, my voice grew a little steadier. Each time I walked away from someone who only took, I stood a little taller. I reminded myself, again and again, that honoring my own soul wasn't selfish.

It was sacred.

And maybe, just maybe, it was what I'd been here to learn all along.

It was during a quiet season of healing and self-discovery when I wandered into a small classroom in Santa Barbara. A wooden sign near the door read "Developing Your Psychic Skills." I slipped into one of the plastic chairs near the back, notebook in hand, expecting another curious dip into the unseen.

And then Mary walked in.

She didn't need to speak to command attention. There was something in the way she moved—anchored and calm, like someone who had danced with death and come back softer instead of bitter. Her eyes scanned the room, kind and steady, and when our instructor paired us together for an exercise, I felt it instantly—an invisible thread tugging at something familiar inside me.

We sat across from each other, knees nearly touching, and as soon as we began to speak, the air between us changed. Her voice was honeyed, slow and sure. When she shared that she had survived two near-death experiences, I didn't flinch. I nodded—not out of curiosity, but recognition.

So did she.

We weren't strangers. Not really. There was something ancient in the way we understood each other, something wordless and whole.

As the exercise ended and people began to stir, Mary leaned in with a smile and said, "I organize the local IANDS chapter here. Our speaker for next month just had to cancel. After hearing your story…I think you're supposed to take her place."

Her invitation hung in the air between us. "Yes," I heard myself say before my mind could catch up.

I blinked. Did I really just agree to public speaking?

The girl who once hid behind her notebook at school, the woman who trembled at the idea of taking up space—she had just said yes without hesitation. But oddly, there was no fear. Not even a whisper. It felt like the choice had already been made somewhere deeper than thought.

That night, I sat cross-legged on the living room floor with a pen in my hand and a blank notebook in my lap. The room was still, the kind of still that invites something sacred in. And then it started—the words came, one after another, pouring out of me like water breaching a dam. My pen scratched across the page as if guided by unseen hands, steady and certain.

This wasn't writing. It was remembering.

Over the following weeks, I stood in front of the mirror reading aloud, letting the sound of my own voice become something I could trust. I rehearsed in front of a coworker I felt safe with, her gentle presence giving me room to fumble, to laugh, to grow. I wasn't chasing perfection. I was chasing honesty.

The night of the meeting arrived. I walked into the softly lit room, the chairs arranged in a loose circle, a few early attendees already settling in. My palms were dry, and my breath was steady. Mary greeted me with that same grounded warmth, then introduced me to the group as their speaker.

I stepped forward, notes in hand, and looked out over the expectant faces. A hush fell. I took a breath.

"My name is Heidi," I began, "and this is my first time sharing this aloud."

No shaking. No spiraling. Just presence.

I let the words carry me—my story, my crossing, the return. I explained the difficulty of capturing the experience in language, how the other side was felt more than seen. Still, I tried. And the room met me in that effort with patience, stillness, and reverence.

An hour passed like ten minutes.

When I finished, silence hung for just a beat—and then the questions came. Thoughtful, raw, searching. Faces leaned in. Eyes softened. People wanted to understand, not to challenge.

And more than their curiosity, what I felt was belief.

They believed me.

There were no sideways glances, and no hushed doubts. Just open hearts receiving a truth I had spent years learning how to speak.

I had been heard.

Near the end of the Q&A, I mentioned I was writing a book. I said it lightly, almost in passing, not expecting it to land anywhere in particular. But a woman seated near the front raised her hand and asked, "When will your second book be available to the public?"

I blinked. My second?

A small laugh escaped my lips as I explained that I hadn't even finished the first. That I had only started after my mother passed. That I was still in it. Still unraveling.

After the talk, she came up to me. Her hand found my arm. "I'm a professional editor," she said, eyes clear and kind. "When you're ready, I'd be honored to help—for free."

Her words lodged in my chest like a seed taking root. She didn't want money. She wanted to nurture something she believed mattered. That kind of generosity—the kind without strings, without agenda—was its own kind of miracle.

Driving home beneath a canopy of stars, I rolled the windows down and let the cool night air wash over me. Something had shifted.

Hope stirred—not the desperate kind, but the anchored kind. The kind that rises quietly after a long silence. I had spoken my truth, and the world hadn't crumbled. It had opened.

And for the first time, I knew: this wasn't an ending.

It was a beginning.

Back then, the words *near-death experience* carried weight. Not the kind that opened doors—but the kind that drew long pauses, tight smiles, or sideways glances over the rims of coffee cups. People didn't talk about things like that—not openly. Not without someone shifting in their seat or softening their voice to a whisper, as if even curiosity about the other side required discretion.

So, when the invitations started arriving—first a few local gatherings, then conferences in other cities—I knew what I was walking into. Opportunity and resistance, both waiting at the door. And I stepped through anyway, with my heart wide open.

Each time I stood at the front of a room, that same quiet knowing returned. My palms rested softly on the podium, the hum of the microphone testing the silence. And then the words came—not rehearsed, not memorized, but pouring through me. I was never there to teach or convince. I never needed them to believe me. I simply shared what had happened, and what had *changed* me.

But it didn't always land softly. There was almost

always one person who raised a hand near the end, eyes narrowed not in judgment, but in ache. Their question carried the edge of something personal, something raw.

"Did you really meet God?"

"Why would *you* get to see Jesus?"

"If that's true…then why do bad things happen to good people?"

Their words didn't feel like challenges; they felt like wounds. And they landed not in my mind, but in my heart—like a stone gently placed where I carried my own unanswered questions.

I never bristled. Never deflected.

Instead, I looked into the grief behind their eyes and told them the only truth I could say out loud. "I don't know why you had to go through that. I don't know why your child had to suffer. But I believe with every part of my being that their soul is still with you. And I believe you will hold them again."

That's what I offered. Not theology. Not certainties. Just presence. Compassion. A soft place to set their pain down, even if only for a breath.

Because I *had* seen what lies beyond the veil. I had been shown that our souls choose these lifetimes—that we incarnate to grow, to rise through the hardest things. But I also knew better than to wrap someone's devastation in spiritual theory and expect it to bring comfort. You can't pour philosophy over a bleeding heart and call it healing.

Some questions don't need answers.

They need witnesses.

But it took time for me to understand that. In the beginning, those questions rattled me. Not because I doubted what I had experienced—but because I doubted whether I could carry it well. Whether I was worthy of holding something so sacred in the presence of such deep pain.

And truthfully, that wasn't the only thing unraveling.

I began to notice shifts in the Santa Barbara IANDS chapter. Little things at first—a tension in the air, a clipped tone during meetings, conversations that seemed less about community and more about control. The spirit of shared discovery was being nudged out by ego. Quiet rivalries surfaced. Hierarchies formed. It wasn't about the light anymore—it was about the spotlight.

And then…there was Mary.

The woman who had first opened the door for me. The one whose warmth had once wrapped around me like sunlight. At first, the change was subtle—a missed message here, a vague response there. But eventually, the silence grew too loud to ignore.

Maybe it was jealousy. Maybe something I said had touched an old bruise she hadn't told me about. I don't know. All I know is that where there had once been connection, there was now space, coolness, and absence.

And it hurt.

I had placed her on a pedestal. I had mistaken eloquence for enlightenment. I thought that surviving death meant she had transcended the weight of being human. But no one escapes that weight. Not really.

Even the wise still bleed. Even the awakened still ache.

I had to step back and see her clearly—not as a spiritual giant, but as a woman. A beautifully flawed, deeply human woman. I had to let her down from the pedestal gently, without resentment. I had to hold space for both the gift she had given me and the wound she had left behind.

That became a turning point.

I stopped mistaking spiritual language for spiritual maturity. I stopped assuming that everyone on a path of healing had actually done the work. And most importantly, I stopped outsourcing my truth.

I began to trust my own voice.

And I kept speaking—sometimes in quiet rooms with

folding chairs, sometimes through glowing screens late at night. I wasn't seeking applause or validation. I was showing up for the one soul who needed it. The one person clutching their story in silence, wondering if they were crazy, or broken, or alone.

Every talk became an offering.

And even when the questions got hard…even when discomfort prickled through the room like static, I stayed rooted. I stayed soft.

Because I wasn't just recounting what I'd seen on the other side.

I was becoming who I had seen myself to be.

Since my near-death experience, the feeling of *home*—that place beyond the veil, filled with light and unconditional love—had become less of a memory and more of a presence. Not distant. Not abstract. But close, intimate, and almost familiar.

It would often arrive in the quiet moments: the hush of early morning before the world stirred, or the stillness right before sleep when thoughts fell away and only awareness remained. That's when I'd hear them—my guides. Not with ears, but with knowing. A soft nudge. A clear thought rising from somewhere just beneath the surface.

They had always been there. I just hadn't always known how to listen.

At first, their messages came like whispers—gentle suggestions that floated up through the fog of half-sleep. But the more I trusted, the louder the guidance became—not in volume, but in clarity. A thought would rise, complete and calm, and I would simply *know* it wasn't mine. Not because it felt foreign, but because it felt wiser than anything I could have crafted on my own.

Sometimes, the messages weren't words at all. Just a sudden certainty that settled into my chest like a truth long known—grounding, quiet, unshakable. Other times, I'd catch it in the flicker of light dancing at the edge of my vision, or, once in a while, in the unmistakable presence of spirit in human form. Brief. Surreal. But real. Always real.

And then, there were the signs.

The lights would flicker in perfect rhythm—on, off, on again—whenever my grandfather came close. I'd smile, whisper a hello, and feel his steady love wrap itself around me. Birds showed up like messengers, always just when I needed them—landing on my window ledge or swooping low across my path with impossible timing.

My grandmother had her own way of reaching out. Her perfume—a floral, powdery scent I hadn't smelled in years—would suddenly fill the air around me as I folded laundry or walked through a grocery store aisle. No one else seemed to notice. But I knew.

And my mom…my mom was relentless in the best way.

She loved to wake me up—not with noise or light, but with a gentle push in my energy. A mother's nudge. She sent me the number *143*—her way of saying "I love you"—in every form imaginable. License plates. Digital clocks. Gas station receipts. Always there, like breadcrumbs from heaven.

One morning, after a speaking event, I woke up with a jolt—not from an external noise, but from a voice that felt like it had spoken directly into my soul.

You need to write a book.

Still half-asleep, I mumbled back, "I am writing a book…"

The response came again, firmer this time. *Not that one. You need to write a book of affirmations—based on the three messages you were given during your NDE.*

I blinked into the light seeping through my bedroom

window and laughed out loud. "I don't know how to write a book like that."

But the voice returned, calm and certain: *It doesn't matter how long it is. It just needs to be written. The people who need it will find it.*

I sat with those words. Let them echo through me like bells in a chapel. And then I did what I always try to do when the message feels too big to ignore—I listened.

I opened my computer, dug out the notes from my very first IANDS talk, and started pulling pieces together. It wasn't polished or complicated. It didn't need to be.

Just fifty pages—half of them simple, direct affirmations. No filler. No fluff. Just words spoken from that same sacred place that had brought me back to life.

Within days, the manuscript was done.

And then another nudge: *Call Mandy.*

Mandy was the editor I had met after my very first talk. The one who had offered her help, with no strings attached. I hadn't spoken to her in a while, but the moment her name surfaced in my mind, I knew. The timing was right.

I reached out.

She responded almost instantly: "Send it to me."

I did.

She read it with care, made a few gentle edits, and within two weeks, the book was ready. I self-published it. No fanfare. No launch party. Just quiet love made visible.

It costs four dollars.

That wasn't a marketing decision. It was a promise—to keep it accessible. To make sure no one who needed it would be priced out of receiving a little light. I like to leave copies in neighborhood book boxes—the ones with the tiny glass doors and wooden frames. I tuck them into the corners of the world where someone might stumble across it at just the right moment.

Sometimes I get emails.

Messages from strangers—some who read the book, others who heard a podcast or interview—reaching out with trembling gratitude. "Your words helped me sleep." "I didn't feel alone for the first time in months." "Thank you for reminding me that I'm still connected."

Each message humbles me.

Because this tiny booklet—born out of surrender and divine insistence—was never meant to be big. It was meant to be *true*. It was meant to be found by those who needed it most, quietly. Unexpectedly.

And somehow, it continues to find its way.

That amazes me still.

And I am so, so grateful.

Life didn't suddenly become easier after my near-death experience. The lessons kept coming. The losses didn't pause. But nothing—not even glimpses of the other side—prepared me for what I faced in 2012.

That was the year I said goodbye to Butters.

For nineteen years, he had been my steady companion. Through heartbreak, motherhood, spiritual awakening—he had never left my side. He wasn't just a cat. He was a presence. A soft heartbeat beside mine in the darkest hours. A witness to it all. Longer than my marriage, longer than any relationship, longer than my boys had been alive—he had been there. Always.

He was more than a pet. He was home.

Butters had this way of curling into my neck, purring with the precision of someone who knew exactly where my pain lived. He'd make biscuits on my chest, his little paws pressing rhythmically like he was massaging sorrow right out of me. On the days I couldn't find love for myself, he loved me harder. Unconditionally. Purely.

People who've never bonded with an animal might not understand the grief. But Butters was no ordinary cat. He radiated something sacred—like a little slice of the divinity wrapped in orange fur and gold-eyed wisdom.

He was there for every one of my sons' births. Watchful. Gentle. As if he knew the gravity of what was unfolding. I'd catch him trailing behind feet, curling up on the back of the couch to keep a lookout while chaos reigned below. He became part of our family story—woven so deeply into the fabric that it was impossible to picture life without him.

Still, no matter how much he loved the boys, he was always my shadow.

He followed me from room to room, content to perch nearby as I moved through my day. His favorite spot was the bathroom sink—curled like a cinnamon roll, eyes blinking slowly as I applied mascara or brushed my hair. He made me laugh. He made me feel seen. He made my heart sing.

He passed away on my birthday.

The man I was dating had surprised me with a weekend on Catalina Island. We returned that Sunday, with sunlight still clinging to our skin, and the moment I opened the door, something inside me dropped.

The house was too still.

Butters lay in his bed, his body heavy with exhaustion. He tried to stand, to greet me like always, but his legs gave out beneath him. His meow, once bold and full of sass, came out as a breathless whisper.

Still, even in that moment, he tried to be a good boy—struggling to lift himself toward the litter box.

"No, baby," I whispered, already on my knees beside him. "You don't have to. I've got you."

I lifted him gently, changed the blanket beneath his fragile frame, and laid down beside him. My face close to his. My hand stroking the familiar curve of his back. We talked.

I told him I loved him. Over and over again.

I thanked him—for his loyalty, his love, his light. I told him how much he had carried me. How deeply I would miss him. How proud I was of the way he loved the boys, and how beautifully he had been mine.

And then, with tears thick in my throat, I gave him permission.

"It's okay to go home now," I whispered. "You don't have to stay. I know you're tired."

My voice broke as I said it again and again. *I love you. I love you. I love you.*

The tears came in waves, blurring everything.

Even now, as I write these words, the grief rises. It always does. I know I'll see him again—on the other side, it'll be a blink. But here, in this body, the ache remains. I miss the weight of him on my chest. The sound of his purr rumbling through the silence. The way he made the world feel less sharp.

I carried him to the vet.

They gave him a shot. I held him close. And just like that, with grace and peace, he slipped out of this world.

I wept.

For days. Weeks. Grief swept through me like a tidal wave, wild and unrelenting. I cried until my chest ached. Until my eyes stung. Until there was nothing left to do but surrender.

That night, as I lay curled in bed, grief still thick in the room, I heard it—a soft *thud* from the hallway.

I sat up.

And then, I saw him.

Butters, running up the stairs just like he used to—full of energy, full of light. His fur shimmered, his body whole. He paused at the top, looked at me, and in that moment, I *knew*.

He came to let me know he was okay.

No fear. No pain. Just love.

He had waited for me to come home before he left. That was Butters. Loyal. Devoted. Forever my boy.

He didn't just cross over.

He waited—for me.

It was my birthday—again.

2013.

Just one year after losing Butters.

I hadn't expected the day to feel light, not exactly. Grief still sat quietly in the corners of my life. But I didn't expect *another* goodbye. Not so soon. Not like this.

One moment, Lily was here—tail wagging, eyes bright, curls bouncing with every excited step. The next, she was gone.

No warning. No signs. Just a sudden stillness that knocked the breath from my body.

Lily was only seven. A honey-colored Cockapoo with a coat of soft curls and eyes that sparkled with mischief. She was joy in motion—a little firecracker of love, always ready to leap into a lap or cover your face with kisses. We brought her home just before the divorce, hoping she might cushion the heartbreak for the boys.

And she did. God, she did.

She became their anchor in the storm, their laughter when the world got quiet, and their warmth when everything felt cold. She had this uncanny gift—like she could sense the exact moment someone needed her. A tilt of her head. A nuzzle beneath a hand. Her love was intuitive, and unwavering.

She healed us, one tail wag at a time.

Her loss came like a strike of lightning—bright, brutal, and fast.

That morning, something felt off. I couldn't explain it— just a tug in my gut, a whisper that wouldn't leave me alone.

I got in my car and drove to my ex's house to check on her. My hands gripped the steering wheel tighter than usual. My chest buzzed with unease.

When I pulled into the driveway, the silence greeted me first. A silence that didn't feel natural.

And then I knew.

She was already gone.

A sudden stroke. There was no chance to hold her, and no time to say goodbye.

I sank into the driver's seat, with my body trembling. My hands covered my face as the sobs came hard and fast. I gasped between cries, willing it not to be true. *Not Lily.* Not *my* Lily.

The weight of it was unbearable. She had died alone. I hadn't been there.

The guilt pressed into me like glass shards—sharp and deep. My sweet girl, my loyal companion, had slipped away, and I hadn't been there to whisper, "I love you," to stroke her soft ears, or to help her cross in peace.

And then…something shifted. A gentle flutter outside my windshield caught my eye. I blinked through my tears. A tiny finch had landed on the hood of my car.

It stared straight at me, tilting its head with curious insistence. Then it chirped—a high, melodic note that sliced through the silence. And again. And again. It didn't flinch.

It didn't fly away.

It sang.

I sat up slowly, tears streaming down my cheeks, and met its gaze. The bird hopped closer, dancing, chirping as if it were *speaking*. Reassuring. Reminding. For five full minutes, that tiny creature stayed with me.

And I *knew*. It was her.

That was Lily. Her energy. Her love. Her playful spirit wrapped in feathers and song. She had found a way to reach me, even now. Even from beyond.

She was telling me she wasn't alone, that she was okay, and that she had made it *home*.

A peace settled into my chest—tender, sacred, and undeniable. I could feel her in that little bird's wings. In its bright eyes. In the joy it carried straight into my broken heart.

It was her way of saying: *Don't worry, Mama. I'm still here.*

I will never forget that moment. Never forget the mercy of it.

Grief doesn't follow a straight line. It loops. It spirals. Just when you think the pain has softened, life hands you another goodbye, and your heart cracks open all over again. But sometimes…love finds a way through.

And sometimes, it comes on tiny wings.

Six years after my mother passed, I lost my grandma too.

By then, dementia had already taken her in quiet increments. It didn't arrive all at once. It crept in slowly, memory by memory, chipping away at the sharp-witted, strong-willed woman we had known. Her world became smaller, her thoughts looser, drifting further from us and closer to something unseen.

She spent most of those years in a nursing home, nestled between the familiar and the beyond. One foot here, the other already halfway home.

The last time I saw her was about a year before she crossed over. Before the visit, my sister called me. Her voice was soft and cautious.

"Prepare yourself," she said gently. "She might not remember who you are."

I nodded into the phone, trying to steady myself, but no amount of mental bracing could prepare my heart for what I'd feel when I walked into that room.

She was lying in a twin bed beneath thin white blankets, her frame small and fragile, barely a shadow of the woman who had once ruled our family kitchen. Her hair, once perfectly coifed and set with pride, now lay in wisps around her face, soft like a dandelion gone to seed.

I hesitated at the door. And then, she looked up. A flicker of recognition sparked in her eyes. She smiled.

"My Heidi," she said, her voice cracked but clear.

I pressed a hand over my chest as tears rose behind my eyes. She remembered. In that moment—despite the fog, despite the time—she knew me. It felt like someone had reached into my chest and squeezed, hard and gentle all at once. Bittersweet joy flooded me. For a second, it was like nothing had changed. For a second, she was *there*.

We talked for nearly an hour. The conversation meandered through memories and little laughs. She asked about my boys. I told her stories, watching her eyes crinkle at the corners. Her voice, though raspy and slow, still carried that hint of matriarchal sparkle—the one that had once told everyone what to do in the kitchen without ever raising her tone.

She was tired. But she was still her.

She yawned softly and blinked up at me with growing heaviness in her eyelids. "I think I'll take a little nap now," she whispered.

I leaned down and kissed her forehead, the same way she used to kiss mine. Then I stepped out into the hallway, where a nurse waited with a kind smile.

"She had a good day," she said. "We haven't seen her that happy or talkative in a long time."

I nodded, blinking back the ache.

I flew back to California with a strange, quiet peace in my chest. I hadn't known it was the last time I'd see her in this life—but somehow, I *did* know. She had given me a window. A soft goodbye tucked into a shared hour. A final "I love you" folded into her smile.

She remembered me.

And I will never forget her.

Even now, she still lets me know she's near.

As I said, it begins the same way every time. I'll be doing dishes, folding laundry, or driving in stillness when a familiar scent sneaks into the air—delicate, floral, unmistakable.

Her perfume. The very same one that clung to her sweaters, the one that lingered long after her hugs. No one around me is wearing it. There's no bottle nearby. Just this soft, invisible presence wrapping around me like a shawl.

It always stops me in my tracks.

In the middle of grief. In the chaos of life. In the quiet moments where I feel like I'm losing my grip—she comes. Not with words. Not with signs I need to interpret. But with that scent—her scent.

And in those moments, I *know*.

She's still with me.

She comes when I'm anxious. When I'm overwhelmed. When I'm silently begging the universe for some sign that I'm not alone.

That fragrance wraps itself around me like a whisper: *You're still mine. I'm still here.*

It's her love letter from the other side—unwritten, unseen, but deeply felt.

And I treasure every visit.

13

LOVE, HURT, AND DATING

After the divorce, I did what most people do—I ventured back out into the world and tried to find love again. I dipped my toe into dating, stumbled my way through awkward dinners and hopeful phone calls, and slowly tried to rediscover the woman I was outside of marriage and motherhood.

Two serious relationships followed in the years ahead. Neither lasted, but both carved deep lessons into my heart—not just about love, but about the silent wounds I still carried.

The first came two years post-divorce. He lived in Thousand Oaks, just over an hour from Santa Barbara if the 101 decided to cooperate. He had three kids. I had three kids. Somehow, we shared the exact same custody schedule. That synchronicity meant we could spend most off-weekends together, weaving ourselves into each other's lives between soccer games and school pickups.

For four years, we dated long-distance.

From the outside, it might've looked manageable—even hopeful. But underneath the surface, the foundation was cracked. What looked like compatibility was really a quiet storm. I hadn't yet faced the echoes of my childhood—the unhealed places that still ached for something I couldn't name. And like clockwork, those wounds gravitated toward familiar pain: men who were emotionally shut down, controlling, and just as fractured as I was.

It was as if our brokenness recognized each other, drawing us together like damaged magnets pulled by patterns we didn't yet understand.

Every time I tried to talk about the future—what we were building toward, or what I needed—the air thickened. His eyes narrowed. Conversations spiraled. He treated commitment like a threat, a door he refused to walk through. I kept trying. I tiptoed around his resistance, hoping I could earn the kind of love I was desperate to believe existed.

Until one morning, when I woke up and felt it—a stillness that hadn't been there before. No fireworks. No breakdown. Just a quiet knowing that something in me had shifted. The ache had turned into clarity.

I picked up the phone, my fingers steady, my voice calm. "It's over," I said.

No shouting. No pleas. Just truth. Tired, clean truth.

When I hung up, it was as if a weight I didn't even realize I'd been carrying slid off my shoulders. I exhaled and felt light for the first time in years. Not hopeful. Not terrified. Just…free.

However, freedom can be disorienting.

When the noise of dysfunction finally quieted, the silence that followed was intimate and unrelenting. It was just me now—me and the aftermath. My choices. My grief. My quiet hopes. I didn't regret ending it. Not for a moment. But I had to relearn how to be in my own skin, to stop bending myself into someone else's shape and remember what mine looked like.

I wasn't looking for love. I wasn't even thinking about dating.

I just wanted to breathe. To exhale. To come home to myself.

It was my second year in Solvang when the unexpected happened. I turned a corner in the grocery store, my mind spinning with to-dos and dinner ideas, when I nearly collided with someone from my past—someone I hadn't seen in years.

"Heidi?"

He said my name like it was a question and a smile all at once.

I blinked, momentarily stunned. He looked almost the same—sharp suit traded for weekend jeans, but still put together. I knew him from my years at the brokerage firm in Santa Barbara. He was the firm's attorney—confident, composed, and always moving like the hallway belonged to him. We'd exchanged pleasantries back then, shared nods, polite smiles, and brief conversations. There had always been an ease. A quiet, mutual respect.

Now here we were, face to face in the pasta aisle.

We talked for a few minutes—nothing deep, just the warm hum of reconnection. Then he asked if he could take me to dinner. I paused, surprised...and a little flattered. I said yes.

We had dinner that week, and with it came a kind of familiarity I hadn't felt in a long time. The conversation flowed effortlessly, just like it had back at the office—witty, comfortable, and steady. I didn't feel the need to perform and didn't feel like I was tiptoeing into someone else's mood.

After years of uncertainty, that steadiness felt like air.

We started seeing each other. Nothing overwhelming. Just casual, consistent moments that started to add up. When the boys were at their dad's, I'd go to his house—a beautiful place tucked into a quiet street shaded by old oaks. We'd cook, laugh, and decompress from the long weeks. He was still practicing law. I was grinding out long days as a credit analyst in Santa Barbara. We were tired, both of us, but there was a comfort in collapsing into the same rhythm.

By July, we were running on fumes.

He suggested a weekend away. Huntington Beach. His hometown. Just the two of us, no obligations, no alarms. He booked the hotel, planned the drive. I didn't hesitate.

The drive down was light and full of laughter. Music, stories, fingers brushing across the console. It felt like what a relationship was supposed to feel like—easy, kind, and connected.

When we arrived, we checked in, threw on swimsuits, and headed straight for the ocean. The salt clung to our skin, the sun warming every inch of tension until it began to melt.

That night, we dressed up and walked to a nearby restaurant. I remember feeling open, and grounded. The noise in my head had quieted.

Over dinner, I asked gently, "Tell me about your family."

A flicker. A shift. His posture stiffened. The air changed.

"I'm not close to my mom or sister," he said. His tone was clipped, guarded.

But then, like a dam cracking, something else surged through—bitterness, sharp and sudden. His words turned jagged, his voice rising with a cold edge. The anger he carried for them poured out like poison.

I leaned in, careful. "Why are you so angry with them?"

That's when it happened.

He slammed his fists on the table, his voice exploding, "I'm not angry!"

The room fell silent. Utensils froze midair. Conversations stopped. I could feel the heat rising in my cheeks and could hear the pulse pounding in my ears.

"Please," I whispered. "Please, lower your voice."

But my request only fanned the flames. His voice climbed louder. I tried to de-escalate, to understand, but he wasn't reachable.

Suddenly, I was twelve again—small, invisible, and humiliated.

I stood quietly, willing my voice not to break. "I'll meet you outside," I said.

I walked out, weaving through tables, offering hushed apologies to people staring at their plates, pretending they hadn't heard everything. But I felt their eyes, and their judgment. It clung to me like a second skin.

I wouldn't cry. Not here. Not where no one knew what it had taken just to show up.

When he emerged, we walked back in silence. His stride was calm, and steady. Mine shook beneath the surface.

Back in the room, I finally broke. "Are you okay?" I asked.

He didn't even look at me.

"Yeah," he said, as if the question was an inconvenience.

I waited for something—an apology, a scrap of empathy. Instead, he opened the mini fridge.

"This one's special," he said, holding up a beer. His voice had shifted again; it was light and chipper, like nothing had happened.

"What makes it special?" I asked numbly.

He smiled, that same thin line. "The taste."

I took the bottle. I drank it.

There were two beds. I lay in one. He lay in the other. A movie played, light flickering across the walls. We didn't speak. The silence had weight now—thick, oppressive.

I couldn't shake what had happened. His outburst. The

beer. The numbness. I felt like I was drifting outside of myself, watching everything from above.

And then—nothing.

The next thing I remember was him on top of me.

Everything was heavy. My limbs wouldn't move. My voice wouldn't rise. I tried to understand what was happening, tried to fight, but I was underwater—sinking.

And then, darkness again.

When I woke, I was alone in the bed. He was snoring in the other bed, like it was any other morning. For a moment, I let myself believe it had all been a dream. A nightmare. But my body told the truth.

I was sick. Violently. I barely made it to the bathroom before my stomach gave out. My head throbbed. My vision blurred. I was hollowed out, like something vital had been stolen from me.

He didn't ask if I was okay.

Everything I did irritated him now. I told him I needed to go home.

He didn't argue.

The ride back was silent. He barely slowed the car when we reached my place. Didn't help with my things. Didn't say goodbye.

I went inside and collapsed.

I was sick for days.

A week later, he called—not to check on me, but to say I'd left my beach chair in his car. I asked if he could drop it off.

He said no.

I told him to leave it on his porch.

I drove to his house when I knew he'd be gone. I grabbed my chair. I didn't look back.

I never saw him again.

Six years later, a text appeared.

I was sitting at the kitchen table, hands wrapped around

a mug of coffee that had long gone cold. Emails blurred past, half-read bills and spam stacking into digital clutter. And then, there it was.

His name.

It appeared on the screen like a ghost I had never invited back.

My breath caught. My stomach twisted in an instant, a hard knot of dread curling low. I stared at the notification; my hand was trembling as I clicked to open it. My thumb hovered, suspended in hesitation, as if it somehow knew this message would shatter me.

"My apologies, Heidi. I would like to sit down and talk as well as make reparations. It was date rape..."

The words hit like a punch to the face.

I blinked. I read it again. Then again.

And then the world tilted.

A high-pitched ring flooded my ears. My heart slammed against my ribs, each beat louder than the last. The kitchen around me dimmed and spun. I couldn't tell if I was about to vomit or faint.

Date rape.

He named it.

My brain scrambled to catch up with the truth unraveling in front of me, but everything inside me was already breaking open. A trapdoor had been pulled from beneath me, and I was freefalling—back into a nightmare I hadn't even realized I'd been suppressing.

I always knew something had happened that night. I could never explain it, but the way my body reacted afterward—the confusion, the sickness, the way my skin recoiled from memory—told me what my mind wasn't ready to hear. Still, I buried it. Dismissed myself, before anyone else could. I told myself I was emotional. Exhausted. Overreacting.

And now, there it was. In writing.

From him.

My fingers hovered over the screen as if another message might follow. A retraction. An apology. Anything to make the words vanish.

Nothing came.

I sat there for hours, frozen, with the glow of the screen washing over me.

In the days that followed, I moved like a stranger in my own life. I brushed my teeth. Washed clothes. Opened the fridge. But I wasn't really there. I was somewhere else—adrift in the haze of unraveling memories, lost in the echo of what I now knew.

And then came the rage.

How dare he send that. How dare he package it in the language of healing and call it reparation—like it was some sacred offering. Like he was doing me a favor.

That message wasn't for me. It was for him. For his conscience. His redemption arc.

I didn't owe him that.

Instead, I called the police.

My voice wavered as I explained. I read the message aloud, clinging to the hope that this time, someone would believe me.

They didn't.

They told me it would be complicated. Another jurisdiction. No rape kit. No report at the time.

"Are you sure?" they asked.

Was I sure?

He confessed. In writing. What more did they want?

Then came the warning. If I pursued it, he might lose his law license.

So what? I wanted to scream that I didn't care about his title. I cared about the truth. About my voice. About finally being heard.

But I hung up that call feeling smaller than I had in years.

As if pain needed to arrive wrapped in a bow to be worthy of justice. As if truth had an expiration date.

Still, I wasn't done. I called attorneys. I told them everything. I read the text through tears that refused to stay tucked inside. But the moment I said he was an attorney, the energy shifted.

They didn't say it aloud, but I heard it anyway. He's one of us.

And just like that, I was alone. Again. But this time, I was done staying silent.

I decided to tell my boys.

They were grown now—old enough to understand a version of the truth. I didn't want them hearing it through court documents or whispered speculation. They deserved to hear it from me.

We sat in the living room, the three of us. I held my phone in my hand, the message still lit on the screen. I felt like I was holding a live wire. My palms were slick. My chest ached.

But I told them what happened. What he admitted. What I planned to do. They sat in silence. Still. Processing.

Then one of them looked up, eyes searching mine.

"Are you sure it really happened?"

The words sliced through me like glass.

He didn't mean to hurt me. He was trying to understand. Trying to make sense of something unthinkable. But still—it broke something sacred. And just like that, the doubt crept back in. Even with the message in my hand. Even with the memory in my bones. Even with my truth sitting raw in the center of the room.

I started questioning myself again.

And in that fragile space, I folded.

I didn't respond to the message. Didn't go back to the police. Didn't call another attorney.

I buried it. Again. I told myself it was too late. That it wouldn't matter. That maybe I was overreacting. I told myself I needed peace more than justice. That letting go was strength. Not surrender.

But the truth was—I let it go because I didn't know how to hold it anymore. Because sometimes, when the world tells you again and again that your pain is inconvenient, you start to believe them.

But even in that silence, I knew—

I still had more healing to do.

I started turning inward, slowly, like a tide pulling back from the shore. I stopped chasing love in places that only left me empty. Instead, I began tending to my own roots—setting boundaries, learning how to be with myself without shrinking under the weight of loneliness.

I went on a few dates—casual coffees, polite conversations—but nothing ever stuck. I wasn't ready. Not really. It would be four more years before I'd find myself in another serious relationship. And that one…that one cracked me wide open in an entirely different way.

By then, the boys were young men. They had their own cars, and their own lives, and spent most of their time in Santa Barbara. I was basically living alone. The house was still and quiet—so quiet that every creak and groan of the floorboards felt like a reminder of what was no longer there.

At first, I convinced myself I was fine. This was the natural rhythm of life, I told myself. Children grow up. The house empties. Life moves forward. But no one prepares you for the echo of your own thoughts bouncing off walls that used to hold so much laughter.

No one tells you how deafening the silence becomes when there's no one to cook for, no one to wait up for, and no one to share the silly little details of your day with. I kept the house clean, the fridge full, and the routines steady. But everything around me felt like it had been frozen in time—like I was walking through a memory that didn't quite know how to fade.

Their absence lived in everything. In the quiet of their bedrooms. In the unopened box of Cocoa Puffs I couldn't bring myself to throw away. I moved through the house as if it might collapse under the weight of what used to be.

I was proud of them. God, I was proud. But their absence hollowed me out in a way I wasn't ready for. I had spent decades anchoring our family, holding everything together, pouring myself into the role of mother.

And now…no one needed anything from me.

I didn't know who I was without that.

The days stretched long. I went for walks. I wandered the aisles of Target. I tried to stay busy. But beneath it all, I was drifting—untethered. I had spent so long caring for everyone else that I didn't know how to care for myself.

I didn't know where to start.

There's a certain kind of vulnerability that creeps in when the nights stack up one after another, the bed stays cold, and no one says your name out loud. I didn't realize how hungry I was for connection until I caught myself scanning rooms—searching for a spark, a glance, some flicker of familiarity that might make me feel alive again.

I wasn't looking for love. I wasn't even looking for companionship. I was just trying to remember what it felt like to be seen.

That's when I met him. Carlos.

It was New Year's Eve. I was out with girlfriends, champagne in hand, pretending to be excited for the year ahead. The bar buzzed with celebration and glittered with noise. And then I saw him. Ten years younger. Lean. Confident. There was something about him that made me pause— maybe it was the way he carried himself, or maybe it was just my own loneliness, curling up and tugging at my sleeve.

I walked over. Introduced myself.

And just like that, he came home with me.

Honestly? He never really left.

At first, it was fun. He was attractive, charming in that intoxicating way some people are when they've perfected the art of saying exactly what you want to hear. He told me I was beautiful. That I was smart. That I made him feel like he could finally be himself. And I ate it up like a starving woman.

He told me he had a plan. Said he'd moved home from San Jose to care for his sick father. That he was temporarily crashing on his sister's couch. That they shared a car. That he wanted to be a firefighter.

And even as red flags fluttered in the background, I zeroed in on the potential. I chose to believe the story because I wanted to believe it. I wanted to feel chosen. Desired. Loved.

The age difference gave me pause, but we agreed to keep it light. "No expectations," we said. "We're just having fun. When it stops being fun, we'll walk away."

And for a while, it really was fun.

Until the cracks started to show.

A tiger can't hide its stripes forever. And Carlos—well, his began to show.

It started with small asks. "Can I borrow your car to get to work?" he'd say, flashing that boyish smile. "Just trying to save on Uber." At first, it felt harmless. I wanted to help. I always wanted to help.

But before long, it wasn't a question anymore—it was an expectation. When I said no, the smile vanished. He'd sulk. Sometimes argue. Sometimes just shut down entirely, icing me out with a silence so cold it left frost on the walls.

The balance shifted beneath me. What began as companionship started to resemble dependency. I covered the rent.

The groceries. The utilities. Nights out, weekends in, birthdays, breakdowns—all on me. I did his laundry, too. Folded his clothes like I used to for my boys. Only this time, I wasn't raising a child. Or at least, I wasn't supposed to be.

He came home later and later. Always with a story—traffic, overtime, a coworker in crisis. The details didn't line up, but he said them with such conviction I tried to believe him. Tried to believe *me*. But the gut never lies, and mine was twisting tighter by the day.

His phone never left his side—always on silent, always buzzing, always flipped face-down. When I asked questions, he deflected. Shrugged. Mumbled something vague. I wanted to trust him. I *wanted* to. So, I ignored the pit in my stomach and smiled through the cracks.

Then, one night, he left for work and forgot his phone on the kitchen counter.

It buzzed. Again. And again.

I stared at it like it was ticking. My hand hovered, heart hammering. And then I picked it up. The screen lit up. Messages. Dozens of them. Two women. Different names. Different threads. But the same tone—flirty, intimate, and knowing.

My stomach dropped. I couldn't breathe. The blood drained from my face. The room spun. He walked through the door hours later like nothing had happened. I confronted him, phone in hand, shaking with hurt and disbelief. He blinked, then launched into damage control. Excuses. Deflection. Lies layered with more lies. Even with the truth glowing in front of us, he tried to rewrite it.

But I didn't leave. Not yet.

Because I *loved* him.

Because I still saw the version of him I had fallen for—the man I believed he could be, if only I loved him hard enough.

So, I stayed.

And I was miserable.

When I get quiet—when I truly listen—I can hear them. My guides. My loved ones. They've always been there, whispering truth from the other side. But I have to choose to listen. One morning, I woke up with a thought so clear it rang in my ears like it had been spoken aloud: *You need to move.*

Not to a new neighborhood. Not even a new city.

You need to move—across the country.

At first, I brushed it off. I thought it was wild, drastic, and impulsive. But the nudge didn't fade. It planted itself in my brain and hummed like a tuning fork every time I tried to ignore it.

I knew what it was.

My spiritual team was calling. And this time, I was ready to answer.

I sat the boys down and told them. "I'm thinking about moving…to Florida." Florida. A thousand miles away. A whole new coast.

I waited for protest. For hesitation. But instead, I got love.

"Mom," one of them said, smiling softly, "we can't believe you didn't move sooner."

They were right. They were already out there—living, thriving, and building their own lives. My oldest had graduated from university. My middle and youngest were in community college. They didn't *need* me the way they once did. And I had raised them for this moment—for the day I could finally reclaim *me*.

Still, the decision wasn't easy. Uprooting everything never is. But Florida kept pulling at me. I didn't know much about it—just the headlines, the humidity, and the memes. But my friend had just taken a job in Tallahassee. It made the leap feel less terrifying, knowing someone I knew would be nearby.

Once I had the boys' blessing, I sat down with Carlos. I had rehearsed the conversation. I was ready to let him go. But before I could even speak, he looked at me with those wide, unreadable eyes and asked, "Can I come with you?"

And just like that…I said yes.

Because I wanted to believe. That maybe a new place would change everything. That maybe he would rise to the occasion. That maybe he'd finally become the man I believed he could be.

That was a mistake.

Carlos didn't come with hope in his suitcase. He brought manipulation. Lies. Promises so shiny they distracted me from their hollowness. He talked about building a life, about marriage and roots. He spoke like a man with vision, but he moved like a ghost—always just out of reach.

And I believed him. I wanted to believe him.

But beneath the charm, something darker lived.

What I didn't know at the time was that, under the guise of wanting to move to Florida with me, he was stealing from me. By the end of it, nearly ten thousand dollars would be gone.

Money I had tucked away, carefully saved, scraped together over time for a down payment on a home. Money that was supposed to ground me.

And he took it.

He lied, manipulated, and gaslighted me until I couldn't tell which way was up. I kept looking for the man I had fallen for. But he wasn't there. He never had been.

It was all an illusion—and it nearly broke me.

He almost shattered my spirit beyond repair.

By then, the wheels were already in motion. I had notified my landlord. Given notice at work. It was still the COVID era, and thankfully, my company had adopted a permanent remote work policy. When they offered the choice—return to the office, go hybrid, or stay fully remote—I didn't hesitate.

I chose me. I chose remote.

That daily commute from Solvang to Santa Barbara—two hours round-trip—had been slowly bleeding me dry. The traffic, the energy, the politics. Working from home gave me space to breathe, to focus, to *be*.

Another gift? The company didn't penalize remote employees for moving. My salary stayed the same.

It meant freedom.

It meant I could leave California—and everything I'd been carrying there.

And I could finally chase a dream I'd tucked away for years: buying a home in Florida.

So, I started packing.

That little apartment had been home for almost a decade. The boys and I had grown up there together. It felt like a blink. It felt like a lifetime.

Carlos was still living with me. Still rent-free. Still borrowing my car like it was his.

A month before the move, I asked when he planned to start packing.

He looked up, casual as ever, and said, "I'll need a few more months to work and save before I can join you."

And just like that, the red flags weren't fluttering anymore.

They were waving.

Carlos had lived with me for a year—no rent, no help with bills, nothing. And now, suddenly, he needed time to save? The logic didn't land, but I didn't press. I wanted to believe him. I wanted to believe we were building something real.

When my original moving plans fell through, he offered a solution—said his cousin had a truck and trailer we could borrow. He'd drive them cross-country with me for five thousand dollars, plus food and hotel expenses.

I hesitated.

But the moving quotes I'd gathered—especially with the cost to transport my electric car—were closer to seven grand. His offer felt like a lifeline.

There was just one catch: space.

The trailer could only hold the essentials—my bedroom, bathroom, and office furniture. The rest—kitchen table, dining set, and everything from the living room—would stay behind in storage. He promised he'd rent a U-Haul and bring it all to Florida in June, once he had the money.

So, I boxed up the apartment, one memory at a time. Every drawer emptied. Every picture frame wrapped. Every corner swept. I stood in the middle of it all—the quiet shell of the home we'd lived in—and let my eyes wander.

It felt like the walls were holding their breath.

The boys came to help with the last load. They moved through the apartment like they belonged to it—because they did. I watched them walk the same hallway they used to race down in sock feet. I pictured us dancing in the kitchen, with dinner burning on the stove. The couch was gone, but in my mind, I saw the four of us piled together, laughing at the same old movies.

We didn't say much. We didn't have to.

The weight of goodbye filled the room.

I hugged them too long, memorizing the shape of their arms around me. They told me they were proud. I smiled through the sting in my eyes.

And then, with the trailer hitched and my car packed tight, Carlos and I pulled away from the curb.

We left the last week of February—chasing something new, something unknown. And in the silence between songs on the radio, I whispered the kind of prayer only a mother understands: *Please let what I'm going toward be worth what I'm leaving behind.*

The drive was a disaster. We bickered constantly—about

directions, music, snacks. Little things that somehow carried sharp edges. There was no rhythm. Just friction. Three tires blew out. The trailer hadn't been loaded properly. We pulled over on the side of the road more times than I could count—sweating, cursing, and exhausted. One night, in a cheap roadside motel, we woke to a crash. A drunk driver had sideswiped the trailer.

The damage was mostly cosmetic—scratches, dents, bent metal—but it felt like another blow in a journey already frayed at the edges. It took us seven grueling days to reach Florida.

By the time we arrived, I was a shell—physically depleted and emotionally unraveling. Still, I held onto hope. Maybe it was just the rocky beginning of something better.

Carlos helped me unload. Quietly. Efficiently. Too quietly. A distance crept in behind his eyes, but I didn't know how to name it yet. He stayed that night. In the morning, as he packed up the truck and trailer, he cried. Real tears.

It caught me off guard—it was sweet and strange all at once.

He was supposed to be moving in with me in a few months.

He promised to call every day. And for a while, he did. The texts, the calls, the good mornings and good nights— they kept coming. I let myself believe again. Maybe the worst was behind us.

But like everything with Carlos, the effort faded. The calls slowed, then stopped. Voicemails went unanswered.

My stomach twisted in that familiar way—tight, heavy, and whispering truths I didn't want to hear.

Still, I tried to stay grounded. I focused on what I *could* control. I started house hunting—something modest, something mine. Carlos had promised to reimburse me twenty-five hundred for the move and contribute half the down-payment for our future home.

I found a place. It had charm. Potential. I could see us there.

I made an offer. It was accepted.

Carlos actually answered when I called. He sounded present. I sent him a video walk-through.

"It's perfect," he said. "I can see us building a life there."

I paid the deposit. Spent five hundred on inspections.

Then the roof report came in—full replacement needed. Thirty-five thousand.

I countered. The seller offered twenty-five hundred. I walked away.

I lost the deposit, the inspection fees, and the house.

I tried calling Carlos. Nothing. The next day—nothing. A week. Silence. Then, two weeks later, he called.

Not to check on me, nor to ask how I was. He called to ask for money.

He said he needed five thousand to rent a U-Haul and finally bring the rest of my furniture to Florida.

And I gave it to him.

No hesitation. No questions. Because I still believed him. Still believed *in* him.

And then—he disappeared.

Just like that.

No apology. No closure. Just…gone.

He never repaid me and never showed up.

I ended up spending another four thousand to get my things shipped to Florida.

The down-payment I'd saved so carefully? Gone.

The dream of homeownership? On hold. Again.

But the real cost wasn't money. It was the betrayal.

I had trusted him. Loved him. Let him into my life, my home, and my heart. I thought we were building something real.

But to him, I was a convenience. A resource. A stepping-stone.

A few months later, I found out he'd been arrested for drug possession and carrying firearms. Then I learned about the longtime girlfriend. The kids. A whole life he never once mentioned.

He had told me he loved me. Told me we had a future. But it was all a lie.

How could I have missed it?

How could my intuition have been so wrong?

I kept asking myself, looping through the same questions like a broken record.

I'd done the work. I'd dug through trauma, survived darkness, and clawed my way back to myself. I thought I'd healed. Thought I knew my worth. And then came Carlos—charming, magnetic, and full of promise.

And just like that, I was back in the spiral. Back in the high of being chosen. Back in the free fall of betrayal. That heartbreak was the final straw.

I couldn't unknow what I knew. And I couldn't unsee what I had seen.

And the worst part wasn't that he fooled me—it was that I let him.

However, in the silence that followed, something else began to rise.

Not guilt. Not shame. Not even anger.

Grace.

I took a deep breath. And I chose to look back—not with bitterness, but with softness. I flipped through the memories like old photographs. Some edges torn. Some stained. All part of the same story.

And the truth is—I love who I've become.

I am kind. I am empathetic. I am fiercely loyal. I love deeply. And yes—I am nice.

Unapologetically, truly nice.

I used to think that made me weak. Now, I know—it's my strength.

I'm not perfect. But I'm proud.

And for that, I thank every love, every loss, and every lesson.

14

I'M FREE

"Just when the caterpillar thought the world was over, it became a butterfly."

—Chuang Tzu

Here I am. Tallahassee, Florida. My new home.

The words didn't quite fit at first. They rolled around in my mouth like something foreign or borrowed. I wanted to love it. I wanted to land on both feet. But the truth is that the move was hard.

I hadn't even unpacked my last box before the doubt came rushing in.

Carlos still lingered—his memory clinging like smoke after a fire, curling around the quiet corners of my mind. The emotional wreckage, the financial strain, the exhaustion from pulling my entire life across the country—it weighed on me, thick and suffocating.

And this wasn't California anymore.

Everything here felt slower and softer. More polite but wrapped in a rhythm I didn't understand yet. People waved in parking lots. Strangers struck up conversations in line. There was kindness in the air, but also a cultural undercurrent I hadn't quite learned to navigate.

And my boys…

God, how I missed my boys.

Some nights, I'd lie in bed staring at the ceiling fan spinning in slow, hypnotic circles, wondering if I had completely lost my mind. What was I doing here? Had I made a huge mistake?

The silence in my home was different to any silence I'd ever known. It wasn't peaceful—it was hollow. A reminder of all I'd left behind. But somewhere deep inside me, a small, steady voice whispered: *You chose this.*

Even when everything felt uncertain, I held onto that truth. I had followed my gut here. And even if the landing was rough, something told me I was still on the right path. So, I shifted my perspective.

This is an adventure, I reminded myself. *Everyone here has a story—and if I'm brave enough to share mine, maybe I'll find the connection I'm craving.*

Still, I didn't want to explore the city alone. I started searching online for a walking group, a hiking club—something low-pressure and not soaked in small talk or singles-scene energy. I wasn't looking to date. I wasn't looking to network. I was just looking for *people*.

Most of the groups I found were either defunct or didn't feel like the right fit.

So, I created what I was looking for.

A women's-only social group. Casual. Heartfelt. Real.

I wrote a short intro, clicked "publish," and sent it into the universe, with fingers crossed. Maybe I'd meet a few women. Maybe it would fizzle out. I had no particular expectations.

Three months later, the group had exploded—ten members had turned into over one hundred-sixty.

Clearly, I hadn't been the only one searching.

I started hosting weekly events—"Friyays," I called them. Every Friday at seven p.m., we'd pick a local bar or restaurant, grab a drink, and decompress.

No pressure. No filters. Just women showing up as they were.

We shared stories about work stress, motherhood, break-ups, hilarious Tinder fails, heavy family dynamics. We laughed. We cried. We passed around tissues and margaritas in equal measure.

And through that group, I found the heartbeat of Tallahassee.

I started posting events I was curious about—art walks, food truck festivals, farmer's markets—and a crew of women, sometimes eight, sometimes twenty, would show up to explore alongside me.

That's how I met Stacie.

My platonic soulmate.

From the first conversation, the connection was electric—but in a grounding way. She saw me. Really saw me. Our lives had moved in similar patterns—trauma, healing, spiritual growth, and a fierce sense of humor that softened the sharp edges of life.

Being with her felt like slipping into your favorite pair of slippers—familiar, cozy, worn-in just right. There was no performance. No code-switching. Just exhale.

She became part of my family. And I became part of hers.

Starting over in Tallahassee had been rocky. But in Stacie, I found something real. Something healing.

She moved to town six months after I did—September 2023. She was searching, too. For peace. For purpose. For the kind of grounding that only comes after years of drifting.

We were both strangers in a city that didn't yet feel like home, both craving connection that wasn't performative or laced with competition. And we found it—in each other.

You could feel her inner work in the way she listened, the way she held space without judgment, the way she let herself be seen—and saw you right back.

Two women on parallel healing journeys. Mirror reflections of grit and growth. With Stacie, there was no competition. No backhanded compliments. No jealousy hiding behind pretty words. Just openness, presence, and safety.

It was the first time I understood what *healthy* female friendship could feel like.

And it was healing in ways I didn't even know I needed.

For years, I had been on edge around other women—bracing for the subtle digs, the side-eyes, the passive-aggressive cold shoulder that always came when I refused to play small. But with Stacie, I didn't have to shrink. I didn't have to censor myself. I could show up messy. Raw. Joyful. Grieving. Unapologetically myself.

And I was met with love.

That kind of friendship is rare. It is also powerful, and freeing.

I'm at a point in my life where I no longer barter with red flags.

If I feel judgment, jealousy, manipulation, arrogance, cruelty, or negativity—I don't pause, I don't rationalize, I don't shrink. I walk away.

I crave peace. Harmony. Stability. And I guard them with the fierceness of someone who's earned them the hard way.

Stacie's the same way.

In February of 2024, the ground beneath her shifted—she was laid off from her job. It rattled her. The foundation she'd been so carefully rebuilding cracked beneath her feet.

Then in August, it was my turn.

After five and a half years as the Senior Credit Analyst at Sonos, I experienced my fourth lay-off in my career. I got the news. My position was eliminated.

No warning. No soft landing. Just the unmistakable jolt of *again?*

We hadn't seen it coming. Neither of us had.

The grief came in waves—sharp, unexpected. Shock. Fear. A deep, aching anxiety. The kind that wakes you up at three a.m. and doesn't let you go back to sleep.

But we showed up for each other. We sat on the couch, wrapped in blankets, clutching mugs of tea that had long gone cold. We cried. We laughed through the absurdity. We took turns reading each other's résumés out loud and practicing mock interviews like awkward theater.

"I hate this question," one of us would groan. "Tell me about a time you overcame adversity? Right now, Stacie. I'm in it. I *am* adversity."

The job market was a battlefield.

No more quick interviews and handshake offers. Now it was a digital minefield.

Scams lurked in inboxes disguised as recruiters. Bots sent rejection emails that sounded like they had been written by ghosts. And the AI filters? Ruthless. One missing buzzword, and your résumé might as well have been hand-written in crayon.

We joked, we screamed, we coped the only way we knew how—together.

Thank God for severance. And for retirement accounts we didn't have to cash out—yet.

But that didn't mean it was easy.

There were nights when Netflix played in the background while tears rolled quietly down our cheeks. Nights when silence wrapped around us like a second skin. Nights when hope felt just out of reach.

And then, finally, there was light.

Before our severance checks ran dry, we both landed new jobs.

I never imagined starting over again at this stage. But here I am.

Now I work as a legal assistant for a local commercial real estate attorney. It's new. It's challenging.

And it's mine.

Just like this life I'm building—messy, honest, and resilient. Rooted in the kind of love that shows up even when everything else falls apart. Now that the dust has settled, I feel a new kind of hunger. Not just for stability—but for joy. For alignment.

I don't want to just *exist* anymore. I want to *live*. I want a life that doesn't just look good on paper, but one that feels good in my soul. One that reflects who I am now—after all the heartbreak, all the healing.

Stacie and I travel every chance we get—even if it's just a spontaneous road trip or a lazy Saturday spent exploring a town we've never been to. She makes everything feel like an adventure—even the grocery store.

We crank up the music, roll down the windows, and sing off-key like no one's listening. We laugh until we cry and find meaning in the most unexpected places. With her, I feel safe. Seen. Light.

The boys and I talk often—sometimes daily, sometimes just a check-in. Their voices still center me, even from afar. When we manage to meet up, time slows. I soak up every hug, every laugh, every shared meal.

It's one of the hardest parts of this new chapter—being far away. Even as they become men, charting their own lives, a piece of me still sees them as little boys asleep in the next room.

Motherhood doesn't end. It just shifts.

Work keeps me grounded. I'm still learning—every week a crash course in contracts, closings, and deadlines. But I'm not afraid of starting over.

In fact, I've gotten good at it.

And because creativity has always been a part of who we are, Stacie and I started something together—a little side project that turned into something special. It began as an idea over coffee—what if we created something that brought intention and joy to people's lives? Something playful. Magical.

We started making manifestation wish kits.

Little bundles of hope.

Each one handcrafted with care—mini scrolls, tiny crystals, charms, pens, mesh bags, magnets. Everything you'd need to make a wish, to name a dream, and to believe in possibility again.

We bring them to local festivals and markets, set up our booth, and invite strangers to pause, breathe, and choose an intention. Some close their eyes. Some laugh nervously. Some tear up.

It's beautiful.

It's sacred.

And it's ours.

It brings in a little extra money—but more than that, it gives us purpose. Play. A reminder that even in uncertainty, we can still create something meaningful.

But the work that lives closest to my heart doesn't happen behind a desk.

It doesn't sit in an inbox or live inside a meeting agenda.

It breathes quietly in the stillness of hospice.

I recently began volunteering with Vitas, a hospice care organization here in Tallahassee. From the very first phone call with the volunteer director, my heart stirred with a feeling I couldn't quite name—but I knew it mattered. A calm clarity that whispered, *You're exactly where you're meant to be.*

This was more than a role. It was a return.

I had carried this vision in my heart since 2011, the year I lost my mom.

It's called *Susurrus,* Latin for *a whisper.* And that's exactly what it is meant to be. A whisper at the edge of life. A breath of grace in the silence between heartbeats.

Susurrus is a program built to bring comfort to the dying—and to those keeping vigil beside them. We offer stories from those who've had near-death experiences—not as proof or persuasion, but as soft reassurance.

Not doctrine. Not dogma.

Just possibility. The possibility that maybe death isn't the end. That maybe, just maybe, something waits on the other side of the veil. Something kind. Something full of love.

We don't come in to teach. We come to witness. To sit. To hold hands and share what we've seen in the in-between. Because *Susurrus* isn't really about what comes after death.

It's about what happens when the fear of death begins to dissolve.

And when that fear softens—something beautiful opens.

Regret fades. Resistance loosens. Peace enters.

That's what *Susurrus* is.

A whisper of remembrance.

A breath of grace at the threshold of goodbye.

My mother passed in hospice.

I still remember the warmth of her hands in mine. The quiet hum of the room. Time slowed. There were no more clocks. Just presence. Breath. Love.

Those final days with her changed me in ways I still don't fully understand. There was something holy in the silence. Something sacred in the stillness that wrapped around us as we said goodbye.

That space marked me. Branded itself into my bones. And I knew, even then, that I would find my way back to it. Not just to honor her. But to honor what that space had given me.

Susurrus is that offering.

It is my way of turning heartbreak into healing.

Of transforming loss into legacy.

Of being the whisper I once needed—and now have the privilege to pass on.

•   •   •

Sometimes, when I sit quietly and look back—really look back—it's like flipping through a faded album of someone else's life.

I see her there.

That girl with downcast eyes and a voice like a whisper. The one who tiptoed through rooms, afraid to take up space. Who twisted herself into impossible shapes just to earn a nod of approval that never fully came.

She lived on the edge of her own breath, unsure if she was allowed to exist.

And yet...she never gave up. She kept going. Kept showing up. Kept hoping. I barely recognize her now, and still—I love her. Fiercely.

Because she laid the first stone. She was the foundation. The quiet, trembling beginning. She didn't know her worth then, but she carried me to the place where I could finally claim it.

And for that, I honor her.

Writing this book has been a mirror.

A sacred reckoning. A reckoning with memory, with grief, with growth.

And when I compare the girl I used to be with the woman I've become, I feel nothing but tenderness. She was so small. So unsure. So eager to be loved that she bent herself into silence.

But I'm not her anymore.

Not entirely.

I'm not perfect. I've long stopped expecting myself to be.

I am real. I am raw. I am a work in motion—unfinished, and still, somehow, whole.

I no longer shrink to fit spaces that ask me to go silent.

I no longer dim my light just so others don't have to squint.

It's been a long road. A painful, beautiful, messy, miraculous road.

But I wouldn't trade a single step.

I've made mistakes. I still do. But now, I listen.

To my Guides.

To my body.

To that sacred wisdom that hums beneath the surface of every quiet moment.

My growth hasn't always been graceful. My lessons have come slowly, painfully at times.

But I grow.

I rise.

I trust myself now.

I don't contort for love anymore.

Not for family. Not for friends. Not for work. Not for romance.

If something asks me to become less—then it's not for me.

Some may read this and call me naïve. Let them.

I know the truth.

My love is not weakness.

It is sacred strength.

Pain hasn't hardened me.

Bitterness hasn't made a home in me.

I am still open. But now—I am open with wisdom.

Kind with boundaries.

Generous with discernment.

For years, I attracted people who clung to the safety I offered.

My presence was a balm to their chaos. My steadiness, a lighthouse to their storm. But they didn't come to rest. They came to extract. And when they realized I couldn't carry both of us—when my energy stopped pouring into their void—they left.

They weren't ready for coherence.

Not with me.

Not with themselves.

I've learned that love does not equal access.

My energy is not a resource to be mined.

It is a sanctuary to be respected.

Now, when I ask myself—*Why did that fall apart? Why did it unfold that way?*

I don't ask to blame.

I ask to reclaim.

Because when I meet those questions with curiosity instead of self-punishment, I begin to break the pattern. And every broken pattern brings me closer to home.

This journey—this brutal, beautiful journey—has brought me back to myself.

And I can say now, with certainty, with softness, and with unshakable power, I have finally found my voice.

A NOTE TO SURVIVORS

To every person carrying a story that feels too heavy, too complicated, or too painful to name—this page is for you.

There is nothing wrong with you.
What happened to you does not define your worth, your future, or your identity. The shame you've been holding was never yours to carry, and the silence you learned to live inside was a survival skill—not a flaw, not a failure, not a weakness.

You deserve safety.
You deserve peace.
You deserve a life that feels like your own.

Healing is not a straight line. Some days you will rise. Some days you will rest. Both are part of becoming whole.

If no one has ever told you this plainly:
You did not imagine it. You did not exaggerate it. You did not cause it. And you are not alone.

Your voice matters. Your story matters.
And you matter.
More than you know.

ACKNOWLEDGMENTS

To my sons—
you are the brightest chapters in every story I tell.
My life has been beautiful, messy, chaotic, and breathtaking
because of you.
Thank you for giving me purpose, for seeing me,
and for reminding me that love can rewrite the ending.

To my mom, my grandpa, and my grandma—
the ones who poured love, resilience, and truth into me.
Your lessons carved the woman I am today.
Your spirits still steady my feet.
Your love has been a quiet shelter through the hardest storms.

To my editor, Hugh Barker—
thank you for honoring my voice
and lifting this manuscript into something
that feels like truth laid bare on the page.
Your care, your notes, your heart, and your skill
helped me bring these memories home.

To every fur-baby who curled beside me in my darkest nights—
thank you for loving me without conditions,
for the warmth against my ribs when the world felt cold,
and for reminding me that gentleness can save a life.

To my abusers, my bullies, and every storm I survived—
Strangely, painfully, sincerely—thank you.
you taught me who I refused to become.
from the ashes you left behind,

I built empathy, compassion,
and a heart that chooses love every single time.

To every person who has ever held space for me, believed in me, supported me, or simply stayed—thank you.

RESOURCES FOR SURVIVORS

Healing from trauma is not a journey you have to walk alone. Below are organizations, hotlines, books, and supportive communities that offer guidance, safety, and hope. Please reach out whenever you need support. Your well-being matters.

National Hotlines & Organizations

RAINN—National Sexual Assault Hotline
1-800-656-HOPE (4673)
Online chat & resources: **www.rainn.org**

Childhelp National Child Abuse Hotline
1-800-4-A-CHILD (422-4453)
www.childhelphotline.org

National Domestic Violence Hotline
1-800-799-SAFE (7233)
www.thehotline.org

SAMHSA National Helpline
1-800-662-HELP (4357)
Support for mental health, trauma, and substance use
www.samhsa.org
Florida & Local Resources
Florida Council Against Sexual Violence (FCASV)
Statewide support & crisis centers
www.fcasv.org

Refuge House—Tallahassee, FL
Support for survivors of sexual assault & domestic violence
24/7 Hotline: (850) 681-2111
www.refugehouse.com

Florida Abuse Hotline
1-800-962-2873
www.myflfamilies.com

Online Communities & Trauma-Support Platforms

Pandora's Project
Support for survivors of sexual assault
www.pandys.org

1in6
Resources for male survivors of sexual abuse or assault
www.1in6.org

Survivors Network
Online support space
www.survivorsnetwork.org

Mental Health & Professional Support

Psychology Today Therapist Finder
Search trauma-informed therapists
www.psychologytoday.com
TherapyDen
Inclusive, accessible therapist directory
www.therapyden.com

EMDR International Association (EMDRia)
Find EMDR-trained trauma therapists
www.emdria.org

Books for Healing & Understanding Trauma

The Body Keeps the Score—Bessel van der Kolk, M.D.
What Happened to You?—Bruce D. Perry, M.D.
& Oprah Winfrey
The Deepest Well—Nadine Burke Harris, M.D.
Untamed—Glennon Doyle
Know My Name—Chanel Miller
It Didn't Start with You—Mark Wolynn

Holistic & Complementary Healing

National Center for Complementary and Integrative Health
Mind-body approaches: meditation, breathwork, yoga
www.nccih.nih.gov

Trauma Sensitive Yoga (TSY)
Research-supported healing modality
www.traumasensitiveyoga.com

Insight Timer
Guided meditations for anxiety, grounding, and sleep
App & website
insighttimer.com

If you are in immediate danger or feel unsafe, please contact your local emergency services.

Reaching out for help is a sign of strength, and you deserve support every step of the way.

BOOK CLUB QUESTIONS

1) What moments in the memoir resonated with you most deeply and why?

2) How did Heidi's experiences with silence and secrecy shape your understanding of trauma?

3) What did you observe about the ways childhood coping mechanisms show up in adulthood?

4) Which relationships stood out to you and how did they influence her healing?

5) What role did motherhood play in Heidi's journey toward reclaiming her voice?

6) How did the themes of shame, resilience, and identity show up throughout the book?

7) What surprised you or challenged your assumptions, as you read?

8) Where did you see moments of transformation or empowerment?

9) How does this story invite conversations about generational patterns and breaking them?

10) What lessons or insights are you taking with you after finishing the memoir?

ABOUT THE AUTHOR

HEIDI CRAIG is a writer and survivor whose work centers on truth-telling, emotional healing, and reclaiming identity after trauma. Her debut memoir, *Finding My Voice: Thriving Beyond Pedophilia*, chronicles her journey from childhood silence to adult self-reclamation, exploring the courage it takes to break generational patterns of secrecy and stand firmly in one's truth.

With a background in legal work and trauma-informed communication, Heidi brings a unique blend of resilience, clarity, and compassion to her writing. Her storytelling is grounded in lived experience and fueled by a lifelong commitment to choosing love, honesty, and emotional growth. She believes in writing from the heart—openly, bravely, and without apology—so that others may find pieces of themselves in the stories she shares.

A mother of grown sons who are now out in the world living their best, fullest lives, Heidi celebrates their independence and strength as one of her greatest joys.

Heidi is also the creator of Little Light Stories, a children's series born from her desire to spark hope, kindness, and emotional resilience in the next generation. Through gentle themes, hidden "friends" in the illustrations, and uplifting messages, her stories aim to remind children that they are never alone in their feelings or experiences.

She lives in Tallahassee, Florida, where she continues her work in the legal field while writing, supporting others on their own healing journeys, and building a life rooted in authenticity and hope. She is currently working on future books that continue exploring truth, healing, and the power of using one's voice.

NOTES